# THE RYUKYU KINGDOM

# THE RYUKYU KINGDOM

*Cornerstone of East Asia*

MAMORU AKAMINE

TRANSLATED BY LINA TERRELL
AND EDITED BY ROBERT HUEY

University of Hawai'i Press
HONOLULU

Paperback edition 2019

Printed in the United States of America

24 23 22 21 20 19 6 5 4 3 2 1

**Library of Congress Cataloging-in-Publication Data**

Names: Akamine, Mamoru, author. | Terrell, Lina, translator. | Huey, Robert N., editor.
Title: The Ryukyu Kingdom : cornerstone of East Asia / Mamoru Akamine ; translated by Lina Terrell ; and edited by Robert Huey.
Other titles: Ryūkyū ōkoku. English
Description: Honolulu : University of Hawai'i Press, [2017] | Includes bibliographical references and index.
Identifiers: LCCN 2016017733 | ISBN 9780824855178 (cloth ; alk. paper)
Subjects: LCSH: Ryukyu Islands—History.
Classification: LCC DS895.R95 A3713 2017 | DDC 952/.2902—dc23
LC record available at https://lccn.loc.gov/2016017733

ISBN 978-0-8248-7932-7 (pbk.)

University of Hawai'i Press books are printed on acid-free paper and meet the guidelines for permanence and durability of the Council on Library Resources.

# Contents

# Author's Note

Originally, I had thought to complete this work in only one and a half years, but it ended up taking rather longer than planned. I am grateful for all the help and advice I have received during this period. My students at the University of the Ryukyus lent their hands in many tasks, especially in computer assistance, and in building a database for this work. Though I should list the names of each of the many people who helped me, limitations of space mean I cannot do so.

To Mr. Yamazaki Hiroshi of the book selection committee, who gave me the chance to write this historical overview, I wish to express my deep gratitude for his kindness. He waited for more than three years with grace and patience, and I must finish with my thanks to him.

# Translators' Note and Acknowledgments

In 2008, to mark the establishment of a Center for Okinawan Studies at the University of Hawai'i, scholars of Okinawan studies from the United States, Japan, and Okinawa gathered at East-West Center in a symposium sponsored by the Japan Foundation to discuss the direction that the field of Okinawan studies might take. One of the areas of concern the group identified was the lack of English translations of works by Okinawan writers and scholars—works that would reflect how those scholars see the issues. This translation is a step toward filling that knowledge gap. Mamoru Akamine was born and raised in Okinawa. After graduating from Meiji University, he received his doctorate from Taiwan National University and is now a professor of history at Ryukyu University. The perspective he brings—evident in the title of the book and its opening and closing sections—is one that is missing from existing English-language works in the field. He lets Chinese and Korean sources tell much of the story, adding texture and nuance to the Japanese sources that he also marshals.

The bulk of the translation was done by Lina Terrell, supported by a grant from the Japan Foundation's Institutional Support Program. Robert Huey subsequently edited and revised the manuscript in consultation with the author. As a result of those consultations, a few minor changes have been made (errors corrected, difficulties clarified, and so on). Further revisions followed from the useful comments of the two outside readers, for whose input we are very grateful.

This book was originally commissioned from the author with a general, nonspecialist audience in mind and was published in 2004 as number 297 in the Kōdansha Sensho Mechie series. The author, Mamoru Akamine, wrote the book as an accessible narrative, using primary and secondary sources in Japanese and Chinese. The external readers of the translation manuscript, however, felt the book had potential as an important scholarly contribution, so following their suggestion, the author added extensive footnotes in 2015 and updated references in the notes and bibliography to include works published since the original the 2004 edition. We have included page numbers in notes where we could. The editor, Robert Huey, transcribed these footnotes and, with the author's consent, also added several footnotes to English-language resources with an eye to aiding future scholars in the field.

By nature, we have the greatest respect for the diversity of languages. The advent of the modern nation-state has created a myth of language homogeneity that certainly did not exist throughout most of the eras covered in this book. (Portuguese apothecary Tomé Pires, for example, claimed that more than eighty languages could be heard in sixteenth-century Malacca, where he resided between 1512 and 1515.) We would have liked to demonstrate this by Romanizing names and words in ways that approximated how they actually sounded at the time. However, in order to produce a readable text, we had to make choices regarding Romanization schemes, as well as which languages to feature.

As this book so clearly shows, the Ryukyu Kingdom existed in a complex web of cultures and countries and its representatives needed to be proficient in Chinese, Japanese, or both in order to conduct trade and other negotiations with its neighbors. Also as noted in this book, there were times when individuals in Ryukyu might go by various combinations of names that were Chinese, Japanese, or Ryukyuan. The first issue we faced was how to treat Ryukyuan names and places—whether to give them a Chinese reading, a Japanese reading, or a Ryukyuan reading. Though our impulse was to do the latter, we decided against it in most cases for several reasons: (1) we would still have to choose whether to use a reading based on modern Okinawan (most likely Shuri dialect), in which case we would have to choose a consistent Romanization system ("ee," or "ē," for example; in fact, we have decided to follow the Ryukyu University practice of using a macron, thus "ē") and impose that reading on all places and names, regardless of whether they were Shuri or not, or (2) we would have to attempt to reconstruct Middle Ryukyuan readings, as well as regional variations—something well beyond our skill set—and come up with a consistent Romanization; and (3) very few bibliographic resources exist that would allow any but specialists to look such words up in other sources. In fact, it was this last issue that helped guide our decision to use Japanese, Romanized in modified Hepburn, as our "pillar" language when referring to things in or connected to Ryukyu. This would allow interested readers to look more things up on their own, and also recognize people and place names from other works on Japan. Furthermore, as an ironic legacy of Japan's colonial period, the vast majority of Chinese-language sources cited herein can be accessed in Japanese libraries or archives and are usually searchable there either in kanji or in kana readings.

In certain cases, however, we retained Ryukyuan/Okinawan readings, usually when these readings are commonly encountered in other English-language works on the Ryukyus or Okinawa. In the remaining instances, we used the language appropriate to the person or place. In other words, Chinese place and personal names are given their Chinese readings, though in modern Chinese, using pinyin and tone marks as much as possible, except for well-known places and personal names. We did not attempt to reconstruct historical readings.

For a few key Chinese terms and sources that readers may wish to look up in Japanese sources, we have included the Japanese reading. We acknowledge that this is a judgment call. For Korean proper nouns, we have followed the Revised Romanization system.

Reluctantly, but for the sake of readability, we have dispensed with Chinese characters for the most part, though we have included them in the footnotes for a few terms and proper nouns. It is our intention to prepare a separate glossary, with Chinese characters, which will be available at www.ryukyucornerstone.com.

Japanese/Okinawan historian Greg Smits has talked about how "competing nationalisms" come into play when looking at Okinawa-related historiography. There is an interesting example of it in the notes and bibliography of this book. Since the late 1980s, Okinawan and Chinese scholars have been holding bilingual symposia periodically in which scholars present papers in Chinese and Japanese on topics related to historical relations between the Ryukyus and China. Most of these gatherings have produced proceedings publications, and Akamine cites many of these papers in his work (starting from the second symposium, in 1989, through the sixth and seventh, in 1999–2000). In years when the symposium is held in China, the study group that edits the proceedings, and the title of the publication itself, uses the phrase (in the Japanese reading) "Chūryū rekishi kankei kenkyū" (literally, "research into historical relations between China and Ryukyu"). However, in years when the event is held in Okinawa, the syllables of the first word are reversed—"Ryūchū" rather than "Chūryū"—so the name would be translated "research into the historical relations between Ryukyu and China." (Nationalism pervades even the databases in which these proceedings are listed. For example, in CiNii, the massive bibliographic database kept by Japan's National Institute of Informatics, *all* the proceedings are given as "Ryūchū"—even those that were published in China and actually titled "Chūryū.")

If we cited some of these proceedings in Chinese and others in Japanese, their relationships with one another would be obscured. So we decided to follow CiNii and cite them all using Japanese readings, while keeping intact the Chūryū/Ryūchū distinction. The titles of articles within these publications, however, are given in the language in which they were written. It is a small point, but one that researchers should be aware of when trying to track down sources. (*The Chicago Manual of Style* does not deal with this anomaly!)

For the most part, we have followed Smits, *Visions of Ryukyu,* when translating offices, titles, and so on.

We have also used the following conventions throughout the book:

1. Reflecting the lunar calendar, as well as Asian practice, we give premodern dates as "First Month, 1st Day" (rather than "January 1st"). The lunar month is usually four to six weeks later than its contemporary counterpart. In other words, the lunar First Month usually begins in about mid-February. Japan formally adopted the Gregorian calendar from Meiji 5, Eleventh Month, 9th Day (November 9, 1872), so for dates after that, or dates given in Western sources, we follow the Gregorian calendar.
2. In the case of years, we give the equivalent Gregorian year for the sake of clarity, but where relevant add the Chinese, Japanese, or Ryukyuan year name for scholars who may need that information.
3. Items that the original author put in parentheses appear here in parentheses. Items that the translator or editor have added appear in brackets.

Finally, it is important to recognize those who have supported this endeavor. As noted previously, a generous Japan Foundation grant sponsored the initial translation. The following have provided subvention support to ensure the publication of this book: the Worldwide Uchinanchu Business group, and, at the University of Hawai'i at Mānoa, the Center for Okinawan Studies, the Center for Japanese Studies, and the Department of History. The Kama and Kamato Akamine Endowed Fund for Okinawan Studies provided support for the maps. We are grateful to Byron Inouye at the Curriculum Research and Development Group in the University of Hawai'i at Manoa's College of Education for designing, on short notice, these excellent maps, based on drafts provided by Akamine Mamoru. Professor Akamine joins us in expressing our gratitude to all the above for their generosity.

*Lina Terrell*
*Robert Huey*

# THE RYUKYU KINGDOM

# Introduction

## *What Do We Mean by the "Ryukyu Kingdom"?*

### GEOGRAPHICAL LABELS APPLIED TO OKINAWA PREFECTURE

A look at Map 1 shows that present-day Okinawa's prefectural borders extend from Iōtori (or Iwo Tori) Island in the north to Hateruma Island in the south; this is a distance of about 600 kilometers [372 miles]. Its easternmost island, Kita Daitō, lies 900 kilometers [560 miles] from the westernmost, Yonaguni. Clearly, Okinawa Prefecture is an archipelago of many islands distributed across a wide area of ocean.

Several terms are commonly used to indicate the islands of Okinawa Prefecture, such as the "Ryukyu Archipelago" (Ryūkyū Rettō) or the "Southwestern Islands" (Nansei Shotō). Generally, "Ryukyu Archipelago" is an academic term used in geography or geology, and it includes the Ōsumi Island group near the southernmost tip of Kyushu, as well as the Tokara, Amami, Okinawa, and Sakishima island groups. "Southwestern Islands" refers to the exact same set of islands, with the difference that it is commonly used in official and government circles. Thus, this is the term appearing on maps produced by the Geographical Survey Institute, which creates all the official maps of Japan. Even the terms "Ryukyu Islands" (Ryūkyū Shotō) and "Ryukyu Archipelago" may be distinguished, with the former referring only to the Okinawa and Sakishima island groups. Finally, the archipelago encloses the East China Sea in an arc with its back to the Pacific Ocean, and so sometimes it may even be called Ryūkyū Ko, or the Ryukyu Arc.

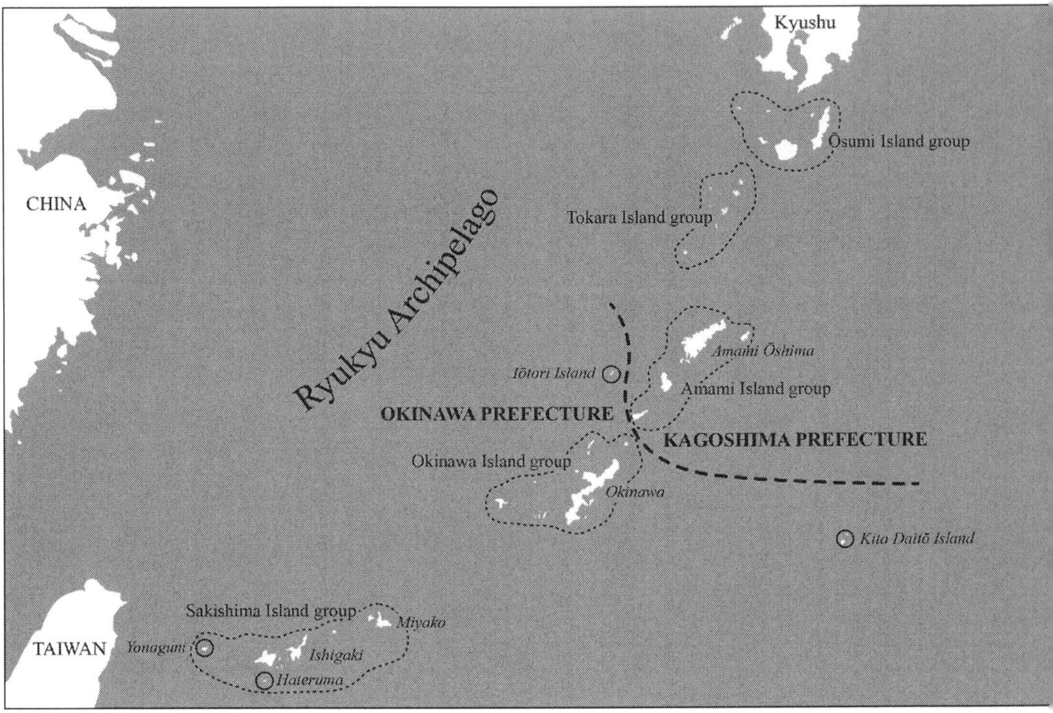


*Map 1.* The Ryukyu Archipelago. The islands marking the north, south, east, and west extremes of present-day Okinawa Prefecture are encircled.

## SHIFTING NATIONAL TERRITORY

Present-day Okinawa is just one of Japan's forty-seven prefectures, but there was a time when, as the Ryukyu Kingdom, it was an independent nation playing an important role as the "cornerstone" of Asia. As such it had a history very different from that of mainland Japan. The territory of this kingdom once stretched from Kikai Island in the north to Yonaguni in the south, encompassing three groups of islands: the Amami group, with Amami Ōshima as its largest island; the Okinawa group, consisting of the island of Okinawa and its nearest neighbors; and the Sakishima group, of which the largest islands are Miyako and Ishigaki. Its influence reached as far as Gaja, the northernmost island of the Tokara group. However, after the invasion, conquest, and subsequent takeover by the Shimazu clan of Satsuma in 1609, the kingdom was forced to cede territory. Thereafter, its actual borders encompassed only the Okinawa and Sakishima island groups, with all the islands north of a line drawn from Iōtori to Yoron falling under the direct rule of Satsuma.

Today, the Daitō and Senkaku island groups fall under the purview of Okinawa Prefecture and are included when we refer to the Okinawa and Sakishima island groups. However, the Daitō group was officially annexed by Japan only in 1885, and the Senkaku group [near Taiwan] was part of the territory ceded to Japan by China after the Sino-Japanese War of 1895. Thus, neither of these island groups was ever part of the Ryukyu Kingdom.

## TWO DISTINCT CULTURES IN THE PREHISTORIC PERIOD

The current view of the Okinawa Archaeological Society is that before the so-called Gusuku Period in the eleventh and twelfth centuries CE, which was marked by the advent of true agriculture, the three island groupings that we now call Amami, Okinawa, and Sakishima could, in fact, be divided into two distinct groups.[1] Based on ceramics and stone tools found throughout the islands, a "Northern Ryukyu Culture," in the Okinawa and Amami Islands, may be distinguished from a "Southern Ryukyu Culture," centered on Miyako and Ishigaki in Sakishima. The northern group shows a connection to Japan's Jōmon period cultures. Moreover, archaeological finds such as pottery, Neolithic stone tools, and burials with stone box coffins and jars characteristic of Yayoi culture and commonly found in Kyushu show that the islands were influenced by the Yayoi culture as well. However, in the southern group, separated from the northern by two or three hundred kilometers of ocean, there are few if any signs of these Japanese cultural influences. Many pots and stone tools, as well as axes made with sharpened shells, similar to those often seen in the prehistoric cultures of Taiwan, Indonesia, and the Southeast Asian islands, have been found there. These justify a separate "Southern Ryukyu Culture" classification for Sakishima.

## THE YAMATO POLITY AND THE SOUTHERN ISLANDS

Around the middle of the seventh century, at the time of the founding of the earliest Japanese polity, the islands south of Kyushu were known as the "Southern Islands." Texts such as the *Nihon shoki* and the *Shoku Nihongi* mention "tribute" sent by the people of southern islands with names like Amami, Shigaki, and Kumi. We may surmise that "Amami" referred to modern-day Amami Ōshima; "Shigaki" to our Ishigaki; and "Kumi" to our Kume Island. After the eighth century, ships headed to Tang China no longer followed the northern route along the Korean coast. Once the southern island route via Amami Ōshima in the East China Sea had been established by explorers sent out in every direction to find the islands of southern Japan, signposts naming the islands, landing sites, and sea-lanes were set up throughout the archipelago. The people of Amami, Shigaki, and Kumi may have been connected with these missions, but from the time of their tribute as recorded in the *Nihon shoki* and the *Shoku Nihongi* through the end of the tribute convoys to China, all mention of them disappears from Japanese historical texts.

## UNCOVERING CHINESE ARCHAEOLOGICAL FINDS AND THE "ACCOUNT OF THE LIUQIU KINGDOM"

The oldest archaeological finds of Chinese origin found in Amami and the Ryukyus consist, among other items, of Warring States Period (403–221 BCE) coins, known as *meitōsen* [Ming knives], from the Kingdom of Yan [before 222 BCE]; Han dynasty [206 BCE –220 CE] bronze arrowheads; *wǔzhū* [J. *goshu-sen*] coins, widely used in China from the Han until the Sui dynasty [581–619 CE]; and old coins of the Tang dynasty inaugural currency. In addition, charms and clothing accessories decorated with shells carved with the Chinese bronze-ware motif known as *tāotiè* [J. *tōtetsu*] have been found in many excavations of sites that date from Japan's Yayoi period.

The first mention of the kingdom in written records appears in the "Account of the Liuqiu Kingdom" in the *Book of Sui* (*Suí shū*, 636 CE), published during the Tang dynasty. It records that in 607 CE, Emperor Yang of the Sui dynasty sent Zhū Kuān on an expedition to Ryukyu, and Zhū Kuān returned with captives in tow. The next year, Zhū Kuān was dispatched once again, but only to return the armor the Ryukyuans had worn.[2]

Currently, we do not know the circumstances under which Ming knives, Han-style arrowheads, *wǔzhū* coins, and Tang dynasty currency arrived in the islands, and we can only note the similarity of the motifs on the excavated shell carvings to *tāotiè* designs. As for the "Ryukyu" mentioned in the "Account of the Liuqiu Kingdom," there is debate about whether it refers to Okinawa or to Taiwan. Thus, neither archaeology nor written records clearly provide any specific people or events showing a historic link between China and the prehistoric Ryukyus.

## THE PLACE OF AMAMI AND THE RYUKYUS IN THE EAST ASIA TRADE SPHERE

In 960 CE, the Song dynasty established its control over a greater geographical area of China than any of its predecessors. A new tax code encouraged overseas trade and promoted its unprecedented growth. Positioned in the middle of the sea-trade routes connecting the lands around the China Sea, Amami and the Ryukyus were affected by these changes as well. First Muslim trade ships, soon joined by ships from Japan and Southeast Asia, visited ports along the coast of China. For their part, Chinese merchants emigrated to Korea, Japan, and Southeast Asia and set up trading centers in every area. They established a Chinese trade network, with the Song dynasty at its center enjoying soaring economic growth. All movement in East Asia belonged to a trade system that encompassed the entire area, with each country's seaborne merchants acting as its carriers. The new East Asian economic structure represented by the international trade conducted by these sea traders is known as the "East Asia Trade Sphere."

Exports from China to Japan included such wares as porcelain and coinage, as well as incense and spices from Southeast Asia. Japan in its turn sent to China gold, pearls, abalone shells, mother-of-pearl inlay, sulfur, and mercury. Among these exports from Japan, many, such as the shells and sulfur, were from Amami and the Ryukyus. The mother-of-pearl inlay was manufactured using thin slices of the iridescent interior of *yakōgai* [*turbo marmoratus*] shells set into lacquerware. The "Silk Road of the Sea," with trade ships linking the far-flung communities of East Asia, brought increasing numbers of merchants and their goods to Amami and the Ryukyus, and soon they joined the greater East Asian trade network as important trade centers.

## THE KINGDOM ATTRACTS PIRATES

In the second half of the fourteenth century, when the heretofore unnoticed "Ryukyu" burst upon the stage of history like a comet to become the cornerstone of East Asia, the island of Okinawa was, in fact, divided into three rival domains. Based in the northern, central, and southern parts of the island, the rulers were known as King of the North [Sanhoku-ō]; King of the Middle [Chūzan-ō]; and King of the South [Sannan-ō]. The first to recognize the Ryukyu Kingdom, and who by doing so created its historic role as cornerstone, was Zhū Yuánzhāng [reign title Hongwu], founder of the Ming dynasty and, as emperor of China, the leader of East Asia.

At the time of the kingdom's recognition by China, the Chinese coast had been suffering from the savage depredations of the so-called *wakō* pirates, whose numbers were augmented by opponents to the newly established Ming dynasty.[3] Because among those coastal residents who were conducting legitimate trade there were also those who joined in with the pirates, Zhū Yuánzhāng forbade overseas trade and travel by all Chinese, imposing a total sanction on all sea travel. The foreign trade necessary for the tribute system came under the control of the imperial court, and foreign travelers and merchants were prohibited from freedom of entry into China. Other countries had to submit as vassals to be recognized, and all trade was restricted to tribute missions only. While Zhū Yuánzhāng was creating this new international system for East Asia by prohibiting travel on the seas and reorganizing the tribute system, the kings of Chūzan, Sannan, and Sanhoku were eagerly seeking overseas Chinese to serve as tribute emissaries, and one after another they sent tribute missions to the Chinese court.[4] In response to this initiative from the Ryukyus, Zhū Yuánzhāng set no limit to the number or frequency of their tribute missions and even went so far as to allow the Ryukyuans to use large ships as their tribute vessels. This was a degree of preferential treatment not extended to any other nation engaged in the tribute system.

The background for this preferential treatment lay in the unceasing pirate attacks along the Chinese coast. Despite one-thousand- and five-thousand-man military encampments stationed there as safeguards, these pirates, beyond the control of the tribute system, showed no signs of slowing their activities. In a move intended to eradicate the pirates and their rapacious pursuit of Chinese trade goods from the coast, Zhū Yuánzhāng designated his new vassal, Ryukyu, as his official "carrier of goods," in place of Chinese carriers who were prohibited from sea travel. The emperor provided the ships on which the Ryukyuans were to transport Chinese wares and thus established for the new state a wide marketplace in which its merchants could ply their trade freely. In so doing, he hoped to deflect at least some of the pirates' attention away from the Chinese coastal areas.

## BRIDGE TO THE WORLD

The age-old oceangoing trade that had plied the China Sea in such high volume suffered a heavy blow from the Ming dynasty's strict enforcement of the tribute system and ban on sea travel. In contrast, Ryukyu seized upon the opportunity provided by the Chinese prohibition of private foreign trade and the vassal tribute system. Ryukyuan merchants became the middlemen in a profitable system in which their ships carried Chinese goods to foreign lands, where they were exchanged for merchandise to sell to the Chinese market.

The end of unrestricted overseas trade and travel, and the resulting collapse of the East Asia Trade Sphere, which had been built on the ability to conduct commerce freely, meant the demand for foreign goods in China could not be met. Also, the Ming dynasty's strict new timetable for tribute missions, to which its client states were compelled to adhere, severely limited the supply of Chinese goods in all areas of Asia, and demand for them reached new heights. Given that Japan could send only one mission every ten years, and even Annam (Vietnam) and Java could send only one every three years, this new scarcity of highly desirable goods, combined with the limitation on how often a nation could send tribute missions, was a real hardship. These circumstances wrought great change upon trade in East Asia. With its steadily growing fleet of trade ships, Ryukyu emerged as a central figure in regional commerce in its role as merchant middleman between Japan, China, and Southeast Asia.

The Ryukyu Kingdom benefited hugely from China's policy of preferential treatment. With China granting sea passage to Ryukyuan ships, the kingdom built the magnificent Silk Road of the Sea by engaging in energetic commerce with the many port cities in the South China Sea and Southeast Asia. As it became the link between these and Japan and Korea on the East China Sea, Naha was transformed into the greatest port of the region. Thus the people of this tiny kingdom, through a myriad of experiences and contacts with Asia's nations, succeeded in building a unique culture tinged with diverse influences.

## RYUKYU, VASSAL OF JAPAN, AND RYUKYU, VASSAL OF CHINA

Unified in the fifteenth century under the king of Chūzan, by the sixteenth century the Ryukyu Kingdom extended from the Amami island group in the north to the Sakishima group in the south. In 1609, however, the kingdom was invaded and quickly defeated when Kabayama Hisataka, a samurai of the Satsuma *han* in Kyushu, landed with more than three thousand men on one hundred ships. Thereafter, the kingdom came under the control of the Tokugawa shogun's *bakuhan* administrative system; treated as a "foreign land" [*ikoku*], it was ruled by Satsuma with the backing of the shogun.

Although the government of the Ryukyu Kingdom during the early modern period was subject to the restrictions and regulations imposed by both the Satsuma *han* and its overlord, the Edo *bakufu*, both of these latter tacitly recognized that the kingdom was still a vassal state of China. The royal government at Shuri Castle regarded China as its "silent backer" and maintained a certain distance from the *bakufu* in an attempt to retain the kingdom's standing as an independent nation. Satsuma's policy of allowing the kingdom to retain its client-state status with China even after its takeover by Satsuma proved useful for Ryukyu (see Chapter Five). To survive, the kingdom deliberately intensified the degree to which it sinified and increased its commitment to the diplomatic protocols and tribute exchanges required of a client of the powerful Chinese Empire. In this way, the Ryukyu Kingdom established a subtle safeguard and built a resistance that slowed its extinction by the overweening power and cultural influence of Satsuma and the *bakufu*.

The border between Japan and China in the early modern period was not a line, but a zone, and the royal government in Shuri, from the center of that zone, tried to strike a balance between its two powerful neighbors. It maintained a double orientation after the Satsuma invasion of 1609, as both "Ryukyu, vassal of Japan," submitting to the *bakuhan* system while maintaining a façade of independence, and "Ryukyu, vassal of China," participating in the Chinese tribute system. Thus it established itself as a buffer zone, creating a unique identity that was neither completely Chinese nor completely Japanese.

## VANISHED DOCUMENTS PERTAINING TO THE KINGDOM, AND NEW RESEARCH

The Ryukyu Kingdom was dismantled in 1879 by Japan's Meiji government, and in the so-called Ryūkyū Shobun [Disposition of Ryukyu] was annexed by Japan, coming to a sad end as just another part of the "national polity."[5] A large number of royal documents were confiscated and sent to Tokyo to be kept by the Department of the Interior; the bulk of this collection was destroyed by fire in the Great Kantō Earthquake of 1923. Additionally, many precious royal treasures and papers, including the original *Rekidai hōan* [Treasury of Successive Generations], the kingdom's record of its trade and diplomatic relations with China, Korea, and all the various East Asian nations its trade ships visited for the period from 1427 to 1867, were lost when Shuri Castle was destroyed in the terrible Battle of Okinawa at the end of World War II. The postwar period has been a time of unceasing labor and diligent research, attempting to recover the history of the kingdom, with extensive searches for papers within Japan that may have survived earthquakes and fires, and wide-ranging overseas travel to search in foreign archives.

In 1972, a copy of the *Rekidai hōan* made in prewar Taiwan at the Taihoku Imperial University [now Taiwan National University] was published. This document, fundamental to the advancement of research on the kingdom's trade and diplomatic relations network, shed new light on the subject. The Okinawa Prefectural Board of Education is currently working on a new, collated edition with detailed annotation, which is referred to herein as the "revised edition."[6] Furthermore, several foreign archives, including the First Historical Archive of China in Beijing, as well as the Palace Museum, the Institute of History and Philology, and the Institute of Modern History, all in Taiwan, have unearthed numerous *tōan,* administrative documents connected to Qing-period Ryukyu. With these contemporary Chinese documents, combined with the royal government's own record of its international relations in the *Rekidai hōan,* the kingdom's history takes on a whole new shape. Add to these the many important documents that have been found within Japan, such as the Shuri royal government's *Hyōjōsho monjo* [Proceedings of the Judicial Council],[7] and it is clear how much surprising research is taking place and revising our understanding of history.

This book, benefiting from such recent research, begins with a look at the birth of the Ryukyu Kingdom, then moves through the period in which it was the cornerstone of East Asia. The "royal authority" of the "kingdom" was first recognized by all of East Asian society in the fourteenth century after the Gusuku (lit., "fortification; castle") Period, and it is during this period that it begins to appear regularly in the historic documents. Thus we will begin with a review of the Gusuku Period.

CHAPTER ONE

# The Gusuku Period

## THE EAST ASIA TRADE SPHERE AND THE EMERGENCE OF *GUSUKU*

### *Gusuku* on the World Heritage List

On November 30, 2000, UNESCO's World Heritage Committee, meeting in Cairns, Australia, added Okinawa's "Gusuku Sites and Related Properties of the Ryukyu Kingdom" to the World Heritage List. The designation applied to five *gusuku* sites, including Shuri Castle, Nakijin, Katsuren, Zakimi, and Nakagusuku (see Figure 1.1), as well as to Sēfa Utaki shrine, the Tama Udun Royal Mausoleum, the Sunuhiyan Utaki stone gate, and the royal residence and garden at Shikinaen, for a total of nine World Heritage sites.

Distributed throughout the area from Amami to Miyako and Yaeyama in Sakishima, with the heaviest concentration on the island of Okinawa, *gusuku* (sometimes called *gushiku* or *suku*) resembled the type of walled fortified castles built with stone that were developed in Japan during the Warring States Period [ca. 1450 to 1603 CE]. There is debate as to whether originally they served as sacred sites, dwellings, or forts, but the five *gusuku* at Shuri, Nakijin, Katsuren, Zakimi, and Nakagusuku are known to be representative of the fortified stone castles built during the time when the kingdom was emerging.

*Gusuku* may be categorized into two groups, either as small, single-enclosure structures, or as large, multiple-enclosure structures. All five of the sites admitted to the World Heritage List are large, multiple-enclosure *gusuku*. Currently, more than three hundred *gusuku* sites in Amami and the

*Figure 1.1.* Ruins of Nakagusuku castle. Photograph by R. N. Huey.

Ryukyus have been confirmed, and the era in which they were built is known as the Gusuku Period. There is extensive discussion on the exact time of the period's beginning, but it was sometime in the eleventh or twelfth centuries.

### The Birth of *Gusuku* and the Appearance of the *Aji*

In the era prior to the Gusuku Period, the inhabitants of the Ryukyus and Amami led a primitive lifestyle centered on fishing, hunting, and gathering. At some point—and this is what marks the beginning of the Gusuku Period—they shed this lifestyle and began cultivating crops in earnest, eventually forming a stratified society of agricultural villages, each within recognized geographical boundaries and usually populated with people related by blood or marriage. A leading class known as *aji* (lord) emerged in every village during this period. Early on, the *aji* built the smaller single-enclosure *gusuku* to mark the sphere of their political power, but by the thirteenth century liege lords appeared who built the large, multiple-enclosure *gusuku* and began a process absorbing their smaller neighbors and consolidating ever-greater power.

A manuscript in the archives of the Imperial Household Agency, the *Hyōtō Ryūkyūkoku ki* [Account of a Passage to the Land of Ryukyu], describes the experiences of a party of travelers who set out for China from Ojikajima in 1243. They were shipwrecked on "Ryukyu" during a fierce storm and at one point found themselves in the midst of a battle between two groups of Ryukyuans. The text includes a realistically drawn picture of the fighters, depicting men armed with spears and shields.[1] The *Omoro sōshi*, a collection of ancient religious songs (*omoro*) compiled by the royal government in the sixteenth and seventeenth centuries, contains some "regional *omoro*" that were sung in different parts of the islands in the period before the *aji* were gathered together in Shuri. In those *omoro, aji* who led other, more junior, lords, and who were based within the largest *gusuku* in each area, are referred to in such terms as *aji-osoi* [lord attached, i.e., leader of lords], *aji no mata no aji* [lord of other lords], or *aji-osoi teda* [the sun who is a leader of lords]. The *Hyōtō Ryūkyūkoku ki* is the only text we have that gives a visual depiction of thirteenth-century Ryukyuan *aji-osoi* as they commanded and fought with their men. Evidence of trade in the form of large quantities of Chinese ceramics has been unearthed in excavations of the largest fortified *gusuku* built by these *aji-osoi.*

The early Yuan dynasty enjoyed a booming ceramics trade from about the mid-fourteenth century. At that time, Okinawa and its nearest islands were divided into three regions, a northern (Kunigami), a central (Nakagami), and a southern (Shimajiri). The chief lords of each of these regions were based at Nakijin Castle (Sanhoku) in the north, Urasoe (Chūzan) in the central region, and Shimajiri Ōzato (Sannan) in the south, and together their fiefdoms are known as the Sanzan [literally "three mountains," also known as the Three Kingdoms Mountains]. They competed continuously among themselves for supremacy. Finally, in the first half of the fifteenth century, Shō Hashi of Chūzan prevailed over his rivals, unifying Sanzan under his rule and establishing the First Shō dynasty. Soon, however, it fell in a coup d'état to the founder of the Second Shō dynasty. In the latter half of the fifteenth century, the third king of the Second Shō dynasty, King Shō Shin, succeeded in summoning all remaining *aji* to live below Shuri Castle. In their stead, representatives, called *aji-uttchi* [*aji* agents], were sent to administer their domains. Thus the previously independent fiefdoms came under the complete control of the Shuri royal government, signaling the end of the Gusuku Period.

The Gusuku Period was a time when trade grew between the domains, centered on individual *gusuku* and their neighbors. As trade goods circulated throughout the region ever more widely, the islands notably saw the development of a general "Greater Ryukyu Culture," which encompassed the two separate cultural spheres that had long existed in the archipelago, namely, the Northern Ryukyu Culture, shaped by both Jōmon and Yayoi cultural influences, and the Southern Ryukyu Culture, with its links to the societies of Polynesia, the Southeast Asian island groups, and Taiwan. At the same time, the power structure of the Gusuku Period determined the form of government in the kingdom that followed. Well might we wonder what stormy course the newly unified nation followed as it underwent such huge political transformations and the unification of the two disparate northern and southern cultures.

### Keywords for Understanding the Gusuku Period

Beyond helping us in understanding the origins of the Gusuku Period, five important keywords help illuminate the period. These include *ishinabe* [stone cooking pots]; *kamuiyaki* [lit. tortoise pottery, i.e., gray stoneware]; *gusuku* earthenware [*gusuku doki*]; ironware [*tekki*]; and Chinese porcelain [*chūgokusei jiki*].

In the early Gusuku Period, *ishinabe,* or stone cooking pots, made from talc stone mined on the Nishisonogi Peninsula in Nagasaki Prefecture (Kyushu) and used to cook grain, were brought south into the Ryukyuan archipelago. Most frequently found in western Japan, these pots have been found in sites from the Kantō region in eastern Japan to Hateruma Island, southernmost in the archipelago.

*Kamuiyaki,* or gray stoneware, was produced at the ancient kilns excavated on Tokunoshima, in the Amami island group. Frequently consisting of storage containers characteristic of agricultural societies, this type of pottery was of a quality similar to Japanese *sue* ware and is found throughout the entire Ryukyuan archipelago from Amami to Yaeyama. *Gusuku doki,* a type of earthenware that mimics the appearance of *ishinabe,* has the wide, shallow profile characteristic of earthenware produced in the archipelago during its agricultural period.

These wares were widely distributed and commonly used, and the quantities unearthed at archaeological sites dating to the early Gusuku Period serve to convey an idea of the progress achieved by this agricultural society. Simultaneously, numerous ironware products such as small weapons and farming tools *not* produced in the archipelago were also in circulation. The widespread use of *ishinabe, kamuiyaki, gusuku* earthenware, and ironware items, as well as the comings and goings of the people who brought them in, also helped ensure the spread of various farming techniques. Together these phenomena are held to be the primary forces in the formation of the Gusuku Period, with its agriculture-based hierarchical society led by powerful *aji.*

The final keyword may be the most important in capturing the essence of the Gusuku Period. Chinese porcelain (especially *tamabuchi*-style white porcelain, thought to have been used as dishes, has been found in early Gusuku Period sites alongside the *ishinabe, kamuiyaki, gusuku* earthenware, and ironware discussed previously. This porcelain entered the islands after the twelfth century, so Okinawa's archaeological community has begun to accept that the origin of the Gusuku Period may be set in the twelfth century. However, some scholars have proposed that this date must be moved back to reflect the entry of *ishinabe* into the archipelago in the eleventh century; the exact period of the arrival of *ishinabe* remains a topic of hot debate.

Because the Chinese porcelain found at excavations is always found together with *ishinabe,* it probably did not come directly from China, but instead was brought in via Kyushu. The question that remains is just how it was brought in, and by whom.

### Hachirō no Mahito and the Southern Sea Trade

The eleventh-century *Shin sarugakuki,* attributed to Fujiwara no Akihira, gives an account of a merchant named Hachirō no Mahito.[2] According to this text, Hachirō no Mahito was a great trader who handled countless quantities of goods as he traveled from northeastern Honshu to Iōshima or Kikaijima in the Satsunan islands just south of Kyushu. Included in the items he dealt with were *yakōgai* and sulfur produced in the Ryukyuan archipelago.

We know that sulfur was used as gunpowder in Chinese artillery, and the *Wǔjīng zǒngyào* [Essentials of the Military Classics] (eleventh century), a military encyclopedia of the Northern Song dynasty, contains essays on deploying "fireballs" of black gunpowder made from sulfur, saltpeter, and charcoal. Much of this sulfur, also prized for its medical properties, was produced on Iōtori Island in the Ryukyus, as well as on Iōshima in the Satsunan group.

Mention of *yakōgai,* a large conch found in the waters of Amami and southward, may be found in both *Makura no sōshi* [The Pillow Book, by 1000 CE, Sei Shōnagon] and *Utsuho monogatari* [Tale of the Hollow Tree, late tenth century, author unknown]. The Heian nobility laid great value on items decorated with mother-of-pearl inlay from the "south seas," made with thinly sliced *yakōgai.* A technique that had originally come from China, Japanese inlay soon took on a unique style in the latter half of the Heian period. Famous examples of this decorative style include the Buddhist halls Konjiki-dō at Chūsonji [1124, in Hiraizumi, Iwate], Hōōdō at the Byōdō-in [1052, in Uji, Kyōto], and Hōjōji [destroyed in 1053, Kyōto].

We may accept that *ishinabe, kamuiyaki,* iron, and Chinese porcelain were brought into the Ryukyuan archipelago by traders such as Hachirō no Mahito, and that these items were traded for the *yakōgai* and sulfur found in Amami and the Ryukyus. Probably Hachirō no Mahito was a fictional character, but we may trust that the highly regarded *Shin sarugakuki* has provided a fairly accurate depiction of the period's traveling merchants.

The Gusuku Period did not simply come about as a result of naturally occurring phenomena within the Ryukyuan archipelago. Nor can its rise be attributed to the region's physical location within the Japanese cultural sphere of influence. It developed in the midst of a greater East Asian community with China at its center that was also undergoing systematic changes. Ryukyuan society received great stimulation from the movement of people and goods throughout East Asia, and it was this stimulus that brought about the Gusuku Period.

## AMAMI AND THE RYUKYU ISLANDS DURING THE SONG AND YUAN DYNASTIES

### Overseas Commerce during the Song Dynasty and the Overseas Chinese Network

China entered a half century of turmoil known as the period of Five Dynasties and Ten Kingdoms when the Tang dynasty, which had held such sway over all its neighbors, finally fell in 907 CE. By 960, however, order was restored and China reunited with the foundation of the Song dynasty. During this period, nearby nations were undergoing their own political changes as well. In Korea, the Silla Kingdom [57 BCE–935 CE] was defeated and overtaken in 935 by Taejo Wang Geon, founder of the Kingdom of Goryeo [918–1392 CE]; Japan saw the weakening of its Chinese-style legal code [*ritsuryō*] and bureaucracy, and the appearance on the national stage of a new warrior class that would eventually dominate its medieval government.

The Song dynasty was a period of rapidly escalating trade to ever more distant lands. Enormous cities filled with eager consumers were served by well-financed itinerant merchants who traveled throughout the far-flung nation conducting trade. The Song court established a tax code that became an important source of income for its projects, and its promotion of foreign trade resulted in previously unseen heights of wealth and success in commerce. Customs officials oversaw the foreign trade in cities designated as foreign trade ports, such as Guangzhou (in Guangdong); Quanzhou (in Fujian); and Wenzhou, Hangzhou, and Mingzhou [now Ningbo] (all in Zhejiang), all frequently visited by Southeast Asian and Muslim trade ships. These cities also saw the appearance of merchant princes [Ch. *háoshāng,* J. *gōshō*] who possessed vast private capital.

The Song period document *Zhūfānzhì* [J. *Shobanshi,* Records of the Barbarian Countries] describes how compasses and other equipment necessary for sea travel were already in use; it also reports great advances in shipbuilding technology, with the construction of large junks, thirty meters in length and ten in width, that could carry large quantities of trade goods. It was in these vessels that the great merchant princes invested their private capital. The chief imports included incense, spices, aromatic wood, rhinoceros horn, and ivory from the South Seas islands; exports included silk, porcelain, bronze currency, ironware, and lacquerware. Most of the Song merchants involved in this trade did not just live in China but were also stationed at trade centers they built in Korea, Japan, and Southeast Asia. Eventually, they developed a trade network of overseas Chinese that stretched across a wide geographical area.

After the Japanese court ceased to send official envoys [*kentōshi*] to China, Goryeo traders from the Korean peninsula acted as the middlemen for commerce between Song China and Japan. By the eleventh century, however, Chinese merchants had replaced their Korean counterparts and begun dealing directly with Japan.

Groups of Song merchants, called "hawser masters" [Ch. *gāngzhŭ*, J. *kōshu*], influential in trading because of the trading ships they commanded, gathered in the Kyushu ports of Hakozaki and Hakata, forming Chinese communities called "Tang houses" [Ch. *tángfáng*, J. *tōbō*]. A settlement of many traders is said to have gathered around Wáng Shēng [J. Ō Shō], whose Japanese wife gained notoriety.[3] The trade between Japan and Song China accelerated in the twelfth century when Taira no Kiyomori came to power. He supported the China trade and commissioned additional independent Japanese trade ships.

### Establishment of the East Asia Trade Sphere

Under the aegis of the Song dynasty and its soaring economic growth, movement around all of East Asia increased as merchants began to form a trade system that encompassed the entire area. Their international trade activities created an economic order that is known as the East Asia Trade Sphere.[4]

Japan's sea trade with China was based mainly in Mingzhou (modern Ningbo) in Zhejiang Province. Wares imported from China included large quantities of celadon from the Longchuan and Tongan kilns, and as mentioned in the introduction, bronze currency, and incense and spices from Southeast Asia. Japanese exports to China included mainly items such as gold, pearls, *yakōgai* and inlay work, sulfur, and mercury. Of these, sulfur and *yakōgai* were from Amami and the Ryukyus.

Thus Amami and the Ryukyus contributed to the supply of circulating trade goods, and it is clear from the Chinese porcelain found in twelfth-century sites, as well as the prodigious quantities of Chinese porcelain dug up from thirteenth-century *gusuku* sites all over the islands, that Japanese trade ships frequently plied the East China Sea. After the eleventh century, trade on the East China Sea grew at a brisk pace, and this wave of economic activity without a doubt flooded through the archipelago. The movement of both goods and people throughout the lands around the China Sea provided the impetus for its transition from prehistory to the historic period.

The Ryukyu archipelago, slumbering long in the world of prehistory, was rapidly incorporated into the East Asian Trade Sphere to become one of its trade centers. As tools and goods in the once-distinct Northern Ryukyu and Southern Ryukyu cultural areas grew more similar, and as the development of the *gusuku* culture gathered momentum in the archipelago, a single, unified "Ryukyuan culture" emerged.

### Ryukyu in Song and Yuan Dynasty Documents

Many of the Song merchants who settled in Japan had come from Fujian and Zhejiang Provinces. From the eleventh until the late fourteenth century, trade centered mainly on China and Japan. The Chinese porcelain that entered into circulation in Ryukyuan society was of the same type as that in Kyushu, so probably they were not goods traded directly with China, but were imported from the Kyushu area along with *ishinabe, kamuiyaki* gray stoneware, and iron. This was probably the case for everything brought in during this period. There are very few original documents from the Song and Yuan periods, but a few that mention "Liúqiú" do exist.

Such mentions include, for example, a note in *Lìqí-pǔ* [Lychee Register, 1059], by Cài Xiāng [1012–1067], a well-known scholar-official of the Northern Song dynasty (960–1127), that Fujian was a major producer of lychees, very popular in China, and that the fruit was exported to Silla, Japan, and "Liúqiú."[5] Another is in a letter written by Lǐ Fù [1052–1128?] and found in the fifth volume of a posthumous collection of his works entitled *Juéshuǐjí* [Jueshui River Collection]. It reads in part: "If you sail the eastern ocean out from Wenzhou, about 130 *ri* from the coast you will arrive at the country of Liúqiú. In that country they have a special building on the beach where they await visitors from China."[6] This implies that "Liúqiú" had built on its seacoast a building dedicated to the business of conducting trade with Chinese merchants.

In addition, there are the lines in a poem by the famous Southern Song (1127–1279) poet Lù Yóu [1125–1210] (whose studio name was Fàng Wēng):

> Always I'll remember the early autumn storm clearing
> And the oarsmen pointing and saying, "Liuqiu lies there."[7]

Here Lù Yóu is describing a moment when he was gazing eastward from the coast of Fuzhou after an early autumn storm of rain and thunder had cleared up, and a sailor pointed out to sea and said that "Liuqiu" lay out there. Thus we have an example even in literature of a mention of the Ryukyus.

In 1320, Su Tiānjué [1294–1352] compiled a large collection of poems from the Yuan dynasty (1279–1368), entitled *Guózhāo wénlèi* (The Poems of Our Kingdom, Categorized). In volume 4, Folk Songs and Poems, [*yuèfǔ gēxíng*] there appears a poem by Mǎ Zǔcháng [1279–1338], entitled "Shipboard Song" (船上謡 *chuán shàng yáo*). Mǎ Zǔcháng was ordered to go to Quannan (modern-day Quanzhou) in the south of Fujian to investigate cargo shipping in the area. He gives an account of ships setting out from Quannan with destinations that included modern-day Cambodia, Japan, Korea, and Ryukyu.[8]

Another poem, by Yáng Hé [ca. 1367], describes the interactions between Guangdong and Cambodia, as well as Champa (in modern-day Vietnam) and Ryukyu. Finally, *Chóngxiū chóngmíng xiànzhì,* a Yuan-period edition of a gazetteer for the Chongming (Yangtze delta) region, notes how, during the early Yuan dynasty, traders from Japan and the Ryukyus gathered at the offices of the trading company established in Taicang in Jiangsu Province by Chinese maritime entrepreneurs Zhū Qīng [1236–1306] and Zhāng Xuān [d. 1302].[9]

### Formation of Seaborne Trade Routes between the Nations around the East China Sea

After the twelfth century, the East China Sea was frequently traversed by ships from China and Japan. Although they did not achieve the prominence of ports like Dazaifu in Kyushu, Amami and the Ryukyus certainly established themselves as vital centers of trade in the East Asian community. We may be unable to verify that the "Liúqiú" mentioned in these various Song- and Yuan-dynasty documents is the same as our modern Okinawa, but there is no doubt that the same documents clearly show Chinese marine merchants actively engaged in seeking out opportunities for trade.

Additionally, Fujian Province had many iron foundries. There is a very good chance the ironware found in Amami and the Ryukyus dating to before the fourteenth century was part of the wares transported by Chinese merchants and did not come only from sources in Kyushu.

After the twelfth century, we know that many Chinese merchants from local Chinese communities traveled as passengers on the Japanese ships crossing from Kyushu to China. These ships sailed back and forth with great frequency. It seems obvious that the *ishinabe* and *kamuiyaki* gray stoneware brought to the Ryukyus from Kyushu were brought not only by merchants based in Kyushu, but also by these Chinese merchants who traveled so extensively.

During the Gusuku Period, as Amami and the Ryukyus became a part of the new economic order represented by the East Asian Trade Sphere, great numbers of people moved through the area, to a degree never before seen. Even as these people moved through the area carrying their goods of trade, they created the wide-ranging seaborne trade routes that connected the nations encircling the East China Sea.

In the second half of the fourteenth century, Ryukyu, until then in no way a dominant player in the area's maritime commerce, used these trade routes to burst like a shooting star onto the stage of history as the important Cornerstone of East Asia.

CHAPTER TWO

# Founding of the Ming Dynasty and the Rise of the Ryukyu Kingdom

## THE BAN ON SEA TRAVEL, AND THE TRIBUTE SYSTEM

### Purging the Seaways—A Ban on Sea Travel

In 1386, Zhū Yuánzhāng (Emperor Hongwu) quelled the tumult that ended the century-long Yuan dynasty and ascended to the imperial throne in Yingtianfu (Nanjing) as the founder of the Ming dynasty. In Japan, the Kamakura *bakufu* had fallen and the unrest of the Northern and Southern Courts era was peaking. *Wakō* pirates with bases in Kitakyushu and on the islands of Iki and Tsushima were ransacking the coastal areas of Korea and northern China, plundering crops and abducting people whom they sold elsewhere as slaves. Eventually they shifted their depredations southward along the coast of China and sometimes entered into alliances and trade relationships with remnants of the forces that had fought against Zhū Yuánzhāng and that controlled parts of the coastline. These surviving forces represented a real threat to the stability of the new dynasty. This, along with the coastal inhabitants' alliances with the pirates, pushed Zhū Yuánzhāng to forbid foreign trade and overseas travel by private individuals. He instituted this "ban on sea travel" [Ch. *hǎijìn*, J. *kaikin*] to seal off the coastal regions and purge the seas of piracy.[1]

Zhū Yuánzhāng was the first Chinese emperor to use a single era name for his entire reign, a policy called "one reign, one name" [Ch. *yīshì yīyuán*]. His era name of "Hongwu," meaning "great warrior," was an appropriate choice for the powerful general who threw off the rule of the foreign Mongol Yuan dynasty and restored the Han Chinese to power.

In recognition of this return to authority of the Han ethnic group, once he had prevailed in ending the nation's turmoil and restoring order, Emperor Hongwu sought to establish a traditional Confucian nation, its citizens' behavior governed by Confucian values. These values would govern not only China itself, but also its neighbors. Thus the tribute system, based on a Chinese and Confucian ideology of "virtuous rule" [Ch. *dézhì,* J. *tokuchi*] and "correct rule" [Ch. *rǐzhì,* J. *reichi*] that placed China at the center of the world, would be a "proper order" governing China's neighbors, called the "four barbarians." It was to be a system that controlled the surrounding nations and also allowed China and its barbarian neighbors to coexist in a relationship of ruler and subjects, while imposing Confucian order over all its world. With the prohibition on sea travel combined with a strict enforcement of the tribute system giving his government control over all foreign trade, Zhū Yuánzhāng made China the sovereign nation dominant over all East Asia.

### Sending Envoys to Issue the Ascension Proclamation

At the end of 1368, Emperor Hongwu began dispatching envoys to Annam (part of modern-day Vietnam), Goryeo (part of modern-day Korea), Champa (also part of modern-day Vietnam), Java, and others to proclaim his ascension and to demand they submit to his authority and send tribute. When Annam, Goryeo, and Champa all promptly sent legations to offer tribute, Hongwu conferred their rulers with the title of "king." In this way, Hongwu sought to establish the "sovereign and subject relationship," or, in this case, what must be called a "suzerain and dependent state relationship," as required by the Confucian worldview.

The *Míng shílù* [Annals of the Ming Dynasty, J. *Min jitsu roku*] notes that Yáng Zài was dispatched to Japan in the Third Month of 1369. This was during the period of conflict between the Northern and Southern Courts. On his arrival in Kyushu, Yáng Zài went to Dazaifu to present the imperial proclamation to the general of the western campaign, Prince Kaneyoshi, son of Emperor Go-Daigo and the senior representative of the Southern Court in the area. Emperor Hongwu's proclamation reverberates with his anger regarding the devastation being inflicted on the Chinese coast by the pirates, and he demands that Japan suppress them and offer tribute. He desired the pirates be suppressed: they were based in Japan, a part of East Asia's Confucian "proper order" of which the emperor was the head; thus their suppression was the duty of Japan. His strongly worded decree displayed clearly the imposing arrogance of China's "great warrior." It declared, "If you refuse to do this, the gangs of pirates sheltering in the islands around Japan will be condemned, and we will not hesitate equally to condemn the King of Japan."

Prince Kaneyoshi's response was to behead five of the envoys and imprison Yáng Zài for three months. However, when a second legation arrived in 1370, he showed a changed attitude and this time replied to the imperial overture, sending tribute appended with the name "Yoshikane, King of Japan." With this act, it would seem that Japan, too, had joined China's East Asia tribute system. It did not remain long, however, because soon after that Imagawa Ryōshun [1326–1420], deputized as the *tandai* of Kyushu by the Northern Court (controlled by the *bakufu*), arrived in Hakata in the Chikuzen region [modern Fukuoka] and fierce fighting began. When Dazaifu surrendered, Prince Kaneyoshi retreated first to Kōrasan in Chikuzen, and then farther away to Kikuchi in the Higo [present-day Kumamoto] region. Once he lost any chance of victory, Kaneyoshi retired from his position and went into seclusion. At that point, the Japanese king who had acknowledged China as his suzerain disappeared from view.

## THE RYUKYU KINGDOM'S TRIBUTE MISSIONS

### Yáng Zài's Mission and the Chūzan King's Tribute Legation

Yáng Zài, whom the Ming dynasty founder had sent earlier as envoy to Japan, was sent to Ryukyu in 1372 to similarly demand tribute. At that time, the kingdom rested on three pillars: the three domains of Chūzan, Hokuzan, and Nanzan.[2] Yáng Zài chose to present his imperial proclamation to the most powerful of these, Chūzan, with its center of power at the imposing castle of Urasoe, seat and source of royal authority for three successive kings, Shunten, Eiso, and now Satto. King Satto received the decree and at once dispatched his younger brother Taiki to China as his tribute envoy.

The 1372 embassy mission that established the tributary relationship between China and Ryukyu was an epoch-making event. The background to the new relationship went back to five years earlier, when Yáng Zài had heard of Ryukyu during his stay in Kyushu. Rather than returning directly to China, Yáng Zài had stopped in Ryukyu and arranged to meet Satto before returning to Nanjing via Fujian to make his report to Emperor Hongwu. It would not be too much to say that it was Yáng Zài who created the conditions for an oceangoing, sea-trading, outward-looking Kingdom of Ryukyu, located in the East China Sea, though previously there had been no intercourse with China, nor even the royal authority necessary to create a unified polity. In their meeting five years earlier, Yáng Zài had clearly impressed on King Satto the implications of joining the tribute system, and when the imperial proclamation arrived in the fifth year of Hongwu's reign, Satto was prepared to send tribute immediately. Lord Taiki was dispatched to convey officially the kingdom's desire to become a tributary nation. His legation made the ocean crossing with Yáng Zài, and they attended the tribute ceremony at the imperial palace in Nanjing together.

### Recognition of Royal Authority

The *Míng shílù,* in its entry concerning the tribute carried in by the envoy from Ryukyu, notes, "The Local Products given in the Declaration were offered as tribute. The Decree gives to Satto the right to use the Official Calendar [Ch. Dàtŏnglì, J. *daitōreki*], and also gives five lengths each of various types of gold-woven silk brocade." The "declaration" was the official letter celebrating the emperor's virtue, as required by Confucian etiquette, sent by the surrounding nations to accompany the tribute that symbolized their submission. Any legation that entered China without such an official letter was summarily tossed out again. "Local Products" were the tribute goods, and the "Decree" was the document prepared by the court in the emperor's name to award gifts to the tributary nation for its obeisance. The gifts in this case consisted of several lengths of silk brocades woven with designs in gold thread, and permission to use the new calendar established by the Ming court. Thereafter any documents submitted to the court by the Ryukyuans had to note the Chinese year and zodiac.

After Ryukyu had joined the tributary system, it appears marked as "Greater Liuqiu" [大瑠球] on the *Map of the Land of Liuqiu* [琉球国図, Ch. *Liúqiú guótú*] in *Liúqiú túshūo* [琉球図說, J. *Ryukyu zusetsu,* Maps of Ryukyu, mid-sixteenth century] by a Ming-period geographer named Zhèng Rùocéng [1503–1570]. On the lower left of the map, the much larger Taiwan is labeled "Little Liuqiu" [小瑠球].[3] During and after the Tang dynasty, the name Liúqiú (sometimes written with other characters such as 琉求 and 瑠求) was often applied to a wide region that included the island of Taiwan. However, once the Chūzan king joined the Ming tribute system, it became the name of the kingdom based on the island of Okinawa. On maps, what is now the island of Okinawa was clearly labeled Liúqiú Guó [琉球国, J. *Ryukyu koku,* Land of Ryukyu].

### Tribute Envoy Taiki and the Chinese Merchants behind the Tribute Missions

Taiki appears five more times in the *Míng shílù* as envoy for King Satto of Chūzan. He is also mentioned in the *Omoro sōshi,* the Shuri royal government's anthology of Okinawan religious songs:

| | |
|---|---|
| *Oza no Tachiyomoi ya* | Lord Taiki of Uza, |
| *Tau akinai hawerachife* | Fostering the trade with China: |
| *Anji ni omowarere* | Reminiscent of the King. |
| *Ichifeki Tachiyomoi ya* | Superb, glorious, Lord Taiki— |
| *Oza no Tachiyomoi ya* | Lord Taiki of Uza, |
| *Nami ichife* | Setting your ship upon the waves: |
| *Tono michife kiyomon* | Seeing China's fabulous palace, and now returning. |
| *Ichifeki Tachiyomoi ya* | Superb, glorious, Lord Taiki—[4] |

Taiki wielded power in the Uza area of modern Yomitan village in central Okinawa. This *omoro* sings heroic praise of him for his active role as a high-ranking actor in the tributary relationship with China.

However, many people were necessary to deal with the demands of the tribute missions. There were the official documents, such as the one noted in the emperor's decree, which had to be written out in classical Chinese; interpreters to smooth the way during tribute exchanges and tribute ceremonies held at the imperial palace in Nanjing; and skilled ship handlers to sail the tribute ships. It seems doubtful that the people of Chūzan had mastered all these skills themselves. If Chūzan could not have prepared the goods of tribute by itself, then we must assume there were people behind the scenes who made no appearance on the stage we see in the *Omoro sōshi*. These were the Ryukyu Kingdom's Chinese merchant immigrants.

## CHINESE IMMIGRATION TO THE RYUKYUS

### Authenticity of the "Grant of Thirty-Six Families from Min"

The foundation of Okinawa's Chinese community is described in *Chūzan seikan* [Reflections on Chūzan, 1650], an official history of the Ryukyu Kingdom.[5] It tells of the arrival of Chinese people after Emperor Hongwu "granted" the kingdom "thirty-six families of people from Min."[6] Other historical annals with later dates, such as *Chūzan seifu* [Genealogy of Chūzan, 1701/1725] and *Kyūyō* [Chronicle of Ryukyu, 1745–1876], pick up and repeat this information about the 1392 "Grant of Thirty-Six Family Names of People from Min."[7] These "people from Min" (modern Fujian) were professional translators and sailors engaged in the tribute system. The number "thirty-six," commonly used in Chinese idioms implying, for example, a great number of challenging tasks, or several different lines of battle, indicated the variety of responsibilities these people would have, rather than an exact count of the family names involved in the grant.

The *Chūzan seikan* is generally supposed to have been based on the *Dàmíng hùidiǎn* [Collected Statutes of the Ming Dynasty], published in the Wanli period (1573–1619), but its actual source materials are completely unknown. The *Míng shílù,* which is an important catchall history of the Ming period's governmental, social, and economic affairs, makes no mention of the thirty-six families.

### Overseas Chinese in the *Rekidai hōan* and the *Míng shílù*

The *Rekidai hōan* contains hints at the arrival of Chinese people. It records an official letter dated in the Ninth Month of 1431 (Xuāndé 6) and addressed to the Ministry of Rites in Beijing, the office that supervised King Shō Hashi's tribute legations. The subject of the letter concerns a request by Pān Zhòngsūn, a navigator from Changle Prefecture near Fuzhou in Fujian, to retire to his hometown. In 1390, Pān had been officially named as a steersman to serve Ryukyu's tribute legations. He rose to the position of navigator in 1405, but now at the age of eighty-one was no longer able to carry out his duties. Note that Pān was already working as a steersman for a Ryukyuan tribute ship two years before the Grant of Thirty-Six Families in 1392.

Another entry, this time in the *Míng shílù,* dated the Fourth Month of 1411 (Yongle 9), notes that a certain Chéng Fù, from Raozhou (modern Boyang Prefecture) in Jiangxi, a region famous for its ceramics, had been given permission to return to his hometown. He had asked to retire, also at age eighty-one, after serving King Satto faithfully for some forty years. Counting back from Yongle 9 shows that Chéng must have begun working even before King Satto sent his first tribute offering in 1372 (Hongwu 5). Before Satto joined the tribute system, Ryukyu, like Japan and Southeast Asia, had communities of Chinese merchants running private business enterprises. Similar examples of other Chinese merchants in Southeast Asia requesting permission to return home to the villages they were born in show that such requests were not unique to the Chinese community in Ryukyu.

Large quantities of Chinese ceramics have been dug up from *gusuku* ruins dating to the fourteenth century, when the Yuan dynasty was coming to an end. We may understand that the contemporary demand for Chinese porcelain was great indeed. Built as they often were near harbors and at the mouths of rivers, many *gusuku* saw plenty of oceangoing traffic, and Chinese merchants seeking to establish bases for the far-flung Asian trade network had long been on the scene. Thus trade opportunities, so eagerly sought by Chinese merchants throughout their Asia-wide network, were also available in Ryukyu.

There remain some questions as to whether the above-noted imperial grant that is mentioned in the official histories sparked the formation of the Ryukyuan Chinese merchant community, though there is no denying the existence of people, such as Pān Zhòngsūn, who were involved in the tribute system by order of the Ming court.

However, it conforms better to the historical reality to say that the Chinese merchant community (in Okinawa) came into being essentially as a secondary consequence of the establishment and commercial interaction among Chinese merchant communities that were spreading throughout Asia at that time, and that the structure of these communities subsequent to the Ming court's ban on sea travel included the indigenized "smugglers" who could not be fit into the framework of the tribute trade system.

### Toward Tribute and Trade by Means of Alliance with Chinese Merchants

In fourteenth-century Ryukyu, a few all-powerful leaders addressed as *aji-osoi* by their lesser *aji* allies had emerged after a period in which each local lord had competed for dominance. We may surmise that a few Chinese merchants had established trading centers and were conducting their business while at the same time nurturing close relationships with their local *aji-osoi*. When Emperor Hongwu ascended the throne and issued his ban on sea travel, all such private commerce enterprises were forbidden. This brought to a sudden stop the import of quantities of Chinese porcelain and other goods in such demand in Ryukyu, which had been undergoing something of a "Chinese boom." Many of these merchants lost their livelihoods.

Another possibility for commerce did open up for them: handling tribute missions on behalf of the sovereign. Emperor Hongwu was determined to establish a strict tributary system, but it soon became clear that tribute missions would be allowed to carry "supplementary cargo" along with the formal tribute goods. Trade by individuals was not permitted under the tributary system; however, squeezing trade merchandise in as extra cargo on tribute missions was permissible.

Chinese merchants of the time stationed in Southeast Asia's international trade ports had developed a network tying them together and operated as important leaders of the East Asian and Southeast Asian commercial web. With the ban on sea travel and the formalization of the tributary system, these merchants with bases in the various regions of Southeast Asia were on-the-spot authorities on Chinese matters and became deeply engaged in the tribute missions to the Ming court.

In the case of Siam (Thailand), a number of Chinese merchants had been appointed to official positions, and their business acumen had been assimilated into the country's trade system. Thus, on the occasions of tribute missions, these men were tied to the ruling authorities and held positions of great responsibility within the tribute legations. Once exclusively engaged in private business enterprises throughout Southeast Asia, they entered into the public sphere when they assumed positions with the tribute legations. Without holding official authority in the Ming court, they were thus still able to participate openly in trade with China. This relationship between the Chinese merchants and the local governments, as has been pointed out previously by many scholars, was a convenient arrangement for both. The merchants became linked with the official authorities, and joining the tribute legations secured them the means to conduct trade legally. For the local governments, the relationship was a way to strengthen their position within the larger trading sphere. Recruiting among the Chinese allowed them to take advantage of their Chinese-language skills for drawing up official diplomatic letters, their familiarity with the trade customs of China and other foreign lands, and their excellent seamanship skills.

Finally, from China's perspective, having the overseas Chinese merchants join the tributary system gave China control regarding what special privileges, such as imposing no tariffs on tribute goods, would be accorded to them, as well as making it possible to secure a degree of stability as to the type of goods moving through the trade network.

Like their fellows in Southeast Asia, the Chinese merchants who held a central position in Ryukyu's trading community did not fail to jump at the new chance to make profit. However, independent merchants or groups were not permitted to join the tributary system. To join, it was necessary to be a royal authority officially invited by the Ming emperor. In what we now call Okinawa, unity remained to be achieved, with the three principalities still vying for supremacy. Despite this, King Satto of Chūzan sent the first tribute mission in 1372, followed by King Shōsatto of Sannan in 1380, and finally King Haniji of Sanhoku in 1383; each offered their tribute to the Ming court referring to himself as "king." It is highly unlikely that the Chinese merchants, who allied with the three kings to organize their tribute, did not also travel with the legations. Given their monopoly of such important positions as translators and navigators, the heavy involvement in the tribute missions by overseas Chinese was just as necessary in Okinawa as in the other lands of Southeast Asia. Thus all three of the Okinawan kings employed the Chinese merchants to manage their own tribute offerings, and each was recognized by the emperor as holding royal authority.

## THE MING DYNASTY PREFERENCE POLICY

### Most Numerous Tribute Missions

We have seen that Emperor Hongwu followed an unusual policy of preference toward Ryukyu and its tributary status. As soon as the Ming dynasty had been established, Hongwu dispatched his emissaries to the neighboring lands to proclaim his ascension and to demand that tribute be sent to his court. As he was the Virtuous Son of Heaven, the emperor's right to tribute was regarded as a matter of course; the resulting tribute legations to the court became excessively frequent. This annoyed Emperor Hongwu and provoked him to strictly limit how often a country might send legations to the court. Goryeo had sent so many that in the Tenth Month of 1372 (Hongwu 5), the emperor ordered it to limit its visits to once every three years. Similarly restricting schedules were imposed on Champa, Annam (Vietnam), Java, Pattani [in modern-day Thailand], Palembang [in modern-day Indonesia], Siam (also in modern-day Thailand), and Cambodia.[8] Ryukyu, on the other hand, sent its first legation soon after this order was given but was excused from the limited schedule; in contrast, it was designated as having no specific legation schedule. At times two or three ships would make port together, and though visits were limited to the seasons when the prevailing winds allowed passage across the ocean, some years saw the arrival of multiple Ryukyuan tribute legations.

From 1372, when the first Ryukyuan envoy went to China, the three principalities of Chūzan, Sannan, and Sanhoku sent frequent legations. During the Hongwu era (1368–1398) alone, the court accepted 32 legations from Chūzan, 13 from Sannan, and 12 from Sanhoku. In his discussion of these, Akiyama Kenzō provides a table that shows how often each tributary sent legations to the Ming court, based on his reading of the *Míng shǐ* [History of the Ming Dynasty, 1739]: Ryukyu sent 171 legations; Annam (Vietnam), 89; Tibet, 78; Hami, 76; Champa, 74; Siam (Thailand), 73; Turfan, 41; Java, 37; Samarkand, 36; Korea, 30; Cambodia, 14; and Pattani (part of modern-day Thailand), 8.[9] These figures from the *Míng shǐ* reflect only the number of actual *tribute* missions, not necessarily all formal visits, but they give us a good understanding of how many times Ryukyu sent envoys to the court.

### Various Preference Policies

Although the Ming court did provide tribute ships to other client states in order to maintain a degree of control over the tributary system, during the Hongwu and Yongle eras (1368–1424), China granted at least thirty oceangoing ships to Ryukyu. These ships came out of fleets attached to coastal military fortifications in Fujian and Zhejiang Provinces. These five-thousand- and one-thousand-man garrisons were established during the Ming period to protect coastal inhabitants from the incursion of marauding *wakō*. Ryukyu was the only nation gifted with so many ships, and we may understand from this how far the Ming court went in its preferential treatment. Included in the grant of ships were also the personnel, such as navigators, necessary to operate them.

The Ming tributary system controlled and limited the ports of entry and trading posts for tribute legations; each nation had its own designated locations for both. Originally, Ryukyu's port of entry was at Quanzhou, but its legations were not held to this and frequently arrived instead at Fuzhou to the north, or at Ningbo or Rui'an in Zhejiang Province. The Ryukyuans even had a compound at Rui'an, the Tōan Kan'eki [Dong'an Station], built for the use of their envoys and legations. These cities were chosen deliberately over Quanzhou for the convenience of purchasing large shipments of the porcelain from kilns such as Longchuan in Zhejiang and Tong'an in Fujian—porcelain being the trade item that the Ryukyuans needed most.

Additionally, after 1383, China tightened its control over the parallel and mutually reinforcing policies of the ban on sea travel and the tributary system with the introduction of sea-crossing permits [Ch. *kānhé,* J. *kangō*], verifying that ships were legitimate tribute vessels. Any ship desiring entry had to present a permit.

New papers were required, and tribute records wiped clean, every time a new emperor ascended the throne; yet again, however, Ryukyu was exempted from these rules. In Ryukyu's case, the royal government had the authority to issue a "half-seal verification license" [Ch. *bànyìn kānhé zhízhào,* J. *han'in kangō shissō*] that functioned as a sea-crossing permit.[10]

### Decoying the Pirates

Thus Ryukyu escaped from the stringent regulations regarding verification permits and apparently could enter China through any port of its own choosing. But we must wonder why Ryukyu alone was singled out for such preferential treatment.

During this period, the pirates continued to rampage along China's coast. Because they were based in Japan, the emperor viewed it as Japan's responsibility to take its proper place within the structure of East Asian society and take strong action to extirpate the terrible pirate menace. The letter Emperor Hongwu's envoy delivered to the Japanese court [see "Sending Envoys to Issue the Ascension Proclamation" at the beginning of this chapter] first clarified Japan's position in East Asia's international arena, of which China was the center. Second, it demanded that Japan crack down on the pirates wreaking such havoc on China's coasts and find a permanent solution for the problem.

Japan, however, refused, and the attempt at negotiation failed. Japan's entry into the tributary system and formal relations with China had to wait until 1401, when the envoy of Shogun Ashikaga Yoshimitsu appeared at the Ming court. Relations were interrupted after Yoshimitsu's death in 1408 by his heir Yoshimochi's refusal to pay tribute and resumed once again when Ashikaga Yoshinori finally dispatched another envoy in 1434. With a period of some sixty years stretching between the Hongwu emperor's initial ascension proclamation and Japan's permanent entry into the tributary system, it was clearly not an easy matter for Japan to become a part of the system.[11]

The Ming court's diplomatic overtures to Japan were hampered by its insistence that Japan deal with the pirates. Needless to say, throughout the delay, the Chinese coast continued to suffer under the marauders' repeated onslaughts. China's dual policies of enforcing the prohibition on ocean travel and strengthening the coastal defenses were aimed at eliminating both *wakō* and Chinese smugglers, but there was no way for China to force Japan to act on these matters. Thus it became Emperor Hongwu's plan to divert the pirates and the smugglers away from the Chinese coast by assigning its newest tributary state of Ryukyu, flush with new power, the role of decoy.

### Naha as Slave Market

Once Ryukyu had embarked upon tributary exchanges with China, it became a gathering place for pirates in search of Chinese merchandise. Furthermore, Chinese smugglers, circumventing the ocean travel ban in their quest for high profits, appeared in the Ryukyuan archipelago, sailing from island to island and conducting their clandestine business. People taken in pirate raids were also offered for sale at a slave market in Naha. An entry in *Goryeosa* [J. *Kōraishi,* History of Korea, 1451] for the Eighth Month of the first year of the Gongyang era (1389) tells of a group of Koreans captured by pirates whom King Satto of Chūzan in the land of Ryukyu returned to their homeland. There is also a record of Satto sending home thirty-seven Koreans in the Eighth Month of 1390 (Hongwu 23).[12]

These returns continued after the new Joseon dynasty [1392–1910] took power in Korea, and in the First Month of 1416 (Yongle 14) the Joseon court dispatched one Li Gei [Yi Yun] to Ryukyu to secure the return home of forty-four more Koreans.[13] The inhabitants of the Korean peninsula and the Chinese coastal areas were targets for the pirate slavers, and they were transported to many different markets to be sold. Naha was one, and thus Ryukyu was involved in the pirates' trade in human beings. It was the

Ming court's plan that Naha should become a rich trade market that would attract the pirates and encourage them to sell their captives there.

### Important Partner to the Ming Court

For the Ming court, however, Ryukyu was more than just a manager for trade outside its borders. According to a 1394 entry in the *Míng tàizǔ shílù,* at the request of Chūzan's King Satto, Yà Lánpáo, a Chinese merchant serving as a royal minister in Ryukyu, was granted the senior fifth rank, and two court interpreters, one named Yé Xīyǐn, were given official posts as commandants of *qián hù* [thousand-man installation].[14] Ministerial posts in the royal government are discussed in the first section of Chapter Five, but here we should note the placement of Yé Xīyǐn and his colleague at one of the coastal military fortifications.

These *qián hù* were military encampments manned by about one thousand soldiers and officers, established along the Chinese coast to provide some protection against the pirates' invasions. The Ming court appointed Chinese based in Ryukyu to officer positions in these *qián hù* camps, possibly to construct an information-gathering network for news about Japan and the pirates. None of Emperor Hongwu's diplomatic missives remain, but surely the Ryukyuans must have provided the Ming court much information regarding the pirates.

In 1432 (Xuande 7), the emperor dispatched his envoy Chái Shān [J. Saizan] to Japan to invite the Muromachi *bakufu* to send a tribute legation, ordering Ryukyu to act as a mediator in the negotiations. Thus the Ryukyuans bore responsibilities as diplomatic liaisons to Japan, in addition to acting as "decoys" for the pirates, collecting and conveying information on their movements, and guarding against them. That the ships granted to the Ryukyuans ostensibly to carry their tribute legations were in fact naval ships attached to the coastal defense installations has already been discussed; we must also assume these ships were not intended actually to be used only to send tribute, but as part of the effort to suppress the pirates, led by overseas Chinese merchants with appointments as military officers.

Throughout this period, the Ming court was dealing with remnants of the Yuan dynasty and its allies north of the Great Wall, and stationing troops to guard the border area. Ryukyu was additionally valued for its tribute goods, which included the sulfur and horses so important to the Ming's military needs. Thus we see that Ryukyu became a prominent figure on the world stage as an important client state of China, with connections to China's antipiracy policy and its military strategy. With this relationship as a base, Ryukyu ventured to expand its role as Cornerstone of East Asia.

CHAPTER THREE

# Ryukyu in the East Asian Trade Sphere

## THE ADVENT OF THE GREAT TRADE ERA

### Development of Trade in Southeast Asia

The Chinese merchants whose trade ships had long plied the oceans between Japan and the South Seas suffered a heavy blow under the limitations of the Ming dynasty's tributary system and its ban on ocean travel. In contrast, Ryukyu benefited greatly under China's tribute system and its strict enforcement of the ban that effectively ended private Chinese enterprise on the open seas. The Ryukyuans pursued with gusto commerce and trade opportunities in ports all over Southeast Asia, building on the trade network already established in every corner by Chinese merchants (see Map 2). They brought in the Chinese and Japanese goods in high demand and then returned to the markets of Japan and China carrying the products of the Southeast. They profited greatly as the middlemen in a transit trade system they exploited to its fullest.

The *Rekidai hōan* includes records of trade and other exchanges between the Ryukyu Kingdom and the various lands of Southeast Asia, including Malacca, Annam (Vietnam), Palembang, Java, Samudera, Pattani, and Sunda.[1] The earliest connection we know of was with Siam (Thailand) and its port at Ayutthaya, with access to the rest of the world via the Chao Praya River. Samudera had the port city of Pasai about three kilometers [two miles] up the Pasai River in the northeastern part of Sumatra. The main port for Java was at Gresik; Palembang lay about ninety kilometers [fifty-four miles] up the Musi River in the southeast corner of Sumatra. Sunda's port city of Kalapa, modern Jakarta, was in western Java. Pattani, on the eastern coast of

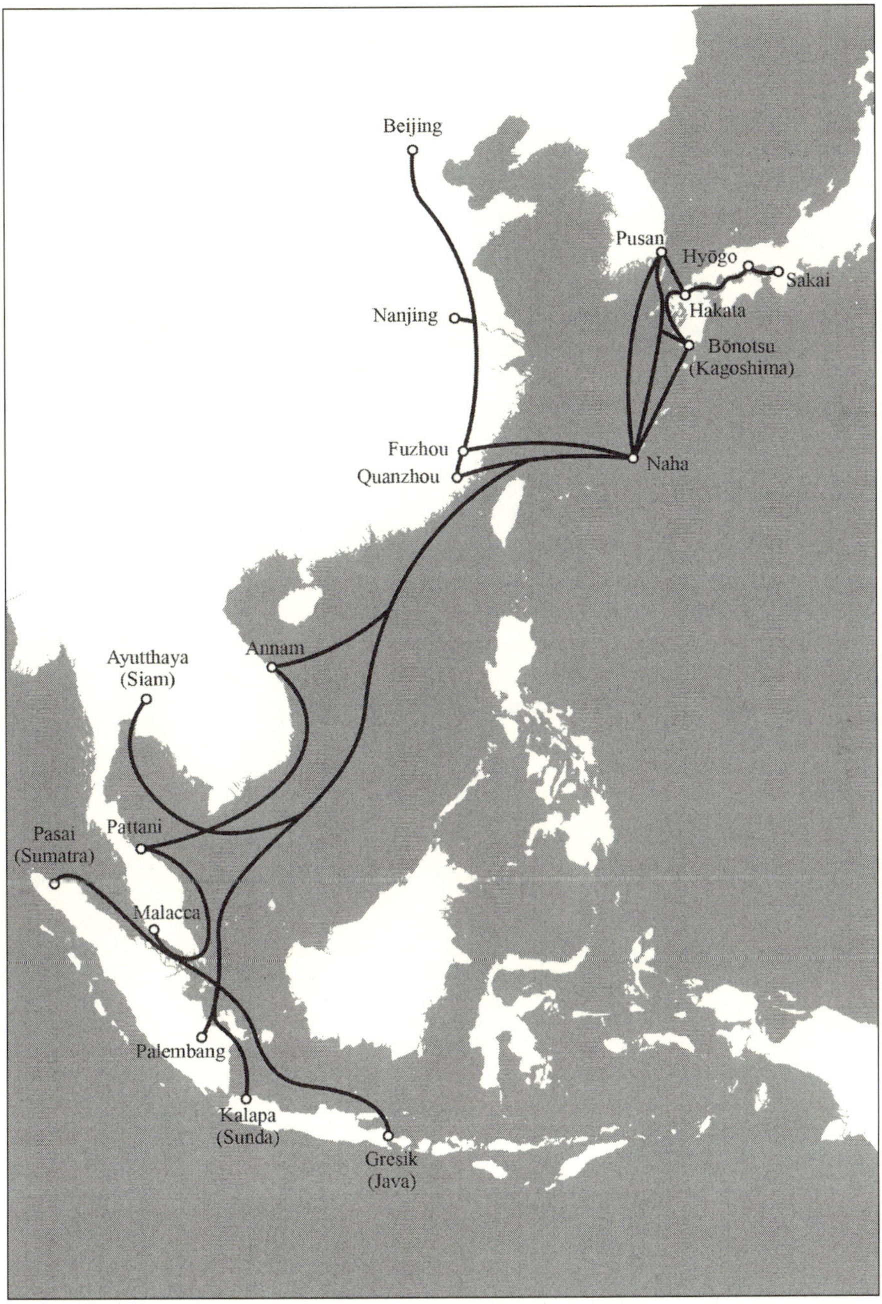


*Map 2.* Trade routes followed by Ryukyuan traders in the fourteenth through sixteenth centuries.

the Malay Peninsula, was a Thai port city once known as Langkasuka. There is also mention of Tonkin [now Hanoi] in the north of Annam, and of Hoi An and Da Nang [both in Champa], in its central region. Malacca, at the southern end of the Malay Peninsula and today one of Malaysia's state capitals, was an international port where traders from both East and West met, and it grew wealthy from its role as the central link in the spice trade between Europe, the Middle East, and Asia. It is evident that Ryukyu's trading grounds covered the entire region of Southeast Asia.

Besides the Chinese celadon that was in such demand in the region, the Ryukyuans' merchandise included Japanese daggers, fans, and copper; also sulfur, horses, mother-of-pearl, summer-weight cloth, oxhide, and other goods produced in their own islands. In exchange they accepted the products of the South Sea islands, such as sappanwood, pepper, cloth, liquor, ivory, and tin. Foremost among these was the sappanwood, used in making a red dye, and pepper, valued for its flavor; these two items were possibly the most important of all the South Seas trade goods.

The Ryukyuan ships carried more of the Chinese porcelain than any other item, but the higher-quality celadon made a very fragile cargo. To reduce risk, the sea traders carried mainly small pieces that were cheaper and sturdier and could be shipped across the rough seas with less breakage.

### Ryukyuans in the Words of Portuguese Traders

In *Commentarios do grande Afonso Dalboquerque* [1774 ed.], the Portuguese nobleman Afonso de Alboquerque described the Ryukyuans, whom he called Gores, who could be seen in contemporary Malacca:

> The land of these Gores is called Lequea; the men are fair; their dress is like a cloak without a hood; they carry long swords after the fashion of Turkish cimetars, but somewhat more narrow; they carry also daggers of two palms' length; they are daring men and feared in this land [of Malacca]. When they arrive at any port, they do not bring out their merchandize all at once, but little by little; they speak truthfully, and they will have the truth spoken to them. If any merchant in Malaca broke his word, they would immediately take him prisoner. They strive to dispatch their business and get away quickly. They have no settlement in the land, for they are not the men to like going away from their own land. They set out for Malaca in the month of January, and begin their return in August and September. The usual course of their navigation is to beat up the channel between the islands of Celate and the point of Singapura, on the side of the mainland.[2]

In a letter to Afonso de Alboquerque, a Portuguese imprisoned at Malacca named Rui de Araújo noted the royal government's trade monopoly when he wrote, "The Gores come every year in junks owned by their king, and the king allows no one but his own vassals to travel."[3] Tomé Pires, who worked at the Portuguese trading station in Malacca, wrote in his *Suma Oriental* [*An Account of the East, from the Red Sea to China,* 1512–1515] that the Ryukyuans were called the Lequios, as well as the following:

> Just as we in our own kingdoms speak of Milan, so the Chinese and people of all the other lands speak of the Lequios. They are truthful men; they do not buy slaves; so they would not sell their own countrymen for anything in the world. They would rather die than do this. . . . The Lequios freely sell their goods for credit. If they find they have been cheated when the times come to collect payment, they will collect it sword in hand.[4]

With these images of successful traders, heroic men of honor with no fear of traveling the distant seas, de Alboquerque, Rui de Araújo, and Tomé Pires have handed down to us a romantic picture of the Gores, the Lequios.

### Sea Trade Routes and Seasonal Trade Winds

The official ships [Ch. *shǐchuán,* J. *shisen*] dispatched to the South Seas from Ryukyu could include crews of more than two hundred men. Among them would be between twelve and thirty officials, including a chief envoy [*seishi*], vice envoy [*fukushi*], interpreter [*tsūji*], captain [*kachō*], cargo master [*kansen chokko*] (or purser [*jimuchō*]), and pilot [*shōsui*].[5] According to the *Xīngchá shèngrǎn* [J. *Seisa shōran,* Survey of Official Voyages, 1436], the tribute ships followed a regular sea route. Upon departing from Ryukyu, they headed first over the horizon to the port of Wuhumen in Fujian, then continued to Champa, taking about ten days; with favorable winds they could reach Siam in about forty-six days.[6] Okinawa lies in the East China Sea, where in winter a north wind blows, caused by a high-pressure front over the continent; in summer, the Ogasawara high-pressure front sends a steady south wind. In April and May, the seasonal winds shift from north to south; the north winds return in September and October. September through November presented the best conditions for ships sailing from Ryukyu to China and the lands of Southeast Asia; the return trips usually relied on the southerly winds of March and April. The conditions for the journey to China and Southeast Asia are described in this *Omoro sōshi* song about a ship called the *Bellringer:*

| | |
|---|---|
| *Mafafe suzunari kiya* | True South-wind Bellringer: |
| *Mafai saramekeba* | When the true South Wind blows |
| *Tau Naban* | From China, from the Southern lands |

| | |
|---|---|
| *Kamafe tsute mioyase* | Carry tribute for the King and offer it up. |
| *Owechife suzunari kiya* | Following-wind Bellringer: |
| *Owechife saramekeba* | When the Following Wind blows[7] |

## TRADE WITH KOREA AND JAPAN

### Relations with Korea

In the Chinese world, in addition to the unequal relationship between the Chinese emperor and the kings of the various neighboring countries, a sort of "protocol among equals" [J. *teki-rei*] had to be observed between these kings, with the assumption of "equality" or "equivalence" between them. That is, the surrounding nations possessing a "patent of investiture" [J. *sappō* or *sakuhō*] from the Ming emperor regarded one another, in principle, as equals in rank. These countries exchanged correspondence in the form of official communiqués called *zīwén* [J. *shibun*]. Such were the circumstances under which the small island kingdom of Ryukyu formed its active and flourishing friendship with Korea and the Joseon dynasty.

The friendly relations between Ryukyu and Korea dated to 1389, when Chūzan's King Satto sent a representative named Okci [Ch. Yùzhī, J. Okuchi] to Goryeo with gifts of sulfur, sappanwood, and pepper, as well as a number of Koreans who had been captured by the pirates. In response, Goryeo began sending agents such as Kim Yun Hwu to sail on the Ryukyuan ships.[8] These ties continued even after the Goryeo dynasty fell in 1392, and Yi Seong-gye ascended the throne and began calling his country Joseon. In general, the exchanges with Joseon consisted of Ryukyu returning people captured by the pirates or rescued while adrift at sea, and of the Korean king sending gifts of thanks in return. The two nations did not really form a commercial relationship based on trade.

According to the *Sejong sillok* [Annals of Sejong, 1454], envoys of the Ryukyuan king had status equal to that of the envoys of the Japanese king.[9] However, when the Ryukyuan king sent an official communiqué, it was answered by the Koreans not with a *zīwén* but with a less formal letter that deliberately disregarded the above-mentioned "protocols." Furthermore, Korea ranked one level above Ryukyu within the Chinese tributary system, so it held itself as the superior in matters of culture and government. There was no sense on the Korean side that the newly emerged nation of Ryukyu was an equal, despite their diplomatic ties. In the 1450s, merchant ships from Hakata, Tsushima Island, and other parts of Kyushu frequently carried envoys back and forth to Korea; Ryukyuan envoys began to replace some of the monks and merchants from Kyushu as passengers. With events such as the dispatch of Ryukyuan envoys to Korea to obtain a copy of the complete Buddhist canon, the Tripitaka, the emphasis for both Ryukyu and Korea was on developing a mutually rewarding relationship of proper formality and good neighborliness, rather than becoming economic trading partners.

### Ryukyu Seen as a Vassal by the Ashikaga Shogun

Relations with Japan were another matter altogether. The famous "Bridge of Nations" Bell [J. *Bankoku shinryō no kane*], cast during the reign of Shō Taikyū (r. 1454–1460), has an inscription praising Ryukyu's prosperity. Part of the inscription reads, "The land of Ryukyu is a lovely place in the South Seas. An admirer of Korea's excellence, cheek-to-jaw with China, and close as lips and teeth with Japan, this legendary island evokes admiration in its neighbors. Traveling by ship, its people form a bridge between the many various countries, filling its temples with the most precious goods and exotic products of foreign lands." Ryukyu was the "Bridge of Nations" because it was a link between the various lands of Asia, with its "cheek-to-jaw" closeness with China, and its "close as lips and teeth" relationship with Japan. We may surmise from these expressions the intimacy of their ties. With its development as a transit trade hub, the kingdom held Japan and China in positions of equal importance.

The oldest document from this period concerning the intercourse between the Ryukyu Kingdom and the Japanese mainland is a missive sent by Shogun Ashikaga Yoshimochi to Ryukyu's King Shō Shishō in 1414 (Ōei 21). The message begins, "We have carefully read your message, having received the above items [on this day] the 25th Day of the Eleventh Month in the 21st year of the Ōei Era. To the King of the Land of Riukiu."[10] This letter is discussed further later in this chapter, but it is worth noting that the language and style used is that of the shogun to one of his vassals within Japan. It differs somewhat in that the date stamp reads *toku yū rin* [neighbor of virtue], which was not used on correspondence within Japan. Thus even as the Ashikaga shogun regarded the king of Ryukyu as a head of state, this hints at his view of the king as his vassal, as well.

### Ryukyu, Korea, and Japan Pursue Independent Diplomatic Courses

Japan was in no way sincere in its professed submission to China, even after Ashikaga Yoshimichi had officially become a tributary state head and received a patent of investiture. As a matter of etiquette, letters to the Ming emperor were dated according to the Chinese imperial era and the shogun referred to himself as "the king of Japan" and a "servant" of the emperor.

Letters to Korea, however, did not use the Chinese calendar, giving instead the zodiac year or Japan's own era date; neither did these letters use the term "king of Japan," required under the "protocol among equals." The Ashikaga shogun's letters to Korea used the same calendar as in communications with Ryukyu, as well as the *toku yū rin* stamp. He took a traditional approach to international relations and held that Japan outranked Korea. As for the upstart Ryukyu Kingdom, the shogun regarded it in part as a foreign country and in part as a vassal to Japan—an approach unique among the East Asian community.

For his part, when the king of Ryukyu addressed a missive to the *bakufu,* he did not use his royal name but instead the idiosyncratic Ryukyuan designation *yo no nushi* [master of the era], indicating that these communications were not equivalent to the *zīwén* sent to other kings in Southeast Asia. The Far East Asian community, consisting of Japan, Korea, Ryukyu, and China, with the last the center of a system of tribute and bestowal of authority, made up a bloc within the larger region of Asia; yet, in fact, China's goal of a "protocol among equals," in which all behavior was regulated according to Confucian ritual ideals, was never fully achieved even there. The three smaller nations did not submit to Ming diplomatic leadership, but instead determinedly pursued their own interests without letting themselves be fully regulated by the tributary system or the grant of patents of investiture.

### Old Ryukyu as a Foreign Land

Although it cannot be said that the Ryukyu Kingdom enjoyed a relationship of equals with the Japanese *bakufu,* neither was its king a "vassal" of Japan. In 1306, Chikama Tokiie bequeathed to his heirs his stewardship rights to land in Satsuma's Kawanabe County, as well as holdings that included Kikaijima, Amami Ōshima, Erabu, and Tokunoshima in the modern Satsunan island group. However, an entry in the *Yijo sillok* [Annals of the Yi Dynasty, J. *Richō jitsuroku*] for 1453 tells of the monk Dōan of Hakata, who, acting as an envoy of Ryukyu, returned home two Koreans who had been shipwrecked. Four people had washed up on the island of Gaja in the Tokara group in 1450, but because at that time control of the island was shared between Satsuma and Ryukyu, two survivors had gone to Ryukyu, and two had been taken in by Satsuma.[11] King Seongjong of Korea had appointed his prime minister, Sin Sukju, to compile the *Haedong jeguk gi* [Annals of the Lands of the Eastern Sea, J. *Kaitō shokoku ki*] in 1471. It included a map of Kyushu, brought to Korea by Dōan, that also showed the island of Gaja as under the shared rule of Japan and Ryukyu and forming the border between them.[12] The *Kyūyō* [1745], an official history of the Shuri royal government, records that in 1466, King Shō Toku personally led troops to conquer Kikaijima in the Amami island group.[13] The kingdom held the island as an independent territory until the late fifteenth century; its influence extended as far as the northern half of the Tokara island group. The region was self-governing, and not under the rule of Japan's feudal government. The Ryukyu of this period, during which the kingdom was created through territorial expansion and military strength, coeval with Japan's early feudal age, is known as "Old Ryukyu" (Ko Ryūkyū). From Japan's point of view, Old Ryukyu was "other"; it was a "foreign land" and thus distinct from all other territories within Japan.[14]

### Establishment of the Ryukyu Magistrates and the Circulation of Yongle Copper Currency

Among the most important trade goods brought to Japan by the Ryukyuans were Chinese satin and licorice root; from Southeast Asia came sappanwood, spices, cinnabar, and ivory; agarwood [J. *jinkō*], sandalwood [J. *dankō*], and costus root [J. *mokkō*] for incense; and prepared stick incense in bundles. These luxury goods from China and the South Seas were in high demand, eagerly sought by the nobility. The ingredients for perfume, dyes, and medicines sold at very high prices, and fragrant woods were used by the Kyoto nobility, the daimyo class, and wealthy merchants in the art of blending and enjoying incense. These goods came into Japan not only on Ryukyuan trade ships, but also on those of merchants (including pirates) operating out of places like Hakata and Tsushima.

The Muromachi *bakufu* installed at the port of Hyōgo [modern-day Kobe] a Ryukyu magistrate [*bugyō*] to oversee cargo that arrived on Ryukyuan ships. These ships followed a route north to Hakata, passing through Akamagaseki (now Shimonoseki) on their way to Hyōgo on the Inland Sea, to acquire the fans, screens, and elegant accessories such as daggers to be used in their trade, or as tribute to the Ming court. The goods brought in by the Ryukyuans were taken to the Kinki region (Osaka and Kyoto) by merchants representing the great merchant houses of Sakai, the merchant community and port for Osaka. The spices and fragrances passed through the hands of numerous southwestern daimyos, such as Lord Tanegashima, Sagara of Higo, Shimazu of Satsuma, and Shibuya Mitsuyori (priestly name, Dōchin), the commissioner for Kyushu, and his son Yoshitoshi. These items were also frequently reexported to Korea.

Finally, Chinese Yongle currency (copper cash) was an important part of the cargo Ryukyu transported to Japan. Known during the Muromachi period as *eidaka,* these coins played an important role in developing the period's monetary economy, circulating in the marketplace and allowing standard prices to be set for commodities. Also in wide use in the port cities of Southeast Asia of the fifteenth and sixteenth centuries, Yongle currency was the common means of payment across a vast area and was key in the development of the regional trade sphere. Ryukyu needed an established and guaranteed currency to ensure smooth trading in Japan and Southeast Asia, and it obtained a large quantity of Yongle coin during the course of its tribute missions early in the Ming dynasty. Thus, in addition to being the instrument of Ryukyu's expansion of trade over a large region, use of this Yongle coin linked China, Japan, and Southeast Asia together and formed the basis of a vigorous economy.

### Japanization of Ryukyuan Culture Begins

Many Japanese people traveled to and from the kingdom during this period. Buddhism is believed to have been brought in by the monk Zenkan during the Kanjun era (1265–1274); King Eiso embraced Buddhism and built the Gokurakuji at Urasoe Gusuku as a residence for Zenkan. Later, around 1368, the Buddhist priest Raijū came to Ryukyu from Satsuma's Bōnotsu Ichijōin and established the Naminoue Gokokuji as a temple where King Satto could offer prayers.

Buddhism's spread through Ryukyu intensified during the reign of King Shō Taikyū of the First Shō dynasty. During this time, envoys were dispatched to Korea to obtain a copy of the Buddhist canon (Tripitaka), and the famous Zen monk Kaiin visited from Nanzenji, one of the Kyōto Gozan temples, the five most important Rinzai temples in that city. He became the founding patriarch of Tenryūji, Fumonji, and Kōgenji and had temple bells cast to bestow on each. Kaiin performed important service in the diplomatic relations between Ryukyu and the Ashikaga shogunate, and King Shō Taikyū named him *kokushi* [nation's teacher] to honor his work. Kaiin is also known as the founder of Enkakuji, the most important Zen Buddhist temple in the kingdom, in the family precincts of the Second Shō dynasty.

Besides these monks connected with the Gozan tradition, other Zen Buddhist monks also came to Ryukyu. Missionary work continued under the patronage of several successive Ryukyuan kings, and envoys were sent out to conduct negotiations with Japan. In addition, Ryukyuan-born monks went to study at the Gozan temples, and relations were especially strong with the Zen monks of Daitokuji, which was outside of the *bakufu*-sponsored Gozan community. These monks introduced Japanese culture and literature to Ryukyu society. They also brought many tales of the origins of Shinto and its shrines. They established shrines of the Kumano sect, and they widely propagated belief in the cult of the "Kumano avatars."[15]

After the fifteenth century, Naha was a center of trade that fell mainly under the purview of well-capitalized merchants from Sakai and Hakata. Sailing on ships dependent on the seasonal winds meant that when they set out on a trade voyage, these merchants also had to spend considerable amounts of time waiting for the winds to change before they could return home. We can assume that residential districts that might be called "Little Japans" came into existence. The establishment of Kumano shrines may well have been connected with the belief in the ocean-dwelling Kumano avatar by Japanese who spent their lives on the sea and who prayed at the shrines for safe sailing. Among the Japanese who flourished in Ryukyu, some settled there permanently, and many Ryukyuan noble families claimed Japanese ancestors as their family founders. The era of Old Ryukyu thus underwent a profound "Japanization" with the frequent arrival of Japanese people, goods, and culture.

## NAHA PORT: HUB OF INTERNATIONAL TRADE

### Naha, Flourishing Transit Trade Port

After gaining control of Chūzan in 1406, Shishō and Hashi, father and son, went on to subdue Sanhoku in 1416 and Sannan in 1429, finally establishing a unified island polity. Theirs was the First Shō dynasty, and it marked the creation of the Ryukyu Kingdom, with a single monarch as its head of state. From that moment, Shuri became a true capital, the seat of an independent king who was the focus of international relations with China and who held a patent of investiture bestowed by the Ming emperor. Naha lay about five kilometers [three miles] to the west of Shuri, and unlike today, it was built on sandbanks in the estuary through which three rivers, the Kokubagawa, the Nohagawa, and the Kumojigawa, flowed into the sea. The area was an estuary in which freshwater and salt water met, preventing the formation of a coral reef and resulting in an excellent natural harbor.

During the reign of King Shō Kinpuku (r. 1450–1453), a causeway with seven sluice gates, called the Chōkōtei, and linking to Shuri Castle, was built along the river inlets. Naha's harbor was renovated during the reign of King Shō Toku, and taking a leading part in the intercourse between the nations around the China Sea allowed the Ryukyu Kingdom to enjoy an unprecedented level of prosperity during the fifteenth century. As the hub for sea routes between Ryukyu and Fujian; Ryukyu and Southeast Asia; Ryukyu and Bōnotsu, Hakata, Tsushima, and Korea; Ryukyu and Hyōgo and Sakai, Naha was an international trade port. The *Omoro sōshi* provides us with a description:

| | |
|---|---|
| *Shiyori owaru Tedako-ga* | The Sun King who resides in Shuri |
| *Ukishima-fa gerafete* | Constructed at Ukishima |
| *Tau Nahan yoriyau Nafatomari* | Naha Port, where ships from China and the South Seas gather |
| *Gusuku owaru Tedako-ga* | The Sun King who resides in the Precinct[16] |

**Naha in Joseon Historical Documents**

A 1453 (Jingtai 4) entry in the *Kaitō shokokuki* (K. *Haedong jeguk gi,* Annals of the Lands of the Eastern Sea) contains the oldest known printed map of Ryukyu, presented to the Korean court by the monk Dōan when he was envoy on behalf of King Shō Kinpuku.[17] On it, the island of Okinawa is drawn to resemble a sea horse. "Naha Port" is written in large characters in the bay defined by the sea horse's curling tail. Smaller characters reading *hōko* [宝庫 treasure house] and *kokko* [国庫 national treasury] are visible. The *hōko* was a warehouse built on an exposed reef and served as the royal government's storehouse for the goods gathered in the international trade; it was later known as *o-mono gusuku* [precinct of royal treasures].

The eyewitness account of Cho Tukseng, a Korean rescued from shipwreck in 1462, said of the *hōko:* "There is a fort built at the side of the river. In its inner rooms are kept large pieces of porcelain; the wine cellar is filled to overflowing with jugs of wine; and the magazine is stuffed with iron armor, javelins, swords, bows, and arrows."[18]

The *kokko* is described in the *Ryūkyūkoku yuraiki* [Origin of the Ryukyu Nation, 1713] as "the place dedicated to selling off public goods," in other words, a marketplace under government management where trade goods were bought and sold.[19] This later came to be known as the *oya mise* [great market]. The section titled *"Ryūkyūkoku ki"* (*Notes on the Ryukyu Nation*) in the *Kaitō shokokuki* records that Chinese, Southeast Asian, and Japanese merchant ships visited Naha's port to conduct business at its commercial marketplace.[20]

On the northern side of the port lay a district called Tōei [lit., Tang flourishing], marked on the old map as Kumeri [久米里] and later known as Kumemura [久米村, Ryu. Kuninda], where many overseas Chinese merchants lived. According to an account in *Yijo sillok* based on the words of a group of Koreans shipwrecked in 1479, this Chinese residential area had "Chinese merchants coming to do business, and some who lived there."[21] The ban on sea travel had been imposed in 1394 and renewed in 1397, 1433, and 1449; these Chinese merchants sailing in "to do business" were smugglers slipping through gaps in the nets spread by the strict ocean travel prohibition policy.

Finally, those who "lived there" were Chinese merchants settled permanently in Kumemura, with no plan to return home. The royal government employed many of these overseas Chinese to develop its commerce, and they developed close ties with the royal government. They did not assimilate to the local culture, but rather maintained their native Chinese customs, wearing Chinese robes, sitting in chairs, and living in Chinese-style houses with tiled roofs and walls ornamented in red lacquer. They joined the royal government's tribute missions, and just as they continued their own trade with Naha as their base, surely they also formed a vivid part of the scenery in port cities throughout Southeast Asia.

### Overseas Chinese Monopolize Ministerial Posts; Kai Ki Enters the Stage

In 1370, the Ming dynasty established a royal government [*ōfu*], also called the royal bureaucracy [*ōshōfu*], for the benefit of the royal princes who had distributed patents of investiture to China's neighbors.[22] This administration included positions for a chancellor [*ōshō*], a chief administrative officer [*chōshi*], and a director of records [*tenbo*]. The chancellor, who was of the upper second rank, counseled the ruler and oversaw the other royal ministries. Ryukyu modeled its own royal government on that of the Ming court, establishing an identical system. The Ming court itself abolished the position of chancellor in 1380 but permitted Shō Hashi to continue using the title for his chief counselor even after he unified all of Sanzan in 1429. The Ryukyuan chancellorship thus preserved was held, in the main, by Chinese immigrants. In the first year of the Ming dynasty, in addition to the king's tribute offerings, the chancellor had also offered gifts that were in turn reciprocated by the court.

In addition to their responsibilities in regard to the tribute missions, these immigrants remained closely linked with the royal government for the duration of its existence. The most famous example of these Chinese residents who were so closely tied to political power (and the royal authority) was Kai Ki [Ch. Huài Jī]. He is first mentioned in the *Míng shílù* as an envoy for the king of Chūzan to the Ming court, where he was given the rank of *chángshí* [chief administrative officer]. According to the *Míng shílù,* the inscription on a "stele at the Ankokuzan Garden" records that in 1427, in his position as prime minister, Kai Ki oversaw the excavation of a pond (the Ryūtan), building of terraces, and planting of trees and shrubs for a pleasure garden on the slopes of Mount Ankoku, just outside the walls of Shuri Castle. Kai Ki was also the motivator behind the construction of the Chōkōtei Causeway, which was intended to connect the royal capital at Shuri with Naha.[23]

A large and influential society of Chinese immigrants had developed in Palembang, in the southern part of Sumatra. They controlled the city under the Ming "Old Port Pacification Superintendency" [J. *kyūkō sen'ishi*, Ch. *jiùgǎng xuānwèishǐ*] and had gained permission from the Ming court to join the tributary system.[24] Trade and an exchange of correspondence addressed "to the Old Port Management Office" developed during this period as Kai Ki, in the name of chancellor, communicated with his equal, a consular official, because Palembang had no sultan at the time. From the end of the fourteenth century and into the fifteenth, the three principalities (Sanzan) centered on what we now call the island of Okinawa were still struggling with one another for supremacy. As Chūzan slowly gained the upper hand in achieving political unification, and as it worked to become the nation recognized by China as the Ryukyu Kingdom, its Chinese population became even more closely tied to the royal government, carrying out ever greater administrative and diplomatic duties.

In 1436, Kai Ki, who had some influence within Daoist circles as a member of the Quanzhen School, and Shō Hashi sent gifts to the grand master of the way of the celestial masters [a Ming authority in matters of geomancy], along with a letter requesting a protective talisman that would ward off bad spirits and bring fortune to the nascent kingdom. Two years later, in 1438, this talisman arrived in Ryukyu.[25] We may see from this request of a talisman, as Kai Ki worked alone with the king, how deep was his connection to the royal authority, and what a high standing he held within the royal government.

## RETREAT FROM THE PREFERENCE POLICY

### Trade Brokers in Quanzhou

Quanzhou is located on the left bank of the Jin River where it enters Quanzhou Bay. During the Tang dynasty, Muslim traders frequently visited the city and conducted a considerable trade from the "foreign quarters," a settlement for the exclusive use of foreigners. The city's population reached five hundred thousand in the Southern Song dynasty, and by the Yuan dynasty it was famous throughout the world as China's greatest South Sea trading port. Marco Polo and Moroccan scholar and traveler Ibn Battuta called the city Zayton and reported it as the busiest and most prosperous port in the world.[26]

The city name Zayton, for Quanzhou, was derived from its Chinese nickname of Cìtóng Chéng [Coral Tree City], for the coral trees that grew all around the city. The Ryukyuan mission had its official residence, the Rai'en'eki, just outside the city's southern gate along a branch of the Jin

River. The Rai'en'eki had to be outside the city walls, because foreigners were generally not permitted to reside within the walls of the city itself. Nearby lay the so-called Treasure Quarter [Ch. Jùbaǒjiēi] where both buyers and sellers gathered to deal in imported merchandise. The Treasure Quarter of Zayton is said to have been the oldest shopping district of its kind, where every possible kind of merchandise of every age, East or West, could be found. The Rai'en'eki stood near the Treasure Quarter, and an appreciable quantity of goods brought in on Ryukyuan ships could be found there. Furthermore, the merchants of the Treasure Quarter offered many of the trade goods required by the Ryukyuans.[27]

All the merchandise brought in by tribute ships was subject to inspection by the Maritime Trade Office; when a ship came in to port, the office would assign a broker [Ch. *yáháng,* J. *gakō*] to oversee its transactions, a process referred to as "commerce" [Ch. *hùshì,* J. *goshi*]. The broker acted as an intermediary in business transactions, bringing together buyers and sellers and negotiating settlements between them. He bought and sold merchandise in required quantities and at required prices agreed on beforehand; for this he took a commission. In the course of his duties, the broker might collude with government officials and merchants, sometimes actively cheating the foreign traders, and sometimes taking advantage of the system to buy merchandise himself, then sell it later at a huge profit. During the Ming dynasty, all brokers were public officials; private brokers, who did not hold a broker's business permit, were not permitted; and it was not possible to circumvent these brokers and engage in trading tribute cargo without them.

Beginning in the fifteenth century, the harbor at Quanzhou began to silt up from deposits flowing down the Jin River. The harbor became very shallow and no longer navigable by large ships, and the city lost its position as the premier trade port to Fuzhou and Xiamen (Amoy). Fuzhou became the port of entry for tribute ships and the starting point of the overland route for tribute legations on their way to the capital, when the Maritime Trade Office was transferred there in 1469.

### Public Disorder in Fuzhou

Tribute ships had frequently docked in Fuzhou, even before the Maritime Trade Office moved there. In Fuzhou, where tribute ships came and went freely, there was a gradual unraveling of public order. Violence would frequently break out after disputes over the foreign trade, and tribute envoys and their personnel often engaged in a remarkable degree of misconduct. In one such incident, what came to be known as the Cài Jǐng [J. Sai Ei] scandal erupted when the Ryukyuan envoy Cài Jǐng was discovered wearing robes embroidered with "python dragons," for which permission had not been granted to the Ryukyuan king. When the police investigated, Cài Jǐng claimed that the king had received permission from the previous imperial court. Emperor Xianzong (r. 1464–1487) commanded the Ministry of Rites to check its records, and its findings made clear that this was not so. However, although the Chinese authorities found that Cài Jǐng indeed possessed the forbidden clothing of ribbed silk, and that he had had the clothes made illegally, they did not immediately move to punish him. A precedent existed in which the Chinese authorities did not intervene directly in such cases, but left up to the discretion of the Ryukyuan king any punishment for illegal actions by members of his legations. In fact, Ryukyu did not impose any punishment on Cài Jǐng, and he even served several more times as chief envoy of tribute legations to China.[28]

In addition to the kind of arrogant behavior displayed by Cài Jǐng, the Fujian government authorities were increasingly troubled by the number of people who arrived with the Ryukyuan tribute missions but who then settled permanently in China, often to establish and run family businesses. In 1472 the court issued an order to the effect that all such persons should return home. The emperor gave his permission for the Ministry of Rites to allow those who obtained a permit from the Ministry of Revenue to add their names to the family registry; all others must return to their native countries as required by the imperial order.[29] Thus, of the Ryukyuans who had once made up that nebulous group of "overseas Ryukyuans," those who were able to list their names in the Chinese family registry were completely absorbed into Chinese society, and the rest were punished with deportation. Probably most of these "overseas Ryukyuans" were in fact "overseas Chinese" immigrants to Ryukyu anyway. After this, Ryukyuans were no longer permitted to establish residences wherever they wished, but, in Fujian at least, were required to live at the Ryukyu House [Ryūkyūkan] in Fuzhou.

### A Murder Case Prompts the Restriction of Legation Residency Periods

The tribute legation members' unruly behavior caused numerous problems. In Huai'an Prefecture, an incident arose in 1473 in which a local was robbed and murdered by a member of the Ryukyuan legation.[30] The punishment for the repeated scandals surrounding the Ryukyuans took the form of the Chinese limiting them to one tribute mission every two years; restricting their meal allowance to cover a maximum of 150 people; and forbidding the inclusion, with the king's tribute and related goods, of private merchandise, the disposition of which had proved the cause of so many problems. In reality, such private merchandise had always been reported as being part of the official tribute goods, making it impossible for the Chinese inspectors to tell any difference between them; it continued to be transported along with the other tribute.

A report from the Ministry of Rites to the emperor in 1478 stated that in recent years, many Ryukyu tribute emissaries were persons who had "fled Fujian" (i.e., had escaped arrest in Fujian).[31] Since the beginning of the Ming dynasty, numerous Fujianese who had broken the law had taken refuge in Ryukyu. However, even given the many complaints about unruly behavior among the emissaries, limiting the tribute missions to once every two years was no small matter.

During the 1430s, under the Xuanzong era (1426–1435), Chinese interest in foreign affairs was very low, and ministers proposed the curtailment of subsidies granted to tribute legations. According to Hu Ying, a secretary in the Ministry of Rites who oversaw accommodations for legations, the size of the legations visiting the capital was far too large. Reasoning that hosting them was ruinous for the government, he requested in 1435 that the emperor set a limitation on the size of legations. In response, Emperor Xuanzong declared that the Ryukyuan mission to the capital would be limited to just twenty people, including the envoy and his vice envoy; any additional persons had to remain in Fuzhou.[32]

In 1439, a legation arrived from Ryukyu and took up residence in Fuzhou. The cost of provisioning the Ryukyu Compound is impossible to measure because by tradition its allowance was paid in kind, with goods such as salt and rice. However, the envoy pressed hard to change this and be paid in coin instead. The report that, as a result, 796,900 in copper cash had been paid out to the legation in less than half a year finally prompted the court to take action.[33] The Ryukyuans' frequent missions presented a considerable economic burden to the responsible ministries in Fujian and the capital. It also became a matter of political importance to reduce the burden put on the localities the legations passed through as they made their way to the capital. The robbery and murder in Fuzhou's Huai'an Prefecture had provided a direct pretext for limiting tribute missions to once in two years, but the motivation on the Chinese side to revise the policy of favorable treatment toward the Ryukyuans came in response to complaints of the heavy burden to communities hosting them along the route to the capital. Also strongly influencing this policy revision was the resumption of steady relations with Japan and its reentry into the tributary system, when Ashikaga Yoshimitsu sent a tribute mission to China in 1434. Hu Ying's application to the emperor that the Ryukyuans' legations to the capital be subject to limitations took place the very next year.

### Cessation of Grants of Sea Passage

Change in the policy of favoring Ryukyu was also evident in the matter of sea passage permits. Thirty ships were granted during the reigns of Hongwu and Yongle; even during the Zhengtong era (1436–1449), ships were frequently given in the same numbers as before. In 1449, however, pressure from the north by nomadic Oirats increased, and Emperor Zhengtong was taken prisoner at the Battle of Tumu Fortress. The Ming court began spending vast sums from the national treasury to strengthen its defenses and to fortify the Great Wall against invasion by the northern tribes. These military expenditures put the government's finances under great pressure, and the coastal defense system, which had been so vigorously reinforced since the beginning of the Ming dynasty, became subject to strict budget allocations, just like all the government ministries. Every local government came under heavy financial burdens, and the volume of shipbuilding fell precipitously.

These circumstances affected the grant of ships to Ryukyu. In 1450, the kingdom received permission to build ships at its own expense; thereafter, ships were built in Fujian with Ryukyuan funds.[34] During the reign of King Shō Sei (r. 1527–1555), the shipbuilding industry shifted to Ryukyu itself, and Ryukyuan-built hulls came to be used in the tribute trade. The policy of extreme favoritism toward Ryukyu as seen under Emperors Hongwu and Yongle faded under the straitened public finances and budgetary austerities of the Ming government, and this change was compounded by the decision of Ashikaga Yoshimitsu to rejoin the tributary system and finally to control and suppress the pirate menace.

## THE SHADOW OF DECLINE FALLS OVER THE ONCE-PROSPERING KINGDOM

### Prosperity of the Transit Trade and the Development of Centralized Rule

Just when Ryukyu was being limited to only one tribute mission every two years, its relations with the Muromachi shogunate were also changing. As mentioned earlier, all cargo brought into Hyōgo port (modern Kobe) in Ryukyuan ships was managed by a Ryukyu magistrate appointed by the Muromachi *bakufu*. The Ryukyuan royal government deeply resented the rigorous inspections conducted by this magistrate. Further, conditions became turbulent in 1467 when the Ōnin War broke out in Kyoto, and pirates began terrorizing the Inland Sea. As a result, Ryukyuan ships stopped making the passage to the Kinai region. The cessation of Ryukyuan shipping meant that the merchants of Sakai had difficulty obtaining the South Seas products, such as dyes, incense, and medicines, brought in by the trade ships and on which they depended for their highly profitable businesses in the Kyoto area. Some of these Sakai merchants did not possess the trade licenses issued by the *bakufu* to control trade and, bypassing regulations, made frequent journeys to Ryukyu.

In 1471, the *bakufu* declared that such travel to Ryukyu without the proper papers was forbidden. The ruling clan of Satsuma, the Shimazu, was given orders to apprehend these merchants, especially if they were found traveling with quantities of copper cash, and to forward the confiscated goods to Kyoto.[35] The Lord of Satsuma was the logical choice for the duty of controlling unauthorized ships because he already ran inspections on the numerous Ryukyu-bound ships that came into port at Bōnotsu in Satsuma, as well as controlling the important sea routes along the coast of his domain in southern Kyushu.

The Ryukyu Kingdom did not come under the rule of Japan's feudal government during this period, clearly retaining its status as an independent state and a "foreign land." Even if the Shimazu clan retained the control of the seas that allowed them to crack down on undocumented ships, the kingdom had no obligation to comply with these regulations. Authority over the Ryukyuan ships that docked at Naha Port belonged solely to the royal government.

The year after the Shimazu clan was charged by the shogunate with cracking down on illegal shipping, Shō En, strengthened by his close ties to the resident Chinese representatives who oversaw Ryukyu's international trade, toppled the First Shō dynasty in a coup d'état and founded the Second Shō dynasty. Three years later, China issued its order limiting tribute missions to once every two years, and the kingdom saw a great change in its trade environment. The kingdom covered the reduction in tribute missions by simply increasing the number of ships in each tribute fleet. The period during the reigns of King Shō Toku (r. 1461–1469), last king of the First Shō dynasty, and King Shō En (r. 1470–1476), founder of the Second Shō dynasty, showed a steady growth in Ryukyu's transit trade as its ships, joining the unauthorized Sakai traders, linked the merchants of Hakata with the feudal clans in or near Kyushu, including the Sō of Tsushima, the Sagara of Higo, the Tanegashima of Tanegashima, the Ōtomo of Bungo, the Ōuchi of Suō, and the military governor of the western provinces.

Continuing the expansion begun with the First Shō dynasty's campaign to take over Kikaijima in the Amami group in the late fifteenth century, in the spring of 1500, the third king of the Second Shō dynasty, King Shō Shin (Figure 3.1), sent a large army to the island of Ishigaki. There they suppressed

*Figure 3.1.* King Shō Shin (1465–1526, r. 1477–1526), who played a key role in centralizing and stabilizing the Ryukyu Kingdom. Painting by Shō Gen Kō, 1796.

the rebellion led by Oyake Akahachi, and the kingdom as a result achieved control of territory from the Amami island group in the north to Miyako and the Yaeyama island group in the south. Shō Shin's reign saw extraordinary changes in the nation's internal administration, even as trading conditions were getting tougher. All remaining *aji* were gathered to live in Shuri, the government's organization was reorganized and strengthened, and the hierarchy of priestesses who conducted the kingdom's religious rites and ceremonies was formalized. Shō Shin built a centralized government stronger than any seen before and laid the groundwork for a stable kingdom.

### Dispatch of the Royal Ship and Satsuma's "Red Stamp License" for the Sea Crossing to Ryukyu

Once Satsuma took on the task ordered by the *bakufu* of controlling unauthorized trade ships, the Ryukyuan royal government began to outfit its ships as royal vessels, or *ayabune* [crest ships]: painted on the bows were green swallows and golden dragons, and they flew ship flags showing the king's royal crest of three *tomoe,* comma-shaped emblems, embroidered on a dark blue cotton background. The point was to mark the ships as those sent to Satsuma to carry congratulations to the Shimazu clan for their newly acquired power. These "royal crest ships" were meant to preserve relations with Satsuma. The *Shimazu kokushi* [History of Shimazu, 1802] records that Ryukyu sent its first envoy ship to Satsuma in 1481 and that the Ryukyuan king did not send goods suitable for tribute but insisted on sending only luxury goods suitable for maintaining relations with a good neighbor and friendly nation.[36] Correspondence exchanged between Satsuma and the kingdom also spoke of an amicable "good-neighbor diplomacy," referring to both parties engaging in a perfectly equal relationship.[37]

A further expansion of trade tied to Satsuma's control of the sea lanes came when the Shimazu began seizing unauthorized ocean shipping bound for Ryukyu, and merchants from Sakai and Hakata began avoiding the seas around Satsuma. The frequency with which these illegal ships made the crossing was a matter of great concern to the Shimazu clan.

Finally, at the beginning of the Yongzheng era (1504–1520), the *bakufu* gave the Shimazu clan the right to issue its own permits to ships crossing to Ryukyu. With this, Satsuma began issuing the Ryukyu *tokai kangō* [sea crossing to Ryukyu permit] and Ryukyu *go-kangō* [Ryukyu permit], trade licenses stamped with a red seal. In taking the upper hand in controlling domestic trade with Ryukyu, Shimazu endeavored to reduce the influence of other domains there. In 1508, Shimazu Tadaharu sent a letter to the king of Ryukyu seeking agreement that any merchant ship bound for Ryukyu without the Shimazu seal permit would be subject to inspection on the Ryukyu side, and the ships and its goods confiscated if not properly credentialed.[38] This amounted to an attempt by Shimazu to obtain the Ryukyuans' acknowledgment of its monopolistic rights to the Ryukyuan trade. From the Ryukyuan point of view, Satsuma's intentions were to restrict its freedom to trade overseas; profits for merchants would decrease in the resulting market that did not allow competition; and obtaining quality goods would become difficult. Thus the royal government refused to consider the matter and denied Satsuma's request.

### Trade Brings Trouble

Among all the Southeast Asian countries with which Ryukyu conducted trade, only with Siam (Thailand) did trade continue without any breaks. During the reigns of Shō Toku and Shō En (1461–1476), the loss of its trade quarters in Palembang and Java led the kingdom to seek new trade relations in the rapidly rising centers of Malacca and Sumatra.

In all cases, except for Palembang, which had no king, diplomacy was conducted with exchanges of *zīwén,* letters used by states with rank as vassals of China, suitable under the "protocol among equals." In *zīwén* addressed to the king of Siam (Thailand), Ryukyu would request permission to purchase sappanwood to be sent the next year as tribute to the Ming court; letters to the sultan of Malacca seeking pepper, sappanwood, and other products also explained that these items were intended for the next year's tribute offering. The royal government in this way was taking clever advantage of the tribute system built up in Southeast Asia in part by the efforts of Zhèng Hé, whose seven long voyages on behalf of the Yongle emperor between 1405 and 1433 had laid the foundations of the system. By calling on the friendly relations between the various tributary nations, the Ryukyuans aimed to procure the South Seas commodities they needed. Many of the lands and regions with which they traded were indeed part of the Chinese sphere. At that time, the Chinese were vigorously seeking to exert a Confucian social order even into Southeast Asia, and the Ryukyuans made such lands as were within the Chinese area of influence the chief object of their trade activity. The reality of trade and trade relations, however, is that trouble cannot be avoided, and the Ryukyuans found that their trade dealings did not meet their expectations. For example, in Siam (Thailand) the royal family held a monopoly over foreign trade, and ordinary merchants were forbidden from entering into private deals. Government officials stationed in the port of Ayutthaya exercised their "special right of first refusal" [*senbai tokken*] to buy the shipments of Chinese ceramics at prices in their favor, denying the Ryukyuans any options except the government for buying the sappanwood and spices they sought. The Ryukyuans were eager to find a way around the strict regulations to which their business dealings were subjected by these officials.

Even in Malacca, the most important center of trade, complications abounded, despite public officials called *shahbandar* who oversaw business transactions for foreign traders and mediated in disputes between them.

In his letters to his son, Afonso de Alboquerque (mentioned earlier) wrote, "If any merchant in Malaca broke his word, they would immediately take him prisoner." Tomé Pires wrote in *Suma Oriental,* "If they find they have been cheated when the time comes to collect payment, they will collect it sword in hand."[39] Both of these passages speak of how the *shahbandar* officials handled trouble arising over business matters. In addition, their practice of displaying only a small portion of the goods they had to sell, instead of bringing them all out at once, implies that they took precautions in order to avoid being cheated in business transactions. Behind the public stage of trade in Southeast Asia, trouble was always brewing between powerful local government officials and trade merchants.

### Portuguese and Chinese Smugglers Appear in Southeast Asia

In China during this period (the Hongzhi era, 1488–1505), the supplementary trade goods brought along for private sale by the tribute legation became subject to customs tariffs. Ports also began to allow entry, with certain limitations, to private ships not serving as part of tribute legations, and levying tariffs on such ships became standard practice. Gradually, the trade environment on which Ryukyu's royal government depended grew more difficult. Furthermore, the European nations had embarked upon their Age of Discovery. In 1510, the Portuguese occupied Goa in India; they took Malacca in 1511. They put pressure on the trade spheres in the Indian Ocean and the South China Sea. Ryukyu sought to somehow escape the Portuguese influence by opening new trade ties with Java and Sunda, still unaffected by the Europeans, and cultivating ever closer relations with Siam and Pattani (in modern-day Thailand).

However, a shadow had clearly started to fall over the kingdom's commerce in Southeast Asia, already rather straitened. The weakening enforcement of the ban on sea travel resulted in the rise throughout the region of Chinese smugglers, who began to erode the transit trade that functioned as Ryukyu's foundation.

### Smuggling by the *Wakō* in the Sixteenth Century

Demand from the Japanese ruling classes for high-grade woven silk fabrics meant that raw silk thread from China, called *karaito,* had become a high-value import commodity selling for extremely high profits. Silver production was surging in Japan at the time; simultaneously, silver was the chief currency of China, and the government sought to make up for constant shortages. In the 1540s, as Chinese raw silk thread and Japanese silver became staples of exchange, Chinese smugglers in search of silver began to make the crossing to Japan in increasing numbers. Operating mainly in Kyushu, they formed armed organizations into which they recruited Japanese people, and resisting the efforts of the Ming authorities to control them, they kept bases along every part of the Chinese coast. They engaged in both smuggling and regular trade in response to the huge demand for goods.

The Japan-China trade during the Muromachi period [1333–1573] developed with trade centers in Hakata, managed by the Ōuchi clan, and Sakai, also the port of entry for envoys, under the control of the Hosokawa clan. In 1523, relations between Japan and Ming China were temporarily severed after the Ningbo Affair, during which Ōuchi- and Hosokawa-owned trade ship crews clashed in Ningbo, with Kendō Sōsetsu of the Ōuchi clan setting the Hosokawa ship on fire and kidnapping Yúan Jìn, the Chinese area commander in charge of local defenses, before departing.[40]

The Ming court undertook to restore relations with Ashikaga Yoshiharu through the mediation of Ryukyu. The Ōuchi clan finally secured the monopoly on the licensed trade, and in their case, too, Ryukyu mediated in repairing relations with the Chinese. In 1547, however, shipping to China was interrupted once again, as part of Sue Harukata's strategy to oust his overlord, Ōuchi Yoshitaka; he succeeded in 1551. After this, trade between Japan and China became mainly the domain of the so-called late [Muromachi] period pirates [J. *goki wakō*], Chinese smuggling groups that proved to wield extraordinary power. These well-organized pirates, under the direction of their famous leaders Wáng Zhí [J. Ō Choku] and Xú Hǎi [J. Jo Kai], carried the bulk of the Japan-China trade out of their bases in Kyushu.

In about 1556–1557 both Wáng Zhí and Xú Hǎi were killed, either arrested and executed, or assassinated. The remnants of their gangs indulged themselves by turning to pillage in their territories and were finally eradicated only in 1563. With the lifting of the ban on sea travel in 1567, and the designation of the port of Yuegang in Fujian's city of Zhangzhou as a trade port for Chinese merchant ships on top of that, the rampages of the pirates began to lose momentum. The pirates came under even more pressure in 1588 when Toyotomi Hideyoshi ordered their eradication from Japanese waters. Additionally, a newly effective defense by China started a sweeping campaign to clear them out of the Chinese and South China coasts. The effectiveness of these government actions, as well as the release of Fujian coastal residents from the ban on sea travel, meant that the age-long pirate problem was approaching a resolution. However, though the Ming court now permitted ships departing from Yuegang to embark upon international trade voyages to both western and eastern Pacific regions, including the Philippines and south to Borneo and Indonesia in the east, and Annam (Vietnam), Siam (Thailand), and the Malay Peninsula in the west, ships remained strictly forbidden from making the crossing to trade with Japan. Trade with Japan continued to consist, as it had before, of illegal smuggling.

### The Decline of the Transit Trade

The Ryukyu Kingdom's tribute trade was clearly falling off. During the reigns of Shō Toku and Shō En, the average yearly shipment of pepper and spices included as supplementary cargo with the regular tribute reached 2,857 *kin* (one *kin* being roughly equivalent to one pound). Under Shō Shin, the yearly shipment fell to 1,600 *kin;* and by Shō Sei's reign, it was down to 250 *kin.* Where originally twenty-four brokers had been called on to handle Ryukyu's business in the Chinese port, trade dropped each year under Shō Sei until the number was only five brokers and four local translators. In 1546, only three brokers were needed.[41]

On the other hand, in 1517 Portuguese traders and explorers had appeared in Guangdong Province demanding trade. Though failing to establish formal relations with the Ming court, they gained permission to conduct business. In 1557, after they had managed to expel pirates from their base in Macao, the Portuguese were rewarded with the right to reside there and thus established a commercial foothold on the Chinese mainland. Their goal as they extended their trade activities north along the Chinese coast was to open direct trade relations with Japan. Ryukyu, so long the primary transit trade carrier linking the nations of the East and South China Sea trade spheres, felt the basis of its economy shaken by the rise of the Chinese smugglers and Portuguese traders. Though Portuguese ships did stop in Ryukyu during this period, they did not use it as an entrepôt in their trade. In 1571, the Christian convert and daimyo Ōmura Sumitada opened the port of Nagasaki, and Portuguese traders established direct trade between Nagasaki and Macao. Thus going around the Chinese prohibition against direct trade with Japan to carry Chinese raw silk thread and Japanese silver, the Portuguese secured their access to the cash box that was East Asia's single most profitable trade route.

In this way, Ryukyu's trade with Southeast Asia met with one setback after another, falling in the fierce competitive race between Chinese merchants and Portuguese traders. First Sunda, then Pattani (part of modern-day Thailand) broke off relations; in 1570 the Siam (Thailand) trade ended, and Ryukyuan ships never reappeared in those ports. Spain, from its base at Manila in the Philippines, entered into trade with southern China. In 1565, a trade route across the Pacific linked Manila with Mexico in the New World; before long, Manila was visited regularly by Chinese trading junks from Fujian and Guangdong. Ryukyuan ships were also dispatched to the Philippines, but unable to establish a firm position for conducting trade, they soon withdrew.

### Satsuma Gains Ascendancy

In the Third Month of 1570, a Kōsaiji monk named Sesshin arrived in Ryukyu, sent from Satsuma to inform King Shō En that Shimazu Yoshihisa had become daimyo after Shimazu Takahisa and to demand that a royal tribute ship be dispatched in Yoshihisa's honor. At the same time, a senior retainer of the Shimazu clan reaffirmed the ban on any trade with ships that did not carry the required documentation. Two years later, in 1572, and again in 1574, Satsuma repeated its demand for tribute and its warning regarding proper ship documentation. Originally, the royal ships had not been expected to pay tribute; however, in the Third Month of 1575, the royal government finally bowed to Satsuma's demands and sent tribute and official congratulations for Takahisa's ascent to his position as clan leader. At the same time, the government conveyed its acceptance of Satsuma's demand regarding ships' papers.[42]

Shō En died in the Fourth Month of 1572. The following year, his successor, Shō Ei, informed the Ming court of his father's death, and soon imperial envoys bearing the new patents of investiture made the crossing to Ryukyu. Members of the Chinese legations always brought quantities of trade goods with them, and by long-established custom, the Ryukyuans bought these goods, paying in silver. The legation ships, as always, brought a large contingent of officials and soldiers who came expecting trading opportunities, and the royal government was hard-pressed to complete this business before the ships departed for the return trip to China. From the standpoint of the kingdom, Japan loomed ever larger as its source for the silver needed to purchase these goods and the supplies for the legation, and as a market for reselling the Chinese goods. However, with the increase of Chinese smugglers and Portuguese traders in Kyushu, merchants in Hakata and Sakai were no longer limited to the Chinese goods Ryukyu wanted to resell. Furthermore, they were wary of entering into trade with Ryukyu, carefully watchful of Shimazu's increasing possessiveness toward the kingdom. The trade environment around Ryukyu had certainly changed, given the kingdom's dispatch of tribute to Satsuma and its acceptance of Satsuma's policy to deal only with properly authorized ships.

When the Chinese court sent envoys carrying patents of investiture to attend a royal enthronement ceremony in another country, the occasion was referred to as a "promulgation grant" [*bānfēng*, J. *hanpū*]; on the other hand, when no envoys were sent, and the emperor issued a decree directly to the tributary nation's envoy in China, thus avoiding the ceremony necessary to grant a patent, the occasion was a "dominion grant" [*lǐngfēng*, J. *ryōfū*]. A dominion grant relieved Ryukyu's royal government from having to host an envoy delegation and from the expense of purchasing the goods the delegation members would expect to sell. In 1560, in regard to Shō En's patent of investiture, the royal government requested a dominion grant. However, this request had been denied on the pretext that it ran counter to custom handed down from ancient times. The dealings regarding this Chinese patent of investiture also contributed to the weakening of the royal government in its diplomatic relations with Satsuma.

A delegation of Chinese envoys arrived in Ryukyu in 1579; Satsuma also had trade ships make the crossing. The Chinese chief envoy on this occasion, Xiè Jié [J. Sha Ketsu], reported on his return to Fuzhou, "Ryukyu has a Japan Quarter, and several hundred people who gather there waiting to trade our cargo. They go about wearing their swords, and the Ryukyuans are intimidated by them."[43] It is not clear whether the Japan Quarter was occupied only by men from Satsuma. In any event, what we see is no longer the "ceremony of exchange between good neighbors," as Ryukyu referred to its relations with Satsuma. After Ryukyu's submission to Satsuma's pressure in the matters of tribute and ships' papers, we can see clearly that the Shimazu clan had achieved political dominance in the relationship.

CHAPTER FOUR

# The Ryukyu Kingdom under the *Bakuhan* System

## THE SHIMAZU INVASION OF RYUKYU

### Ambition and Frustration: Satsuma's Domination of Kyushu

In 1578, the Warring States Period daimyo Shimazu Yoshihisa, having secured his control over the three provinces of Satsuma, Ōsumi, and Hyūga, turned his attention north. He defeated the Sagara clan at Minamata Castle in Higo (Kumamoto) in 1581; the Ryūzōji clan of Hizen (Nagasaki) was destroyed in the Battle of Shimabara in 1584; and the Ōtomo clan in Bungo reached the verge of collapse in 1587. Within just ten years of establishing his control over the first three provinces, Yoshihisa's rule had spread over all of Kyushu like wildfire.

However, the leader of the Ōtomo clan appealed to Toyotomi Hideyoshi, claiming that the Shimazu's aggression violated the ban against private wars as agreed under the Warring States Period territorial pact among allied clans. Hideyoshi, who had successfully consolidated his control over most of Japan, declared that the Shimazu had not complied with the "division of territory," that is, the agreed-upon territorial demarcations in Kyushu. He decided to mount a large-scale military offensive to contain the Shimazu, and his army set out from Osaka in the Third Month of 1587. Hideyoshi set out to subdue the Shimazu by either diplomacy or warfare: he offered negotiations on the basis of the original "division of territory," even as his general, Hashiba Hidenaga, led forceful military movements. Hideyoshi personally joined the campaign, and the Shimazu clan faced its greatest challenge since the establishment of its domain. In the Fifth Month, Yoshihisa heard that Hideyoshi's forces were moving toward him. Before this huge force moving on him like the surging waves of a stormy sea, he surrendered without even a battle, and Shimazu Yoshihisa's ambitions for hegemony in Kyushu were crushed.

Yoshihisa's campaign to dominate all of Kyushu came to a standstill at Hideyoshi's intervention; he did not, however, abandon his plans to control Ryukyu, though there, too, an obstacle arose. After the Honnōji Incident on the Sixth Month, 2nd Day, 1582, which left him in control of the field, Hideyoshi was at Himeji Castle when he received a request from Kamei Korenori, the daimyo of Shikano Castle in Inaba, to be granted Ryukyu to commemorate the unification of the whole nation. In response, Hideyoshi gave Kamei a fan inscribed with the words "Kamei, Lord of Ryukyu." To ensure their own control over Ryukyu, the Shimazu had to somehow foil Kamei Korenori's political ambitions there.

After Hideyoshi's inauguration as regent (*kanpaku*) to the emperor, he required all daimyo, including Ryukyu, to come to the capital and declare their loyalty. In the Eighth Month of 1588, Shimazu Yoshihisa sent a letter to Ryukyu's King Shō Ei, demanding that he send a delegation to congratulate Hideyoshi on his inauguration.[1] His letter implied that not only would a long drawn-out confrontation with Hideyoshi result in being blocked out of all trade with Japan; raising the banner of revolt against him would certainly soon lead to the destruction of Ryukyu. Shortly after this, Shō Ei died; Shō Nei ascended to the throne in 1589. In the Ninth Month of that year, at the Jurakudai, his palace in Kyoto, Hideyoshi received the envoy of the king of Ryukyu sent through the offices of Shimazu Yoshihisa: Tō'an, a Tenryūji monk. Hideyoshi accepted Tō'an's visit as a sign that Ryukyu had given him its allegiance.

In 1590, with the intention of eventually securing his hold on Ryukyu, Kamei Korenori sent a large warship with a force of thirty-five hundred men to Nagoya in Hizen (near Karatsu in present-day Saga Prefecture, Kyushu), in preparation for a campaign to take the kingdom. News of this reached Satsuma the following year, when Yoshihisa was in the midst of dealing with the military demands laid on both Satsuma and Ryukyu, in anticipation of Hideyoshi's invasion of Korea. He informed King Shō Nei that they had been ordered to provide fifteen thousand men but that Ryukyu would be exempted from this burden if instead the kingdom provided Hideyoshi's army with a ten-month supply of rice for seven thousand men and sent money and rice for building Nagoya Castle (now Karatsu). Shimazu's display of control over Ryukyu impressed Hideyoshi and served as a check to Kamei Korenori's scheme of possession. Kamei made an appeal to Hideyoshi, who had earlier promised Ryukyu to him, that this display of control was almost certainly a bluff.

However, the ruse succeeded, and Ryukyu came to be incorporated into the feudal ranking system of the Warring States Period according to Satsuma's wishes. This incorporation meant that Ryukyu fell under the command of the Shimazu clan. Hideyoshi ordered Kamei to give up his campaign on Ryukyu and focus on the invasion of Korea and Ming China and promised instead to let him have Taizhou [J. Taishū], a district of Zhejiang Province. The title "Kamei, Lord of Taishū" appears on a red-stamped trade license from Hideyoshi dated Third Month, 13th Day, 1592.[2] It was Ryukyu's incorporation into the feudal ranking system, under Shimazu, that provided Satsuma their justification for requiring military service from Ryukyuans.

### The Royal Government Distances Itself from Hideyoshi

The Shimazu sent another message to Ryukyu to remind the king of Hideyoshi's order levying military service and of his offer to accept, in exchange for soldiers, provisions for seven thousand men. In addition, Ryukyu was not to reveal to other countries the plan to invade China.[3] However, Ryukyu immediately sent, with the following year's tribute legation, an urgent report to the Ming government. China responded with a request that Ryukyu obtain more information on Hideyoshi's activities and sent secret messengers to slip into Japan to gather information directly. At that moment, Hideyoshi's forces were ready to invade Korea, and starting in the Fourth Month of 1592, an army of 158,000 men began moving up the Pusan River. The Ryukyu royal government was well aware that the kingdom faced annihilation if it refused to meet Hideyoshi's demands for supplies. As a way to sidestep direct confrontation with Hideyoshi, the kingdom provided a little more than half of what Satsuma demanded, and then waited to see how the war would progress.

In the First Month of 1593, the Ming general Li Rusong came with forty thousand soldiers at the request of Korea's King Seonjo, and the fighting reached a stalemate. In the Fourth Month, a cease-fire was declared, the Japanese troops withdrew to the south, and Japan and Ming China entered into peace negotiations. Hideyoshi listed seven requirements for a peace agreement in the terms he gave the Ming ambassador on the Sixth Month, 28th Day, 1593.[4] Of these, two were of greatest importance to Japan: first, that there should be legal trade between Japan and China without the requirement that Japan pay tribute; and second, that Korea's southern provinces of Gyeongsang, Jeolla, Chungcheon, and Gyeonggi be ceded to Japan.

The Ryukyu royal government took the opportunity provided by the truce between Japan and China in the Fourth Month, 1593, to separate itself from Hideyoshi's influence. It took a clear and conscious stance as a vassal state toward its suzerain ruler, the Ming court. Behind this shift in the government's policy lay Ming China's military intervention against Hideyoshi's invasion of Korea. King Shō Nei anticipated China's protection as its vassal and, on the Sixth Month, 10th Day of the next year (1594), sent a letter in response to Satsuma's renewed demand for support that claimed the kingdom was too weak to send anything. The breakdown of peace negotiations in Korea ended with Japan mobilizing 140,000 men and ordering another invasion in the Second Month, 1597. However, Hideyoshi's death in the Eighth Month of 1598 resulted in Japan's withdrawal from Korea that December, and the seven-year-long invasion of Korea was finally over.

### Tokugawa Ieyasu Seeks to Revive Trade with China

Tokugawa Ieyasu, a member of the Council of Five Elders formed by Toyotomi Hideyoshi, in 1599 sought to restore diplomatic relations with Korea through the Sō clan of Tsushima. The following year, after his victory at the Battle of Sekigahara consolidated his control of the entire country, Ieyasu pursued a policy of encouraging international trade and normalizing relations with Japan's neighboring nations with "good-neighbor diplomacy." He was especially interested in reopening the trade with China that had ended with the last tribute mission in 1547, and he hoped for Ryukyu's mediation to improve commerce.

In the midst of all this, in the winter of 1602, a Ryukyuan ship wrecked on the coast of Date Masamune's domain in the Mutsu region (modern Tohoku). The Ryukyuan crew was sent to Edo (Tokyo), and then on to Osaka, to be delivered to the Shimazu clan by Honda Masazumi, one of Tokugawa Ieyasu's retainers. Ieyasu gave a strict order that if even one of the Ryukyuans died during their repatriation, the five Shimazu retainers who were escorting them would be punished. Ieyasu sought Ryukyu's goodwill by providing this courteous escort to the shipwrecked crew and anticipated winning King Shō Nei's cooperation in acting as a mediator in the negotiations to reestablish formal trade relations between Japan and China.[5]

In the Second Month of 1604, Shimazu Yoshihisa demanded that Shō Nei, sometime that summer or fall, send an envoy to formally thank Ieyasu for the return of the shipwrecked crew. He held that Ieyasu had ordered the return of the shipwrecked crew to Shimazu because Ryukyu was viewed as a dependency of Satsuma. By "dependency" he meant "vassal." Yoshihisa may have based his views on Hideyoshi's 1592 recognition that Ryukyu held rank within the feudal system; however, Ryukyu would not accept his demand, since the dispatch of an envoy to Ieyasu would serve as Ryukyu's acknowledgment of itself as a vassal territory. Ieyasu had great expectations of Ryukyu, but the likelihood of their realization was very small.

### Ryukyu Conquered by the Shimazu Clan

In the Seventh Month of 1605, a Ryukyuan tribute ship returning from China was shipwrecked in Hirado, Kyushu. The *bakufu* conveyed to Nagasaki's governor, via its magistrate in Nagasaki, Ogasawara Ichi'an, that the entire party aboard the ship should be returned home. Moreover, Ryukyu was requested, through the feudal lord of Hirado, Matsuura Shigenobu, to follow the precedent that had been set the previous year with the shipwreck victims in Mutsu, and send a gift of thanks to the *bakufu*. On the Eighth Month, 15th Day, Shigenobu wrote to Shimazu's chief retainer informing him of the contents of the letter Ieyasu had sent on the matter. Knowing the *bakufu* had requested the Matsuura to deal with Ryukyu, and that it was diversifying its points of contact with the kingdom, the Shimazu clan began to feel some urgency. If things continued like this, they were at risk of losing their monopolistic hold on the kingdom.

In the Fourth Month of the following year, the various taxes, tributes, and assessments on all of Shimazu's fiefs had reached roughly 20 percent of its assessed value and had become a clear burden given the devastated state of the land at the time. The new daimyo, Shimazu Tadatsune, therefore decided to break the deadlock of economic stagnation by playing his trump card—sending troops into Amami Ōshima to take it over. On the Sixth Month, 17th Day, having used as his pretext Ryukyu's misconduct in not sending a gift of gratitude, Tadatsune requested and received permission from Ieyasu to dispatch soldiers to Ōshima. On the same day, he was granted the right to change his name to Iehisa, using the "Ie" portion of Ieyasu's given name. The invasion was set for the following autumn. However, in the Sixth Month, Shō Nei received a patent of investiture from an envoy of the Ming government; in addition, the negotiations between Japan and Korea, taking place under the auspices of the Sō clan in Tsushima, had reached their final stage. For this reason, the invasion of Ōshima was postponed, perhaps as a precaution against possible Chinese and Korean reactions.

Korean-Japanese diplomatic relations were finally restored with the visit to Japan of a Korean ambassador in the Fifth Month of 1607. Once again, Ieyasu commanded Satsuma to negotiate with Ryukyu on the matter of sending a formal envoy to express its gratitude. In the Eighth Month, when Ryukyu showed no signs of sending such an emissary, he ordered Satsuma to prepare troops for an invasion of Ryukyu and try one more time to negotiate with them on the matter of the formal expression of gratitude. By the Ninth Month, the Shimazu began calling up military forces for the crossing to Ryukyu and sent retainers to the kingdom on one last diplomatic mission. On that mission, Satsuma pressed the royal government to either pay its portion of the expenses owed for the invasion of the mainland or hand over Amami Ōshima in payment instead. Shimazu Yoshihiro and Shimazu Tadatsune had both participated in the invasion of Korea, but their troops had starved and sickened due to insufficient provisions from their home base; they harbored an understandable anger toward Ryukyu for defaulting on its military obligations. The Ryukyuans, however, did not accept this judgment.

The Shimazu's justification for its invasion of Ryukyu may have ostensibly been the kingdom's disloyal refusal to send a formal envoy to express gratitude for Ieyasu's efforts in negotiating the reestablishment of trade relations with Ming China, but its real object was to make up the difference between the deficits it had incurred over the years dealing with the Ryukyu Kingdom, and the assessed value of the Satsuma *han* as reported to Edo. In the Third Month of 1609, more than three thousand men commanded by the Shimazu retainer Kabayama Hisataka shipped out from the Yamakawa River in Satsuma aboard one hundred vessels. Along the route, they subdued Amami Ōshima and Tokunoshima; in the Fourth Month, they attacked Shuri and Naha. Given that the Shimazu's army had been seasoned in the fierce fighting in Kyushu during the Warring States Period, and that its samurai had shown great courage during the invasion of Korea, the outcome in this face-off was obvious. The Ryukyuan defensive forces crumbled, and Shō Nei surrendered. In the Fifth Month, the Shimazu army arrested the king and his *sanshi* [three ministers], the top officials of the royal government, and, departing from Naha, made a triumphal return to Satsuma. In the Fifth Month of the following year, Shimazu Iehisa, accompanied by Shō Nei, set out from Satsuma. In the Eighth Month, Shō Nei, wearing the robes and crown bestowed upon him by the Ming court, visited the castle at Sunpu (now Shizuoka) and presented Ieyasu with a gift of thanks. Next he proceeded to Edo Castle, where he was given an audience with the second Tokugawa shogun, Hidetada. Thus, finally, Ryukyu presented its gifts to the shogunate.[6]

## RYUKYU AND THE SHOGUNATE'S FOREIGN POLICY

### Shō Nei Returns to Ryukyu

In the Seventh Month of 1609, Ieyasu praised Shimazu Iehisa for the successful subjugation of Ryukyu in a personal letter over his own signature, and ordered punitive measures.[7] When Shō Nei, accompanied by Shimazu Iehisa, was given an audience and a banquet at Edo Castle, Tokugawa

Hidetada informed him, "As for Ryukyu, because the kings of Chūzan have ruled there for so many generations, we will not order a change of leaders, but will allow the present line to continue as in the past."[8] Hidetada also expected Ryukyu to continue as an intermediary in negotiating peace with China in its capacity as a tributary state of the Ming court. Ryukyu's continued existence separate from Satsuma was dependent on just this role as intermediary between Japan and China, and this was precisely the premise for the invasion in the first place. Shō Nei left Kagoshima for his home country in the Ninth Month of 1611, ending the two years and six months of exile in Satsuma. Upon his return, Shō Nei sent a written pledge to Satsuma.[9] Such pledges, also called oath bonds, had been customary between members of the samurai class in swearing loyalty to a master in medieval Japan. In the case of Ryukyu, the bond was a written pledge of loyalty to the daimyo of Satsuma invoking the names of gods and the Buddha. Later generations of Ryukyuan kings, as well as the top ministers of the royal government, including regents and the king's council, followed the custom of sending their own written vows of loyalty to Satsuma upon taking office.

### The *Bakufu*'s Ming China Trade Ploy Fails

Ordered to intercede in the trade between China and Japan, Shō Nei sent tribute legations to the Ming court in two consecutive years, 1612 and 1613. However, after Japan's successive invasions of first the Korean peninsula, then Ryukyu, China became more vigilant than ever before. In the matter of this tribute from Ryukyu, China's suspicions had been raised that it was, in fact, some sort of Japanese ploy. Though it is not clear whether the tribute envoy told the Ming court of how matters were trending between Japan and Ryukyu, China could hardly miss the fact that Ryukyu had exceeded its limit of one tribute mission every two years, as well as the number of personnel for which its legations were authorized. Additionally, besides the usual offerings of sulfur, horses, and cloth, a large quantity of goods manufactured in Japan were included in the tribute cargo. China tightened its defenses and determined not to give Japan any room for maneuvering.

As a result, and entirely contrary to the *bakufu*'s desires, Ryukyu's tribute schedule was reduced from one legation every two years to one every ten years. The court's stated reason for changing the schedule was to give the kingdom time to recover from the economic hardship imposed by Satsuma's invasion. This was just a front, however, because the Ming court had become alerted to the *bakufu*'s desire to pursue direct trade with China by the increased frequency of the Ryukyuan envoy legations and by the negotiations of the Sō clan of Tsushima to procure a trade route with China via Korea. The change to the tribute schedule indicated the sense of crisis that the *bakufu*'s scheming awoke within the Ming government. During this period, Ming China suspected that Ryukyu was conspiring with Japan in regard to China but allowed Ryukyu to retain its status as a vassal nation all the same. Besides reinforcing the stability of its East Asian system, which relied on its relations with its barbarian neighbors, China felt that preserving its influence with Ryukyu was a necessary part of its defensive strategy.[10]

In the fall of 1614, the *bakufu,* in its continued negotiations for direct trade with China, ordered Ryukyu to dispatch another tribute mission and deliver the *daimin fukken gunmon ni ataeru sho* [letter addressed to the governor of Fujian, China, usually known as the *gunmon sho*], which the Shimazu had been asked to draft. The *gunmon sho* conveyed three proposals: (1) that Japanese trade ships would trade directly with Ming China; (2) that Chinese ships would visit Ryukyu for trade; and (3) that Ryukyu would send envoys carrying tribute cargo every year.[11] Thus, even if it turned out to be impossible to establish the direct trade relations as envisioned by the *bakufu,* trade would at least continue with Ryukyu as a trade link.

However, an entry in the *Ikoku nikki* [Chronicle of Foreign Countries] for the Sixth Month, 12th Day, 1621, notes that Ryukyu did not deliver the *gunmon sho* to the governor of Fujian Province.[12] The *Míng shǐ* states that the Ming court denied Ryukyu's request to change its tribute schedule, and the legation was refused entry into China and ordered to return home.[13] From this, we may understand that the *gunmon sho* was not delivered to the Chinese. As far as the royal government was concerned, the Chinese refusal to allow the legation entry was fortunate, because had Ryukyu delivered the *gunmon sho,* it may have invited the distrust of the Ming government toward its tributary state and put at risk the tributary system that ensured the continued existence of the Ryukyu Kingdom. In this way, all attempts by the *bakufu* to use Ryukyu to negotiate direct trade relations with China failed.

### The Perceived Threat of Christianity and the National Isolation Policy

Meanwhile, Christianity had become a serious issue within Japan. There were more than 750,000 Christian converts in Japan by 1605, and missionaries had spread out from Kanto all the way into Tohoku in northern Honshu. The *bakufu* was gripped with the suspicion that such converts might unite and begin to threaten its own and the daimyos' power base. In 1612, Christianity was banned in the area under the direct control of the shogun; by 1614 the ban had been extended to the entire country. The government identified those people it considered a threat to its sovereignty, such as missionaries and prominent laymen, and deported them. To reinforce the ban, the *bakufu* issued a proclamation on the 8th day of the Eighth Month, 1616, strictly limiting European trade ships, once permitted into any port in Japan, to the ports of Nagasaki and Hirado in Kyushu.[14]

The ban on Christianity and the limitation of trade was thoroughgoing. In 1623, England shut down its trading house in Hirado and its agents departed Japan; suppression had only increased after fifty-five missionaries and Christian followers were executed in Nagasaki in 1622. Tokugawa Hidetada's administration expanded the ban in 1624 to forbid any Spaniards from even landing on Japanese soil, because of their close association with Spanish missionaries such as the Franciscans.

In 1635, even Chinese ships were limited to conducting their trade in the port of Nagasaki, as a countermeasure against Christians taking passage on Chinese ships that visited the various ports of Kyushu. Missionaries were barred from entry into Japan, and correspondence with overseas Christians forbidden. In order to prevent Japanese ships from becoming involved in foreign disputes that might damage the shogun's authority, Japanese citizens were prohibited from any overseas travel and not allowed to return if they did leave the country. All international trade came under the purview of the *bakufu*. A rigorously enforced policy of segregating foreigners was further meant to prevent the spread of Christianity; after 1636, upon the completion of Dejima in the Bay of Nagasaki, all Portuguese visitors were confined there because of their deep association with the Jesuits. Then, in 1639, after the Shimabara Rebellion [1637–1638], all Portuguese were denied entry; in 1641, the Dutch trading house was transferred to Dejima and kept under strict surveillance. Given the thorough nature of the *bakufu*'s restrictions on Christians, all of Japan's interactions with the outside world became limited to Nagasaki, and the strengthening of control and regulation of trade set Japan on its course of national isolation, or *sakoku*. Ryukyu's international relations were also subject to control by the *bakufu*.[15]

### Satsuma Is Given the Role of Containing Ryukyu

The policy of suppressing Christianity was also pursued in the Ryukyuan archipelago, where a strengthened coastal guard system scuttled any attempt by Christian missionaries to slip in unnoticed. Satsuma was given the duty of "containing Ryukyu" and relieved of the duty of guarding Nagasaki. The *bakufu*'s motivation in assigning Satsuma the duty of containment was its awareness of Ryukyu's standing as an autonomous nation, and the frequency with which foreign ships were likely to land there.

Satsuma's duties in Ryukyu were a type of foreign defense duty [*ikoku keigo banyaku*] in which both the Satsuma and Tsushima fiefdoms had been involved during the Muromachi period. They had, respectively, to "contain" Ryukyu and Korea; in the event that foreign ships arrived and precipitated a state of emergency, they had to be prepared to dispatch troops in the national defense. It was a simple matter to expand Satsuma's "containment" duties to include the suppression of Christianity in Ryukyu and in guarding its coastlines.

The prohibition of Christianity during the period of *sakoku,* or national isolation, was one of the fundamental laws enforced by the *bakufu* throughout the entire country. The reason for its speedy application directly upon Ryukyu was the kingdom's geographical location as a midpoint on the route followed by missionaries as they traveled north to Japan from the Philippine archipelago. Manila's Spanish Catholic orders sent its Christian missionaries into the Ryukyus and regarded this as a step toward increasing their missionary presence in Japan, as well. The *bakufu* was well aware of their presence and ordered Satsuma to strengthen Ryukyu's coastal defense system. It enforced the suppression of Christianity in Ryukyu by implementing a religious census and the "five households" system [*gonin-gumi seido*].[16] Although the system of requiring commoners to register with a temple in order to prove their Buddhist faith was not established in Ryukyu, registration under the religious census was rigorously implemented.

### Handling of Foreign Ships

Chinese ships had been banned from conducting private trade since the prohibition on ocean travel in the early Ming dynasty, but there remained the possibility that European ships would visit Ryukyu for trade. In 1628, the *bakufu* issued an order that European ships not be permitted to land, thus imposing on Ryukyu a ban on sea travel and trade with Europeans very like that enforced in Japan. The *bakufu* issued an official order via Satsuma on how to handle foreign ships when they did make an appearance in Ryukyuan waters. Included were illustrations of Chinese, Portuguese, Spanish, and Dutch ships, as well as drawings of Portuguese and Spanish people, with descriptions of how to distinguish between the various nationalities and instructions on how to deal with them and report encounters. The *bakufu* provided information for identifying foreign ships, but they also issued a strict order decreeing that Chinese and Dutch ships were to be protected, while any Spanish or Portuguese arrivals were to be arrested and remitted to Satsuma, or even executed if the circumstances warranted.[17]

In 1644, the Ryukyu Kingdom developed a system of signal fires to be used as a means of communication. Until then, the arrival of a foreign ship in the outer islands had been reported only if there was a messenger ship available; now a line of signal fires [Ryu. *fiitatimoo*] on the main island of Okinawa and its outer islands resulted in much faster message transmission.[18] Furthermore, small, fast courier ships called *tobifune* [flying ships] were kept on hand to carry urgent messages. No matter the weather or wind direction, if a Portuguese or Spanish ship came into the area, or there was a shipwreck, these little vessels could make the crossing to report to the royal government. Under the policy of national isolation, the *bakufu*'s handling of foreign ships was careful, even in Ryukyu. Thus the shogunate ensured its feudal laws were observed as far away as the Ryukyu Kingdom.

## SHIMAZU'S GOVERNANCE OF RYUKYU

### Ryukyu Takes Its Place within "Japan"

After the conquest of Ryukyu, the *Land Survey of the Ryukyu Kingdom* [*Ryūkyūkoku kenchi*] was conducted following the guidelines of Hideyoshi's nationwide cadastral survey (*Taikō kenchi*). In determining the kingdom's crop yield, the Shimazu considered the "five islands leading south from Kikaijima" (that is, Kikai, Ōshima, Tokunoshima, Okierabu, and Yoron) as belonging to the Satsuma fief. The royal government was assessed on the islands from Okinawa and south for 89,086 *koku,* of which the royal government was allowed to keep 50,000 *koku.* Records show that due to an error in how Miyako Island had been assessed, the total for the kingdom was revised to just over 83,085 *koku* in 1629; in 1635, the Kan'ei assessment recorded 90,883 *koku;* and the Kyōhō assessment, sent to the Ryukyu Kingdom by Lord Shimazu in 1727, increased the amount by somewhat over 3,346 *koku* to 94,230 *koku.*[19]

At first, the goods sent by the royal government in payment every year were required to include 3,000 rolls of banana fiber cloth (*bashōfu*); 6,000 rolls of fine ramie cloth; 10,000 rolls of coarse linen; 1,300 *kin* [about 1,300 pounds, or 650 kilograms] of ramie grass; 3 *kanme* [about 12 kilograms, or 25 pounds] of cotton; 100 rolls of hemp palm rope; 100 rolls of black braided rope; 3,800 woven mats; and 200 oxhides.[20] These quantities were so high, however, that it was impossible to assemble the full amount, and payment in silver was allowed after 1613. Rice, too, was an acceptable currency, and thereafter began the annual tribute payment of *shinobose mai* (the proceeds from selling tribute rice).

In 1634, Shimazu Iehisa formulated a plan to dispatch a delegation of Ryukyuan envoys to congratulate and show gratitude to Tokugawa Iemitsu when he became shogun. Sashiki Chōeki was sent to Kyoto, and in July he was given an audience with Iemitsu. Before this event, Satsuma had announced for the first time that, including the five islands in the Amami group, Ryukyu's assessment was more than 123,700 *koku*. In May, Shimazu received from Iemitsu, the third Tokugawa shogun, a certificate stamped with the shogun's personal monogram indicating a fief grant: "Satsuma and Ōsumi, and Hyūga together [have brought] 605,000 koku. Beyond this, the 123,700 koku from the Kingdom of Ryukyu are also included as part of our jurisdiction."[21]

According to the jurisdiction grant, the tribute payment of 605,000 *koku* from the regions of Satsuma, Ōsumi, and Hyūga was increased by 123,700 *koku* from Ryukyu (including the Amami group). Thus the *bakufu* publicly recognized that the tribute from Ryukyu was under the jurisdiction of the Shimazu clan. Ryukyu's tribute contribution was publicly handled just like that of other fiefs in Japan, and also listed in the tribute index. This is the first indication of Ryukyu's incorporation into the *bakuhan* feudal system. Ryukyu's special status as an outsider (referred to as "beyond this" in the grant) kept it outside the requirement to provide military support to the *bakufu*. That is to say, although Ryukyu had standing in the feudal system, it was excused from military obligations. Thus the royal government, unlike every other fief in the nation, did not have the burden of keeping up an army in the event of a national emergency.

Four times, in 1605, 1644, 1696, and 1835, the *bakufu* ordered new national maps. Ryukyu was plotted three times, in the surveys conducted during the Shōhō [1644 survey], Genroku [1696], and Tempō [1835] eras. After the Satsuma invasion, it is believed that incorporating Ryukyu, a foreign land, into the national maps was a primary goal of the "Land Survey of the Ryukyu Kingdom." These very large maps are drawn at a scale of 21,600:1, and the Ryukyus are shown divided into three regions: the Amami group, the Okinawa group, and all the islands of Sakishima [the Miyako and Yaeyama groups]. Under each of the three surveys, there were no changes to the amount of 123,711 *koku* assessed on the kingdom and its *majiri,* or village administrative units. The mapping done in 1624 included the Amami group in the territory under the direct control of Satsuma, shrinking the map area of the territory under the authority of the Ryukyuan king. Satsuma, however, as part of its resistance to the *bakufu,* referred to the Amami group as part of the "foreign territory" of Ryukyu, and until the end of the Tokugawa period, included Amami's tax contribution in the 123,700 *koku* assessed on the kingdom and declared the island group a part of the Ryukyu Kingdom, as stated in the jurisdiction grants renewed by each successive *bakufu* administration. As far as the *bakufu* was concerned, Amami remained within the borders of the Ryukyu Kingdom; when maps were made, Amami was always shown as part of the kingdom.[22]

### Journeying to Edo to Perform Diplomatic Obligations

In 1634, when Ryukyu was formally designated as part of the Satsuma *han* under the dominion of the Shimazu clan, the Shō clan, which was now, after all, a retainer of a retainer to Japan's virtual "king," the Tokugawa shogun, was stripped of the title *kokuō* (lit., king of the land), and given instead the title of *kokushi* (provincial governor).[23]

The Edo *bakufu,* after its failure to establish trade with Ming China, maintained its policy of national isolation while also constructing an international order that included Korea and Ryukyu, with the shogun set at its summit. Because the title of *kokuō* [king] was limited to heads of state under the Chinese tributary system's rite of equals, in dealings with foreign countries, the Tokugawa shogun used the title Nihon *taikun* [supreme commander of Japan] to indicate his sovereignty and diplomatic authority. We find the title *Nihonkoku taikun* used by messenger envoys sent from Korea to Japan in 1636; similarly, the "gratitude envoy" (*shaonshi*) from Ryukyu sent in 1644 to announce the succession of Shō Ken (which occurred in 1641) also used this title. The practice of sending "congratulatory envoys" (*keigashi*) from Ryukyu to congratulate a Tokugawa shogun upon taking power, and "gratitude envoys" on the occasion of the enthronement of a Ryukyuan king, had been established by Shimazu Iehisa in 1634.[24]

The missions to Edo were called Edo-*dachi* or Edo *nobori* [going up to Edo]. In their Edo *nobori* (see Figure 4.1), the Ryukyu envoys would accompany the Satsuma domain's envoys when, under the direction of the Shimazu clan, they paid their annual ceremonial visit (called *sankin kōtai*) to Edo to pledge loyalty to the shogun.[25] These rituals in turn were based on the elaborate and formal diplomatic ceremonies conducted by the Korean envoys.

The feudal government's foreign diplomacy was founded under the national isolation policy of the 1630s. By calling Korea and Ryukyu *tsūshin no kuni* [nations of trust, that is, nations with which the *bakufu* had formal, diplomatic communications] and Holland and China *tsūshō no kuni* [that is, nations with which only trade activities were conducted], Japan adapted the Chinese system of classifying its neighbors to fit its perception of its own superiority and viewing its neighbors as barbarian tribes, in an echo of the Chinese habit of referring to surrounding peoples as the "four barbarians." The director of the Dutch Trading Company made the trip to Edo for audiences with the shogun; Chinese traders in Nagasaki conducted the

*Figure 4.1.* Ryukyu Prince Kin proceeds to Edo. Detail from the *Ryūkyū Shisha Kin Ōji Shusshi no Gyōretsu* scroll (1671), University of Hawai'i Library Sakamaki/Hawley Collection.

Ceremony of Eighth Month, 1st Day [Hachisaku no Rei] to commemorate Ieyasu's arrival at Edo Castle on the first of August (by the Chinese lunar calendar).

The phrase "nation of trust" connoted nations that conducted reliable, honest diplomacy, and originally connoted ceremonious relations among good neighbors. The Koreans understood the term in this original meaning; for the *bakufu,* however, the term also implied that there was tribute obligation. Though given the same label of *tsūshin no kuni* as Korea, Ryukyu, under the control of Satsuma, received different treatment and had to understand the term in the meaning of owing tribute. In 1853, the *bakufu* compiled the *Tsūkō ichiran* [Overview of Navigation], a historical survey of the *bakufu*'s international discourses. It distinguishes between different Ryukyuan missions, noting that in 1610 "the Chūzan King came to the Court"; in 1634, however, he "brought tribute."[26] There were exchanges of correspondence between the Tokugawa shoguns and the kings of Korea; in Ryukyu's case, the exchanges were between "the king of Chūzan" and the shogun's Council of Elders (*rōjū*). Although Satsuma made a point of using the title "Ryukyu provincial governor" in reference to the Ryukyuan king, in exchanges with the *bakufu,* as a vassal territory, the kingdom was permitted to use the title "king of Chūzan."

In 1710, Shimazu Yoshitaka presented a Ryukyuan envoy to the shogun and was rewarded with a promotion to lieutenant [*shōshō*] junior fourth rank upper. Again, during the 1714 Edo *nobori,* he was promoted to captain [*chūjō*], senior fourth rank lower. Thus, though not without certain limitations, there developed a custom of rewarding the Shimazu daimyo with a promotion when he journeyed to Edo accompanied by a Ryukyuan envoy. Over the more than two hundred years between that first mission of congratulations and gratitude of 1644, to the last one in 1850, sent on the occasion of King Shō Tai's ascension to the throne, Ryukyuan envoys made a total of seventeen ceremonial journeys to Edo.[27]

## THE EXPANSION OF TRADE IN SATSUMA'S PORT

### The Four Ports

When the three royal ministers who were arrested and transported to Satsuma along with King Shō Nei returned to Ryukyu, they came bearing a document containing fifteen stipulations. This document, known as the Law of Fifteen Articles, clearly laid out the basis of Satsuma's policies in its rule over Ryukyu.[28] Fully five of the articles concerned the regulation of trade. Ryukyu was forbidden from purchasing any Chinese products except those specifically ordered by Satsuma and was prohibited from sending envoys to any Japanese domain except Satsuma; and only traders bearing a license [*go-hangyō*] issued by the Satsuma *han* were permitted to conduct trade in Ryukyu. The *han* would continue to issue directives practically every year regulating trade, and the Ryukyu Kingdom was strictly forbidden from engaging in independent trade. It was clearly the intention of the Shimazu clan to assert exclusive control over Ryukyu's trade economy, and these measures were designed to give Satsuma total control over Ryukyu's tribute trade.

In 1849, the *bakufu* compiled the *Tokugawa jikki* [True Account of the Tokugawa Shogunate], in which the national isolation policy was called the "sea travel ban," in an echo of the Chinese policy forbidding all Chinese citizens from engaging in foreign travel or trade.[29] Unlike in China, however, in Japan's case, the principle of "role/duty" (*yaku*), which underlay the centralized military structure that was a key element to the very formation of the Japanese state also became closely tied to Japan's approach to foreign relations. In retrospect, the establishment within Japan of the Four Ports, each bearing its military responsibility for "guard duty" against foreign incursions, also produced a structure that implicitly recognized the connection between military and trade needs.

Nagasaki Port was representative of these points of contact with the outside world. The others included the port of Matsumae, with its access to the Ainu people in Karafuto (Sakhalin). This northern port served as the main link with the nomadic Shandan people along the lower reaches of the Heilong River [now part of the Chinese-Russian border in northeast China]. The third port, at Tsushima, provided the link with Korea; and finally, the port belonging to Satsuma controlled part of the trade with China through its possession of Ryukyu, now incorporated into the *bakuhan* hierarchy. The *bakufu* recognized the Shimazu lord's right to control foreign trade in Ryukyu by naming it a "house obligation" [*ieyaku*], a service provided for the *bakufu*. The Four Ports thus served dual functions, as part of the *bakufu*'s trade system as well as its coastal defense system.

Obtaining Chinese raw silk thread was a major trade objective. In 1639, after Portuguese ships were forbidden entry into Japanese ports, the import of raw silk thread into the Japanese market fell drastically. To remedy the shortage, the *bakufu* instructed Satsuma to increase the quantity of Chinese silk thread, woven silk, and medicine in the trade goods obtained through the Ryukyuan tribute mission to China. This policy indicates the importance the *bakufu* laid on Ryukyu's role as a window for foreign trade, a role that complemented the state's overall policy of national isolation. In addition to the trade out of Nagasaki, the Ryukyu trade economy was recognized by the *bakufu* as an exchange route with China.

### Satsuma *Han* Administrators Assigned to Control of the Tribute Trade

By 1630, Satsuma was in the midst of a financial crisis. The *han*'s debt included 7,000 *kanme* [about 26,000 kilograms] of rice. Kawakami Matazaemon Tadamichi, a family retainer, recommended that the Shimazu use the profits from Ryukyu's tribute trade to restore their financial affairs;[30] Kawakami was sent to Ryukyu in 1631 to act as magistrate on behalf of the Satsuma *han*. In this way, in a proactive measure to resolve their own fiscal crisis, the Shimazu linked the financial well-being of their domain directly with the Ryukyuan tribute trade. In 1654, the Shimazu seated a senior retainer in the position of Ryukyu *kata* (later, the Ryukyu *gakari*, or overseer). The official residence of this resident administrator was called the Okariya and was located in one of Naha's four wards, near the harbor at Nishimura. The administrative term "Okariya," widely used in the Satsuma domain during the Edo period, indicated a *han* branch office. New administrators usually called *zaiban bugyō dokoro*, "resident administrative officers," were appointed to their positions by Satsuma for three-year terms. A Ryukyu *kariya* was established in Satsuma, and the royal government sent an envoy to take up residence on the first day of every year, with the duties of negotiating and managing exchanges with Satsuma. The Ryukyu *kariya* in Satsuma was redesignated the Ryukyu-*kan,* Ryukyu House, in 1784 and thereafter staffed by the royal government with a resident director [*zaiban uēkata*], a security officer [J. *yoriki*], a storehouse manager [J. *zōyaku*], and a secretary [J. *shoyaku*].[31] (This Ryukyu House is not to be confused with the one in Fuzhou, from which Ryukyu's trade with China was coordinated.)

As Japan pursued its policy of national isolation, China's wariness toward Japan eased. The limit of one tribute mission in ten years imposed on Ryukyu in 1612 was increased to once in five years after 1622. In 1633, Shō Hō's investiture by the Ming court as "king" signaled renormalized relations between Ming China and the Ryukyu Kingdom, and the tribute schedule was restored to its age-old frequency of once every two years. Later, in 1678, the kingdom was permitted to add one tribute ship to the fleet sent to retrieve the envoy to China. Substantial exchanges continued every year, spurred on by Satsuma's pursuit of greater profits.

That said, the *bakufu*'s China trade policy permitted Satsuma to have the Chinese goods it obtained from Ryukyu, but limited it to what could be consumed in its own domain (which portion was called *jitsubushi*); more than that was prohibited. When the number of Chinese ships coming into Nagasaki increased, the earlier practice of Satsuma selling the royal government's goods in the Nagasaki market under the guise of helping the Ryukyu Kingdom was prohibited because it brought them into competition with Chinese ships, though the government did approve sales of Ryukyuan goods through the wholesale stores in Kyoto and in the Kyoto-area markets. However, Satsuma's profits were not solely derived from the *jitsubushi* goods it was allowed under *bakufu* regulations to handle. More than half of its profits came from Ryukyuan goods it cleverly diverted for sale in the publicly administered wholesale markets in the Kyoto area. Even with the regulation of the amount of goods traded and numerous rules and restrictions, Satsuma managed to befuddle the *bakufu* and find ways to sell its imports. The most important of these included the raw silk thread from Huzhou in Zhejiang Province, and silk cloth woven in Suzhou and Hangzhou; the thread from Huzhou was of a quality unparalleled anywhere else in China. Satsuma controlled Ryukyu's trade affairs down to the least details, insisting on protecting its monopoly over the sale of Chinese silk thread and cloth, and thus ensuring its own source of funds.[32]

### Supplying Silver for the China Trade

Trading in China required large resources of silver. Ryukyu did not possess any silver mines; silver was either obtained through Shimazu clan resources or raised from merchants with special privileges, known as *yōkiki* or *tachi'iri,* who frequented the Ryukyu House in the Satsuma domain. Satsuma could not supply enough silver by itself and so had to borrow money from merchants in Kyoto and Osaka, guaranteeing the IOUs with papers stamped with a "reverse stamp" [*urahan*]. Satsuma served as the guarantor for Ryukyu to borrow silver. In 1669, the royal government established its sugar monopoly, and the storehouse manager at the Ryukyu House in Satsuma, in charge of trade affairs, set up a system in which sugar was used as collateral in loan arrangements.[33]

In 1695, the *bakufu* issued the Genroku silver and gold currencies. The new silver coins contained 80 percent of the silver of the earlier Keichō currency; in 1711, when the silver content of the Shihō [also known as *yotsutakaragin*] coins dropped to 20 percent, silver coins underwent great loss of value. The China trade required silver of high purity, and because the lack of such coins was a real hindrance in conducting the tribute trade, the kingdom sent a request through Satsuma to the *bakufu* to be allowed to remint coins with the earlier level of purity. This the kingdom was permitted to do, and the silver content of these royal government–issue coins equaled that of the Keichō mint. This new casting was done at the Kyoto Ginza, or silver mint; after 1799, the coins were made at the Edo mint [in the Ginza of today's Tokyo].

Besides silver, the royal government was dependent on Satsuma for copper and tin, as well as miscellaneous cargo, for use as tribute goods. The sales of sugar and imported Chinese goods in the Japanese market were usually handled by the Ryukyu House in Satsuma. Satsuma's heavy involvement as a mediator in the tribute trade and in regular trade resulted in the development of a tightly regulated economic system.

The Ryukyuan *kai-sen* [junks] and Satsuma's *yamato-sen* [Yamato ships] traveled the sea route between Satsuma and Ryukyu. Their chief cargo included the tribute rice [*shinobose mai*], royal government–controlled sugar, and turmeric, all crops that could be converted to cash in the markets of the Japanese mainland. Some of the *yamato-sen* were called "return cargo ships" [*henjōbutsu sekisen*]. They were alternately known as "silver ships" [*o-ginsen*] when they brought from Satsuma to Naha supplies of silver for use in the tribute trade; on their return to Satsuma, they were "thread ships" [*o-itobune*], loaded with the silk thread and textiles purchased in China.[34]

In this way, the ships dispatched from Ryukyu to China were provided with silver. In 1644, the Chinese Ming dynasty fell, to be replaced by the Manchu Qing dynasty. In 1683, the Qing military forces finally succeeded in suppressing the Ming dynasty restoration movement, based out of Taiwan and led by the Zheng clan. Subsequently, the number of Chinese trade ships coming into Nagasaki Port increased sharply, resulting in large quantities of silver and gold flowing out of Japan. In an attempt to check this flow of silver and gold through Nagasaki's business dealings, the Tokugawa *bakufu* put a cap on the volume of business that could be done with the Chinese and Dutch trade ships. At first this limit was set at about 9,000 *kanme* of silver; in 1687, Ryukyu was given a limit of 1,206 *kanme* of silver for China. In 1715, this amount was further reduced to 906 *kanme*.[35]

Both Satsuma and Ryukyu had an allotment of silver for the China trade, but Satsuma hid from the *bakufu* how much tribute was actually sent to China and when asked simply said it had lent its portion to Ryukyu. For this reason, the silver from Satsuma was called "borrowed silver." In Ryukyu, this silver was known as the "primary silver"; the Ryukyu royal government's silver was the "secondary silver." Primary silver was spent on the raw silk thread, textiles, and medicines desired by Satsuma; the royal government spent its secondary silver on the same kinds of items, as well as on necessities, such as covering living expenses in Fuzhou and Beijing and paying for ship repairs. The China-bound silver arrived from Satsuma on the "silver ships" in August or September; if this delivery was late, it could affect the departure of the tribute ships.

### Nagasaki Trading House Widens Its Market

With the reduction in the kingdom's silver allotment in 1687, there was a huge increase in hard goods such as *tawara-mono* [straw-wrapped goods] and assorted other marine products to make up the difference.[36] *Tawara-mono,* as suggested by the name, were indeed wrapped in straw to protect them in transit, and usually consisted of preserved sea cucumber, dried abalone, and shark fins. The remaining marine products consisted of other fruits of the sea important in the export market, such as *konbu* (kelp), cuttlefish, *keikansō* (a type of seagrass), red algae (for making agar), sliced and dried bonito flakes, and dried shrimp. All of these items were indispensible in Chinese cuisine, and demand for them in China was enormous. From the end of the seventeenth century, the *bakufu,* in its quest to stem the flow of silver, gold, and copper out of Japan, encouraged the export of these goods from Nagasaki Port. Gradually, a collection network for these goods developed, and by 1785 the government-run Nagasaki Trade House was largely devoted to procuring *tawara-mono.* However, in fact, though the *bakufu* held a monopoly over the export of these items, Ryukyu obtained them through the Satsuma *han* and, slipping through the *bakufu*'s control, exported large quantities of marine products to China.

Citing the *bakufu*'s policy of assisting Ryukyu, Satsuma sought during the nineteenth century to increase the share of the trade in Chinese goods moving through Satsuma's port. Hard bargaining ensued with the *bakufu,* which sought to prevent any such increase from threatening its China trade monopoly at Nagasaki Port. In September of 1810 (Bunka 7), Satsuma was given permission to deal in Chinese goods at Nagasaki for the next three years, but trade was limited to the so-called eight kinds of goods in extremely high demand throughout Japan, including fabrics such as silk damask and European woolen cloth; Chinese paper; dye pigments for dark red and navy blue; and lead. Although officially this trade was allowed under the pretext of lending support to Ryukyu, and all these goods were sold as "Ryukyuan products" or "goods of the Ryukyu Kingdom," in fact more than half these Chinese goods had been imported directly by Satsuma. Later, and continuing for many years, Satsuma sold through the Nagasaki market other desirable goods such as medicines, dyes, and Chinese and Western fabrics, all under the label of "Ryukyuan products." In China, the turmoil of the Opium War and the Taiping Rebellion of the 1840s and 1850s gradually reduced the number of Chinese ships coming in to port, and the Nagasaki market waned. In contrast, Ryukyuan products won a greater share of the Nagasaki trade. In addition, the importance of Satsuma's port increased as it became the main window for the China trade.[37]

### News Messengers: Envoys as Sources of Information about China

During Japan's Edo period, news of China came mainly through the *Tōsen fūsetsu-gaki* [Record of News from the China Ships], reports of news obtained from Chinese junks arriving at Nagasaki.[38] These reports allowed some understanding of China's state of affairs, though only to a limited degree. The Shimazu clan took advantage of Ryukyu's tribute missions to China and pressed the tribute envoys to collect as much information about China as possible.

Qing China continued to enforce its predecessor's ban on overseas travel and strictly prohibited the export of weapons; anyone suspected of passing on military information to foreigners in China was harshly punished. For this reason, it was extremely difficult for Japan to gain any military intelligence regarding China. The Chinese news sent to Japan through Nagasaki in general did not include any in-depth information on Qing China's military affairs. The Shimazu, however, were able to obtain such information through Ryukyu's tribute envoys. Upon their return after their stays in Fuzhou and Beijing, and the long round-trip journey between the cities, the "China source envoys" were sent to Satsuma to report. The *han* was quick to send their findings regarding Chinese military forces to the *bakufu*. Officially, these "source envoys" came to the Satsuma *han* to report on the tribute mission; in reality, besides military news, the envoys also brought a wide variety of news about China.

Beginning in 1667, the years between official tribute missions to China had seen the dispatch of ships to offer greetings [*setsukōsen*]. These were often called "ships that listen in every direction" [*sa'ukikibune*], because one reason for this journey was to gather information about China. The custom of sending "China source envoys" began in 1678, and thereafter the tribute envoys were able to collect a varied set of news, in addition to the military information. The envoys' responsibilities were not simply to transport a load of goods to the Chinese court; they also had to serve as messengers carrying news of China to Japan, enclosed behind its policy of isolation.[39]

CHAPTER FIVE

# Reform and Sinification of the Kingdom

## REORGANIZATION OF THE SHURI ROYAL GOVERNMENT

### Distinction of Elite and Commoner Classes

After the Shimazu conquest, the kingdom had been subjected to strict regulations and policing. On the Eighth Month, 20th Day, 1624 (Kan'ei 1), the Shimazu lord issued a "ruling" [*sadame*], in which the Ryukyuan king was given limited authority in juridical matters, in conducting religious observances, and in granting stipends to a selection of government positions.[1] Gradually, the royal government's sense of self-rule rose as restrictions imposed by Satsuma loosened and some autonomy returned. The royal government's political and administrative powers were strengthened as they carried out a structural reform that clarified various administrative duties and functions and brought lines of command into better alignment with the *bakuhan* system.

In Old Ryukyu, there was no formal distinction between the elite and commoners, and in principle people were free to live in any area. After the Shimazu invasion, however, the kingdom adopted the Japanese mainland custom of separating elite nobles and commoners, establishing a class system. In 1689, the royal government founded an Office of Genealogy, charged with the task of tracking and recording family lineages. Noble families generally kept two copies of their genealogies, with one copy stored at the Office of Genealogy, and the other, stamped with the royal government's red seal, kept at the family home (see Figure 5.1). In Ryukyu, the custom of tracking family lineages was called *kafu*. Only noble families tracked their

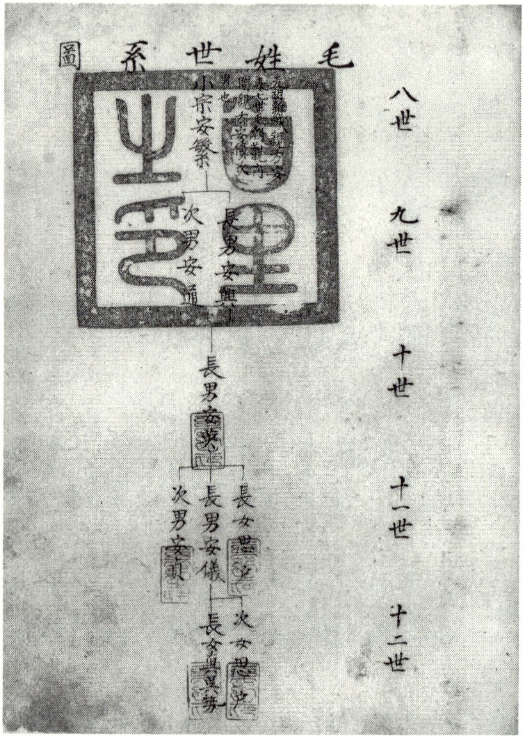


*Figure 5.1.* Title page from the Uchima Family Lineage, descendants of the Mō family. An eighteenth-century document, with the seal of the Ryukyu Kingdom. University of Hawai'i Library Collection.

genealogies, so such families might be known as *keimochi* [lit. lineage possessor]; families without, such as commoners and farmers, were *mukei* [lit. without lineage]. Thus, social distinctions based on the possession of a family genealogy led to the institution of a class-based society of elites [*shi*] and commoners [*nō*].[2] The first compilation of the genealogies sparked such a large number of ex post facto petitions to change family status that in 1712 the government ordered a revision of the family genealogies.

The duties of the elite, despite the label of "warrior," did not include fielding armed forces in times of war. They were not *bushi* such as those found on the Japanese mainland; rather, they were heavily engaged in serving as civil servants in the royal government. Being listed in the revised official genealogy as "elite" guaranteed a family's high status, but a line divided the lineages classified as "elite" into those with ancestral standing and newcomers. Highest ranked were the elite families whose ancestors had held their status since the kingdom's beginning; in contrast, newcomers had latterly secured theirs by successful petition, through distinguished service, or by making contributions to the government. Depending on their histories, families of this class were either *satonushi ke* or one rank below that, called *chikudun ke;* all newcomers were *chikudun ke.* Both the course and speed of promotion for any civil servant depended on which side of this division his family fell. In 1720, the royal government decreed that the official genealogies should be updated once every five years in a process called *shitsugi,* or the "civil service listing." A family inheritance was not passed on intact from one generation to the next as among samurai families in the Japanese mainland; rather, inheritances often gradually diminished over several generations, until finally new appointments restored them. Thus, the preservation of family status hung on public service and promotion in a successful career.[3]

### Court Rank and Administrative Organization of the Royal Government

The royal government's administrative structure consisted of twenty levels, with the king at the top, followed by the *sessei* (royal adviser) and the Sanshikan (royal councilors, lit. Council of Three), who stood above the rank system. These were followed by eighteen divisions of court ranks from senior and junior first rank through senior and junior ninth rank.

The usual titles for the court ranks were *uēkata* (senior first through junior second rank); *pēchin* (senior third through junior seventh, with distinctions within *pēchin* between *satonushi pēchin* and *chikudun pēchin*); *satonushi* (senior and junior eighth rank); and *chikudun* (senior and junior ninth rank). Below these stood the *niya,* those lacking court rank, and members of the commoner class. The titles *pēchin* and *chikudun* did not indicate whether the bearer was an "elite." Some commoners served as *pēchin,* and there were those of the elite who remained *chikudun.* Thus, status as an elite or a commoner could not be determined by the titles of *pēchin* and *chikudun* alone; however, a man's class and rank could be accurately judged by the color and markings of his cap, as well as the quality of his ornamental hairpin.

The highest executive organ of the royal government was the Hyōjōsho (Royal Council); it included the *sessei,* Sanshikan, and two ministries known as Mōshikuchihō (a ministry with responsibilities for police, palace affairs and maintenance, harbors, etc.) and Monobugyō (a ministry responsible for land resources, public employees, taxes, etc.). The *sessei* and the Sanshikan formed the upper branch [*ue no o-za*] and oversaw affairs of state; below them, the remaining divisions made up the lower branch [*shimo no o-za*] of government.

High-ranking officials known as the Fifteen Heads served as the ministers and vice ministers of the Ministries of the Mōshikuchihō and the Monobugyō[4] and formed a parliamentary body to deliberate matters vital to the government. The Monobugyō included the three divisions of Treasury (Shotaihō), Land Management (Kyūchihō), and Preparations (Yōihō). The Treasury Division oversaw the royal treasury and such matters as the remittance of tax to Satsuma; Land Management saw to the collection of rents and their distribution as stipends; and the Division of Preparations handled matters such as short-term special projects and expenses.

The responsibilities of the Mōshikuchihō included conducting diplomacy, managing the Palace Secretariat, maintaining the register of genealogies, and supervising a police force and justice system. In this administrative system, the highest-ranking members of the elite served on the Council of Three (Sanshikan); members of the royal family itself filled the royal adviser (*sessei*) position. Authority over the entire system belonged to the reigning monarch.

## RYUKYU SINIFIES

### Ryukyu, Vassal of Japan; and Ryukyu, Vassal of China

After Satsuma's invasion, its control over the kingdom gradually strengthened. When the Chinese Qing dynasty toppled the Ming and began its reign with a loud assertion of hegemony as Asia's most powerful nation, both the *bakufu* and the Satsuma *han* wished to avoid any friction with the Qing court concerning the Ryukyu Kingdom. Upon the inauguration of a new shogun, all the daimyo were required to submit a written pledge of loyalty [*kishōmon*] to the *bakufu*. Of course, the Lord of Shimazu properly made his pledges; attached to these documents was a promise not to join Ryukyu if ever it engaged in any nefarious plots. He also vowed to be vigilant against any disloyal action taken by the kingdom at China's instigation.

While taking cautious heed of Satsuma's vigilance, the royal government nevertheless aimed at developing an autonomous political system, with the backing of the Qing government. The kingdom maintained its position in the system of tribute exchange with China and simultaneously attended to its duties in the Japanese version of a tribute system under the *bakuhan*, seeking to buffer its own territory with a two-pronged strategy in which Ryukyu played a dual role as a vassal of Japan and also as a vassal of China. The kingdom strove until its final dissolution to preserve its national identity by balancing on this double strategy; doing so became the guiding philosophy of the kingdom's ruling class. And as it executed this strategy of playing two sides, the kingdom created its own unique position.

In regards to the *bakuhan* system, it is important to consider that the royal government, in that system, existed as a subordinate to its overseer, Satsuma, which in turn was backed by the power of the shogun. The administrative structure of the Ryukyu Kingdom, too, was greatly impacted by the rules and regulations of the Satsuma domain, as well as those of the ultimate authority, the Edo *bakufu*. At the same time, the kingdom increased its ritual diplomatic observances of tribute and reception of Chinese imperial envoys, as permitted by the *bakufu*. As it embarked on its path of increasing sinification, the kingdom was deliberately overt in its display of loyalty to Asia's most powerful nation and its imperial court. China's tremendous authority provided a check the kingdom could wield to resist the power of Satsuma and the *bakufu*.

Thus the kingdom increasingly deepened its interest in China. Probably any direct interference on the part of the Chinese in the internal affairs of the royal government would have been a tricky matter to deal with, in the light of the kingdom's real relationship with the *bakufu*. However, as long as the kingdom treated China's imperial envoys with the honors they were due, and correctly observed all the ceremony and ritual required in the tribute offering, the Chinese court asked no questions about the tribute or its origins. The Chinese side was satisfied by virtue of the tributary relationship itself that it "controlled" those who paid tribute—beyond that, China did not interfere. The *bakufu* found this Chinese foreign policy unobjectionable, and the royal government relied on this in conducting the dual policy aimed at ensuring its continued existence. Thus the Ryukyu Kingdom avoided complete absorption into the Japanese *bakuhan* political organization by creating a pseudo-Chinese national identity that embodied the kingdom's supreme effort to retain its autonomy. This was the origin of Ryukyu's increasing sinification.

### "Going Up to Edo": Important Diplomacy

In 1709, the *bakufu* deemed that Ryukyuan diplomatic missions to Edo [Edo *nobori*], in contrast to its ruling in Korea's case, were unnecessary. Satsuma, on the other hand, was required to make the Edo *nobori* journey to reaffirm its pledge of allegiance to the shogun. Since Ryukyu ranked just after Korea among the nations holding tributary status to China, "congratulatory envoys" sent from Ryukyu for an audience in Edo, as had been the past practice, had highlighted Japan's stature in the East Asian community—such was Satsuma's argument when it requested permission, which the *bakufu* eventually granted, to include Ryukyuan "congratulatory envoys" in its Edo *nobori* parties.[5]

Subsequently, Satsuma ordered the members of the Ryukyuan contingent to dress in a Chinese style that emphasized their foreignness and to play up the fact that they were foreign emissaries from one of China's tributary nations. As a formality meant to increase the shogun's standing in the East Asian community, the ritual of Edo *nobori* was of the utmost importance. For Satsuma, the trip to Edo was an opportunity to display its foreign vassals, who were required to wear Chinese robes and play music as the cavalcade advanced along the road, and at banquets and ceremonies along the way. From then on, Ryukyuan envoys who took part in an Edo *nobori* donned their Chinese robes whenever the procession passed through important cities or castle towns, and they performed in parade as a matter of course. In addition, the Chinese-style mustaches and beards affected by the Ryukyuan noblemen only added to their foreign looks in the eyes of any observers, for the custom throughout Japan during the Edo period, unlike during the earlier periods when beards had been common, was for men to be clean-shaven.

In June of 1712, the king discarded the title of Ryukyu *kokushi* [governor of Ryukyu] when Satsuma permitted him to take up once again the title of king of Chūzan.[6] This marked the beginning of the kingdom's policy of emphasizing its status as a foreign nation, and the royal government ranked Edo *nobori* on a par with the dispatch of tribute envoys to China. Together, these diplomatic actions served to emphasize the Ryukyu Kingdom's identity as a sovereign nation. Granted, the kingdom was essentially forced by Satsuma to join the Edo *nobori,* but conversely, the journey had its benefits for the royal government as well. The missions to Edo were another chance to display the "royal authority" required to engage in great diplomatic matters and to improve the kingdom's status among the nations in the Chinese tributary system. Satsuma's demand that the Ryukyuans play up their foreignness acted like a spur to the kingdom's policy of sinification.

### Introduction of Chinese Ritual Ceremony

In another example of adding Chinese style to an existing ceremony, on the first and fifteenth days of the First Month of a new year, the various royal attendants and officials gathered in front of the Seiden, the Main Hall at Shuri Castle, to offer their New Year's greetings to the king in the ritual of *chō no u-mi-hai* [the offering to the court]. An entry in the first volume of the *Ryūkyūkoku yuraiki* [Record of the Origins of Ryukyu] relates that traditionally, three ringing strikes on a *taiko* drum announced the start of this ceremony. On that signal, the king, dressed in Chinese robes, approached a designated worship spot [*yōhaisho,* lit. place to worship from afar] located in the *u-nā* [forecourt] and, facing in the direction deemed auspicious for the year, ceremoniously burned incense as he performed the "three genuflections and nine kowtows."[7] After 1719, this traditional Yamato-style ritual that had once celebrated the selection of a new propitious direction, which changed each year, had undergone some revisions. Starting that year, the new ceremony was performed always facing the direction of the god of the heavens, Hokushin (the North Star). In the revised ritual, a master of ceremonies from Kumemura called commands in Chinese: *Pái bān!* (Stand in line!) *Qǐ guì!* (Kneel!) And finally *Kòu tóu!* (Tap heads!) The assembled participants followed, bending down and kneeling three times, each time leaning forward three times to touch the ground with their foreheads as they intoned the phrase *Wàn suì, wàn suì, wàn wàn suì!* [lit. ten thousand years, i.e., May the king live forever, J. *banzai*]. The ceremony that had been known as *chō no u-mi-hai* later became *ten no go-hai* [the offering to heaven], the change reflecting the Chinese belief that the emperor's power of sovereignty came from a heavenly god. Also from that time, during observances of national ceremonies in every part of the kingdom, the king wore Chinese court robes, called crown robes [Ch. *guān fú,* J. *kanpuku*], as he presided over these newly introduced Chinese rituals.

### Shuri Castle in the Chinese Style

The modern Seiden at Shuri Castle is not that of the Gusuku Period, but a replica of one built in 1768, well after the kingdom had begun to adopt Chinese styles. The dimensions and other details of this building are recorded in *Momourasoe udun fushin ni tsuki miezu narabi ni ozaimoku sunpōzu* [Chart of Measurements, Materials, and Plans for the Construction of the Momourasoe Palace, 1768 (Qianlong 33)].[8] *Momoura* [hundred villages] referred to all the villages of the kingdom; *soe* means "to rule." Thus *Momourasoe udun,* the "Momourasoe Palace," was an honorific reference to the Seiden [Main Hall] at Shuri Castle.

The Seiden at Shuri Castle served as a symbol of the monarchy's sovereignty. Three stories high, its double roof is hipped in the Japanese style, with gables at the ends; the portico in the center-front has a cusped gable, such as those often seen on Shinto shrine buildings. Thus, at first glance, the Seiden seems characteristic of Japanese architecture. A closer look reveals that the larger castle arrangement centers on the Seiden, with an open space (the *u-nā*) to the west where formal events took place, and the living area to the east (behind the Seiden from the *u-nā*) where the royal family and the female courtiers resided. This closely resembles the layout in China's Forbidden

City, with its Outer Court for official events, and the Inner Court where the emperor lived. In addition, bricks are laid out in wide bands perpendicular to the central aisle in the *u-nā*. These lines served as guides for officials attending ceremonies such as the *chō no u-mi-hai* to arrange themselves in perfectly straight rows, and the lines at which they stood reflected their status. In the Forbidden City in Beijing, officials participating in formal ceremonies also arranged themselves in straight lines according to their court ranks. With the difference that in the Forbidden City, the lines were marked with elaborately carved copper ornaments that indicated the rank of those in a given line, this was another point of resemblance shared by Shuri Castle.

Ceramic sculptures in the shape of dragons' heads, symbols of the Chinese sovereign, ornament both ends of the Seiden's roof and the gable over the central portico. Also as seen in the Forbidden City, the portico gable is painted with the motif of two dragons facing each other, reaching for a great gem. The sign of the twin dragons also appears on the wooden framing of the second-floor Chinese-style throne room, the Ōkuri, and a single gold dragon pillar depicting a rising dragon stands directly in front of the throne. The foundation platform of the Seiden is built with stone columns in the manner of Chinese palaces, and dragons are everywhere along the façade banister in the front courtyard, with pillars made in the shape of twisting dragons, and small dragon figures adorning even the handrail portion of the banister. In this way, dragons inhabit all of the Seiden and its environs, giving a strong indication of Chinese influence.

### The *Feng Shui* Cosmology of Shuri Castle

Generally, a "*feng shui* analysis" looks at the topography and compass directions of a site to identify the flow of *qì* energy through the so-called dragon's veins [Ch. *lóngmài*, J. *ryūmyaku*] in the undulations and slopes of a winding mountainside, in order to find "dragon's hollows" [Ch. *lóngxué,* J. *ryūketsu*], places where the *qì* pools. Such places are believed to confer peace and prosperity upon any homes or towns built nearby. In *feng shui,* the good or bad environmental conditions of a site are signs of how the *qì* will directly influence and shape the good and bad fortunes of a person's life. *Qì* that has a beneficial effect is called *shēngqì* [J. *seiki,* vitality]; *qì* with bad effects is *shāqì* [J. *sakki,* death energy]. As might be expected, the search for sites with great sources of beneficial *shēngqì* is continual, and the *feng shui* masters who determine how to create living spaces filled with the flow of *qì* energy have always been in great demand.

Auspicious locations where sources of *qì* are found are called *fēngshuǐ bǎodì* [J. *fūsui hōchi, feng shui* repositories]. Such sites of power are often open only to the front, backed by high mountains and surrounded on either side by heights from which a river flows. As sinification continued, even Shuri's topography was subject to the ideas of *feng shui*.

According to the traditions of *feng shui* as passed down in China, four guardian deities occupy the four directions of any site. These are Black Tortoise [Ch. Xuánwǔ, J. Genbu] in the north; Vermillion Bird [Ch. Zhūquè, J. Suzaku] in the south; White Tiger [Ch. Báihǔ, J. Byakko] in the west; and Azure Dragon [Ch. Qīnglóng, J. Seiryū] in the east. Locations protected by these guardian deities are marked as "sites that suit the Four Deities." Shuri Castle faces west and looks out over Naha's port toward the East China Sea. Normally the positions of the Four Deities correspond to the four directions of North, South, East, West, but in this case, Bengadake, actually to the east of Shuri, is the highest point in the hills around the castle. In *feng shui* reading, it backs the castle and becomes the location for the Black Tortoise (generally associated with the north). The high ground to its left is thus the direction of the Azure Dragon (normally east, but in the case of Shuri, it is to the south); and that on the right, the domain of the White Tiger (normally west, but in the case of Shuri Castle, it is to the north). To the front, to the west beyond Naha, lies the expanse of the East China Sea. Straight out from Naha, the islands of the Kerama group float like a brocaded screen in the middle of the sea, as if to catch the *qì* of the Vermillion Bird. Next, a glance around the environs of Shuri shows mountains such as Torazu and Sakiyama, and lush, thick forest surrounding the castle both near and far, giving the area an air of great natural vitality. From the White Tiger to the left and the Azure Dragon on the right flow the Kanegusuku and Makabi Rivers, both fed with mountain waters rich in *qì*.

The prominence on which the Main Hall (Seiden) of Shuri Castle is built was chosen for its excellent *feng shui* elements. It is the location of a dragon's hollow (*lóng xué*) that collects the vitality (*shēngqì*) flowing through the dragon's veins (*lóng mài*) around it. At the mouth of the dragon's hollow is the "bright hall" [J. *meidō*, Ch. *míngtáng*], regarded as an important place linked with blessings from the gods, and a space teeming with vitality (*shēngqì*). In Shuri's case, the great courtyard in front of the Seiden, the *u-nā*, corresponds to the bright hall. The purity of the bright hall must be carefully maintained, and its size and shape must fit strict rules. It must be neither too narrow, nor too dark; yet if it is too wide, the collected *qì* would simply dissipate. The Rendō, the path leading out from the Seiden to the first front gate, called the Kankaimon, does not follow a straight line, but instead, with a bend to the left and an abrupt right corner, follows a *feng shui* design meant to prevent the *qì* from seeping out.

The beneficial dragon's veins in *feng shui* usually require easily accessible springs and pools of pure, clean water carrying positive *qì*. Just such a spring may be found to the right of the stone stairs at Shuri's Zuisenmon [Auspicious Spring Gate]. The springwater flows from a stone spout carved in the shape of a dragon's head, called the Ryūhi [Dragon Culvert]. The name of the Zuisenmon derives from its proximity to this spring. The dragon, considered an auspicious creature, was the symbol of emperors and kings; here the dragon also refers to the *feng shui* concept of the dragon's veins that poured pure springwater into Shuri Castle. This spring was believed to carry with it good *qì* and was an omen of wealth and luck. When imperial envoys were in residence at the Tenshikan, the hall built for them near Naha Harbor, young men from Kumemura brought them water from this spring each morning. Upon drinking some of the water, the envoy Xú Bǎo Guāng was inspired to write the characters *Zhōngshān dìyī* [J. *Chūzan dai ichi*], meaning the Zuisen was Ryukyu's (Chūzan's) finest spring. A stone monument carved with Xú's calligraphy still stands next to the Zuisenmon, among several other such markers, all celebrating the springwater rising out of this dragon's vein.

Another important consideration in *feng shui* is where the water rising from such a spring flows to; flowing out of an auspicious spring, it must also flow into an auspicious location. A belief that water should be held in the place near the spring from which it flows meant that man-made ponds were often dug near springs to collect the water and prevent the *shēngqì* from dissipating. Given the belief that excavating ponds to hold water encouraged the life pulse of the earth, increasing its *shēngqì*, a pond in front of a spring also became a storehouse for life energy. The pond below Shuri Castle, the Ryūtan [Dragon Pool] Pond, was dug with just such *feng shui* considerations in mind.

Thus, the Shuri Castle that ruled over the *momoura* (hundred villages) was also an emblem of *feng shui* space, a perfect model of the principles of *feng shui* cosmology.[9]

### Sinification in the Kingdom Becomes the Norm

Once the ranks of the members of the elite who ruled as ministers and bureaucrats had been settled, the royal government tackled the issue of formulating a national ideology in accordance with Confucian principles. In order to get firmer control of its ministers, the government made it the ministers' duty to act in accordance with Confucian ethics and morality and promoted Confucianism as the practical political ideology most suited to those who bear the responsibility of governing. The ceremonies that modeled its ideals were regarded with the highest respect.

Confucian ideology was first introduced and fostered in and around Kumemura. However, the latter half of the eighteenth century saw the spread of Confucian education, and elementary education in the Confucian classics became available at academies in Shuri, Naha, and Tomari. Mid- and advanced-level studies were provided at national schools such as Shuri's Mihira Gakkō. The classics of Confucianism became the basis for a national curriculum, and education in the basics of Confucianism reached all levels of Ryukyuan society. The royal government ordered that on the first and fifteenth of every month, its local representatives must read to the commoners in their districts excerpts from the *Articles of Instruction* [*Go-kyōjō*], a text that lays out Confucian philosophy for everyone from elites to commoners. In addition, there was an expansion of the policy of great professional and social rewards for those who conformed to Confucian standards of filial piety, greatly reinforcing the Confucian order of society.

In 1701, a genealogy of the royal family written in literary Japanese, the *Chūzan seikan* (1650), edited by Shō Shōken (Japanese name Haneji Chōshū), was translated into Chinese by the Kumemura scholar Sai Taku, with dates added in reflecting the Chinese calendar. Sai Taku's son, Sai On, edited and updated it in 1725. Even the *Kyūyō*, an official history of the kingdom compiled chronologically in the manner of imperial annals, came under the influence of the general sinification and was transcribed into Chinese.[10]

The adoption of Chinese styles may also be seen in the family genealogies (*kafu*), which only elite lineages were allowed to maintain. The revised genealogy compiled by the royal government in 1690 shows that not only Kumemura residents, but also the elite families of Shuri, Naha, and Tomari, bore Chinese family names (or clan names), such as Ma [J. Ba], Cai [J. Sai], and Mao [J. Mō].[11] For example, in 1700, Ma Tingqi Kōchi Uēkata Ryōshō was a member of the Council of Three [Sanshikan]. Ma Tingqi [J. Ba Teiki] was his Chinese name (family name Ma, given name Tingqi); Kōchi was his Ryukyuan/Japanese family name; Uēkata was his title; and Ryōshō was his given name. Thus, members of the elite had names in both the Chinese and the Japanese styles.

The family names of the Ryukyuan elite differed from those of their Japanese counterparts in that the latter bore their names permanently. In Ryukyu, however, families took their names from the places over which they ruled; a change of domain meant a change of name. Thus linked with territorial changes, some families changed names three or even four times. In Ryukyu, the elite consisted of consanguineous clan groups, tied through their paternal lineages, called *monchū* [Ok. *munchū*]. Given that family names were connected to territory, it was not always possible for, say, the Japanese-style designation "Kōchi clan *monchū*" to include every member of a related group of people under that family name. Instead the clan used its Chinese name to call itself the "Ma family *monchū*." With regard to family genealogy, all members of the Ma clan, for example, were recorded in the "Ma family genealogy" [*Ba-ke kafu*]. Membership in a clan could be clearly determined based on these genealogies using adopted Chinese family names.

At first, the official genealogies were written in Japanese, but as the process of sinification continued, the genealogies took on the style of Chinese family pedigrees, and entries came to be written in Classical Chinese. The Chinese system of religious observances and the social order distinguished between *dà zōng* [comparable to the Japanese term *honke*], the head family or main line of a clan; and *xiǎo zōng* [comparable to the Japanese term *bunke*], a branch family or minor line. Head families held authority over branch families. Though a clan's main line continued unchanging in perpetuity, there could be numerous branch family lines. Blood ties continued through the fifth generation of a branch, after which a new clan group would be established. This system strengthened the ritual of ancestor worship in China's Confucian society and unified family groups; and the system made its mark in Ryukyuan society as well.[12]

### The Spread of *Feng Shui* beyond the Capital

Though *feng shui* was not part of the formal studies relating to Ryukyu's national governance, where the focus was the orthodox philosophy of Confucianism, the royal government dispatched many students to China to study the laws of *feng shui*. A 1667 entry in the *Ryūkyūkoku yuraiki* mentions the studies in Fuzhou of Zhou Guojun [Shū Kokushun], perhaps the first Ryukyuan to receive training as a *feng shui* master.[13] The royal government, fully absorbed in its process of adopting Chinese mores, made a policy of applying the principles of *feng shui* in national enterprises in matters such as planting forests, flood prevention, and village planning or relocations. Thus, the tenets of *feng shui* penetrated to every area of government activity.

*Feng shui* masters began to be consulted in the construction of family homes. Also, many believed that establishing a family tomb in an area judged satisfactory according to the tenets of *feng shui* would ensure the prosperity of the family's descendants. From the end of the seventeenth century, elite families of Naha and Shuri, at the recommendation of their *feng shui* advisers, began to have their tombs built in the *kamekō-baka* [tortoise-shell tomb] style often seen in China's Fujian Province. In fact, there are those who believe that because of the way *feng shui* makes use of mounds and clefts that resemble depictions of female genitalia, the notion of *feng shui* itself grows out of a religious worship of the Earth Mother. These "tortoise-shell tombs," built with space for a *mingtang*, a "bright hall" of collected *qì* at their front, a style strongly influenced by the ideas of *feng shui*, are known to have been sites of this cult of a maternal earth.

Another *feng shui* practice was placing charms against evil spirits in locations where they were known to appear and bring *shāqì*, death energy. As a protection against the misfortunes brought by these evil spirits, small stone tablets carved with the characters *ishigantō*[14] were affixed to fences and walls around the heads of T-intersections and three-forked junctions, locations where such spirits were believed to lurk, to prevent them from entering into nearby houses. The three characters in the word *ishigantō* were believed to hold the power of soothing the multitude of spirits and of fending off calamity. Other protective charms included statues of *shīsā* [J. *shishi*, lion dog] placed on the roofs of houses, and short stone walls, called *hinpun*, that blocked direct access to the front doors of the houses of elite families. These stone walls, known in Fujian as *píngfēng* [J. *byōbu*, wind screen] or *píngmén* [door screen], kept out bad spirits, which could not navigate over or around them. Protective charms such as *ishigantō*, *shīsā*, and *hinpun* were all operated on the concept of *feng shui*. This Chinese tradition of *feng shui*, with its defenses against the mischief of evil spirits, was first brought at an early date to Kumemura by the descendents of Chinese residents there; as the Ryukyu royal government continued avidly to pursue its policy of sinification, it soon gained many adherents as it spread into every part of Ryukyuan society.

Though there were no Daoist masters in Ryukyu, the Japanese translation of the Daoist holy text that describes how a life must be lived, the *Tàishàng gǎnyīngpiān* [J. *Taijō kannō hen*, Essay on the Divine Inspiration of a Daoist Master], was in circulation there and could often be found in the libraries of the elite.[15] Guān Dì [J. Kantei, more commonly known as Guān Yǔ (J. Kan'u)], a Taoist saint believed to protect house and family, also had a following, and his statue frequently stood in the sleeping alcoves of elite houses.

Finally, other Chinese traditions became more widespread as well. Whenever they framed a new house, many families followed the Daoist custom of inscribing the words "Shibi Ranga" [lit. Purple Forbidden City Chariot] on the ridgepole as a good-luck charm and prayer to fend off disaster. These words addressed the prayers of protection for the family to the gods inhabiting the Purple Forbidden City (a group of constellations in the northern sky) and the chariot that carried the palanquin of the Great

Northern Emperor as he rode across the sky. Another deity of Chinese origin with a wide following was Tōteikun, or Tokoten, a "god of luck and happiness" whose statues were frequently enshrined in public spaces for the public to offer up prayers and who was believed to lend protection to certain localities.

### Sinification of the Seafaring Community

The *bakufu* established a system to repatriate Chinese shipwreck victims, through the Satsuma *han*. The *bakufu* ordered that any Chinese ships wrecked on Ryukyu territory be reported to Edo and Nagasaki. Then any survivors were to be transported via Satsuma to Nagasaki, from there to be returned to their homelands. In 1684 (Kangxi 23), the Qing court lifted the ban on ocean travel after it had finally succeeded in suppressing the Zheng family of Taiwan, who had been bent on restoring the Ming dynasty. It issued an order permitting merchants along the coasts to engage in private sea trade once more and officially requested the assistance of the Ryukyu royal government in protecting and repatriating Chinese shipwreck survivors.[16] This request for the Ryukyu government to return Chinese survivors directly to Fuzhou clearly conflicted with the *bakufu*'s instructions, but in response to the renewal of Chinese oceangoing trade, in 1696 the kingdom sent directly to Fuzhou a group of people found adrift on the sea. After that, Korean shipwreck survivors were also sent to Fuzhou, a policy that took into account Ryukyu's status as a vassal of China. Though condemning Ryukyu's stance in accepting the Qing court's request without first consulting with Satsuma, the *bakufu* pardoned Ryukyu for its cooperation with China because it wished to avoid any political conflicts with the Qing government. Behind Ryukyu's disregard of the *bakuhan*'s system for returning shipwreck survivors lay the royal government's political intention of strengthening its relations with China. This demonstrates how sinification gradually affected the kingdom's seafaring community as well.

Originally the ships built and operated by the various villages in the kingdom were Japanese-style ships. Starting in the early eighteenth century, however, the royal government encouraged a change to Chinese junks in the style of *māransen* [lit. horse battleship]. *Māransen* were reliable even in rough wind and waves. Built with several individually watertight decks, even if they took on water there was little risk they would sink, and within limits, they could be sailed against the wind. These ships were much cheaper to build and maintain than earlier models and soon became common. Thus, within the borders of the kingdom, the royal government created a culture on both land and sea suffused with the colors and styles of China.

## REORGANIZATION OF KUMEMURA

### The Kumemura Era

Members of elite families from Kumemura played the most important role in implementing Ryukyu's policy of sinification. The residents of Kumemura not only provided the bulk of leadership in conducting tribute missions, but also served as conveyors of Chinese culture into the kingdom and played a key part in ensuring its secure establishment there. We may surmise from this that the residents of Kumemura gained their high status by being the instruments of sinification in Ryukyu.

When Ryukyu's tribute trade began its gradual ebb in the second half of the sixteenth century, Kumemura also suffered a decline in fortune. In his *Shǐ Liúqiúlù* [J. *Shi Ryūkyūroku,* Record of the Envoy to Ryukyu], Xià Zǐyáng wrote, "The Thirty-Six Families have decayed until only a mere six remain, and [Kumemura] resembles nothing so much as a ghost town."[17] An entry in the *Kumemura nikki* [Kumemura Diary] reads, "By the end of the great Ming dynasty, Kumemura declined until only about thirty elderly residents and children remained."[18]

After the Satsuma takeover, in the interest of reviving the tribute trade, an aggressive policy to reinvigorate Kumemura included filling in the gaps left by the erosion of the Thirty-Six Families by translating into Chinese the entries for families originally from Naha, Shuri, and even Satsuma in the Kumemura family register. In addition, even members of Kumemura's elite who had not been appointed to official positions were given retainers' stipends in rice according to their court ranks, with the result that Kumemura became a special "government official enclave," made up of families different from the elite families of Shuri, Naha, and Tomari, which had formed around the tribute missions. Government stipends for the nobles of Shuri or Naha largely corresponded to their official posts, rather than being based on their court rank. The rice stipend amounted to a special economic privilege granted to the noble families of Kumemura.

With the founding of the Qing dynasty, the aristocrats of Kumemura regarded the change to Manchurian customs with some concern. At first, they changed the style of their clothing from the earlier Ming style to Ryukyuan-style robes, but with the kingdom's increasing adoption of Chinese ways, they became the center from which Chinese culture was spread, and even more so than before, residents of Kumemura steeped themselves in China's ancient traditions. Kumemura bore the primary burden of ceremonial relations with China, and had they not, the kingdom could not have sinified to the degree that it did. For this reason, the eighteenth century is known as the "Kumemura era."

## Kumemura Is Steeped in Confucianism

In 1671, the highest ranking official in Kumemura, the *sōri tōeishi* [director of Chinese affairs] Kin Seishun, was given permission by King Shō Tei to build a shrine dedicated to Confucius, completed in January 1676.[19] By 1678, professional "teachers of recitation" (*kōkaishi*) and "teachers of readings" (*kunkoshi*) were giving instruction on the meanings and wording of the Confucian classics. The royal government had stopped sending students to Beijing during the long period of tumult at the end of the Ming dynasty; in 1686, once the Qing had firmly established itself, students were once again dispatched to the Chinese capital. Four candidates from Kumemura, including Ryō Seishū and Sai Bunfu, were the first "government students" [*kanshō*] sent to the Qing court.[20]

These "government students" studied for three years at the National Academy [Ch. Guózǐjiān, J. Kokushikan], China's most elite academic center. According to the section on foreign students in the *Qīndìng guózǐjiān zhì* [Imperially Authorized Annals of the National Academy], the only foreign students admitted to the National Academy were from Russia and the Ryukyu Kingdom.[21] After returning home, they assumed positions as storytellers and exegetes, taking central roles of responsibility in the Confucian education system. In 1718, with the aim of educating youths, the Meirindō was established in the Confucian shrine as an academy for the study of Confucianism. As the Meirindō also turned out great numbers of graduates trained in Confucian ideas, the people of Kumemura developed an ever more pronounced character as Confucian disciples.

A textbook explaining Confucianism, for use by commoners and translated into Japanese by Muro Kyūsō [aka Muro Naokiyo], was the *Kankoku rikuyu engi taii* [General Explanation of the Six Official Dicta], which explained a set of six rules that gained widespread acceptance in Japan during the Edo period. These were "Obey your parents"; "Respect your elders and superiors"; "Live peacefully in your home-towns"; "Instruct your descendents in morality"; "Be contented within your various livelihoods"; and "Do no harm." The original text in Chinese, the *Liùlùn yǎnyì* [J. *Rikuyu engi,* Six Dicta], had first been brought home from Fuzhou by Tei Junsoku, a Confucian scholar from Kumemura.[22]

## Dispatching "Working Students"

As Kumemura sought to revive its fortunes during this period, besides the government-sponsored "government students," who focused their studies on the Confucian classics, a large number of students from Kumemura studied in Fuzhou as "working students" [*kingaku*]. These students were sent to China as part of the crews of the envoy ships and, once there, were expected to absorb as much Chinese knowledge as possible. The system established to send working students was another result of the royal government's drive to adopt Chinese mores.

Working students crossed to China hidden within larger groups. They came to be included as ship crew, with four accompanying missions in years in which tribute was offered, and eight persons going along in years when the kingdom received gifts. Their presence in the missions was kept hidden from the Chinese. Because the Chinese permitted no long-term students other than the official government-sponsored students, the term "working students" is seen only in documents on the Ryukyuan side; it does not appear even once in Chinese documents. In effect, the working students were illegal, royal government–sponsored exchange students. Initially there was no limit on the length of their stays, and they could stay as long as needed for their studies; however, in 1731, they were limited to a maximum stay of seven years. Certainly, there were those among the working students who focused their studies on the classic texts and ritual ceremony of Confucianism, but many more of them spent their time in Fuzhou studying a wide variety of subjects, including Chinese calendar making, *feng shui,* medicine, the law codes, and Chinese painting and music, and they brought this know-how home to Ryukyu with them. In addition, many among the students who went to China as working students became highly fluent translators of the Chinese language. Truly, Ryukyu's working students became a strongly sinified echelon under the royal government's drive to adopt Chinese ways.[23]

## REINFORCING THE POLICY OF CONCEALMENT

### Takarajima, "Treasure Island"

The royal government's policy of sinification was conducted with the understanding that the reality of Satsuma's control was to be kept hidden from the Chinese, under the so-called concealment policy. The Ryukyuan envoys who made the Edo *nobori* journey occupied an important position in Japan's "diplomacy of sovereigns." It became customary to grant a promotion to the Satsuma lord each time the Ryukyuan envoys made their visit to Edo; thus, as noted earlier, Shimazu was using the Ryukyuans for its own political gains. Lying behind Satsuma's insistence on a concealment policy was their wish to avoid any political interference by the Qing court if it found out how the power relations really worked. However, by far the greater motivation was Satsuma's interest in promoting its own economic interests. Satsuma wanted to control the kingdom's tribute missions and seize all the profits of the tribute trade.

After 1667, permission to send tribute ships spurred new efforts in pursuit of profits. The Shimazu clan, fearing a break in the relationship between Ryukyu and the Qing court if their control of Ryukyu were discovered, named an island in the Tokara island group, just north of the Amami group, Takarajima, "Treasure Island." They concocted a fiction in which Ryukyu carried on a cross-frontier trade with Satsuma via Takarajima, a scheme meant to prevent China from recognizing the presence of Satsuma and the *bakufu* crouching behind the façade erected by the kingdom. With such manipulations to prevent a breakdown in Ryukyuan-Chinese relations, the Shimazu used Ryukyu both politically and economically.

The policy of concealment was not the result of some negotiation or agreement between Satsuma and Ryukyu, but was always entirely the brainchild of the Shimazu clan, their motivation boosted by the reluctance of the *bakufu* to risk political friction with China. Additionally, for the royal government, defeated in war, these steps to preserve the age-old tribute relationship with China represented a way to ensure the kingdom's continued existence. As a result, both sides naturally fell into agreement, and the royal government continued its cooperation into the modern era, conducting the policy of concealment with meticulous attention to detail.

### Concealment Takes Many Forms

In the latter half of the eighteenth century, the royal government issued several written directives to those likely to come into direct contact with Chinese citizens. With titles such as "Instructions for Travelers," "Manual for Handling Ships Crossing to China, and Predicting the Weather," "Instructions for Shipwrecks," and "Handling Wrecks in China of National Ships," the directives denied any relationship with Satsuma.[24]

The handling of ships gone adrift or wrecked in Chinese territory presented some difficulties under the policy of concealment. These ships were most often loaded with Japanese goods and carried Japanese-language documents including correspondence between Ryukyu and Satsuma. Included in the "Instructions for Travelers" and the "Instructions for Shipwrecks" were clear directions that after a shipwreck, any accounting books, letters, or Japanese books that could cause trouble if seen by the Chinese were to be burned quickly before any official inspection could take place. Whenever a Ryukyuan ship set sail, required documents included promissory statements recording the ship's owner, the crew, the pilot, the content and quantity of cargo, and the ship's destination. Once the new orders went out, and fearing that the dates and contents of the promissory statements would reveal Japan's involvement, shipwreck victims were ordered not to use the statements as proof of their own identity, but to burn them before they fell into the wrong hands. Most often the royal government's burn orders were obeyed, since destroying the documents could not conceal the fact that such shipwreck victims were Ryukyuan. Once the Chinese authorities recognized them as such, they always provided crews with help and shelter, delivering them to the Ryukyu House in Fuzhou, from there to be returned safely to Ryukyu.

The concealment policy was consistently upheld even when a ship from Satsuma wrecked along the Chinese coast. According to the *Sasshūsen Shinkoku hyōryū dan* [Stories of Satsuma Ships Wrecked in Qing China], in July of 1741 (Kanpō 1), a Satsuma cargo ship carrying Ryukyu's annual tribute was lost over the horizon from Kume Island. Twenty survivors were picked up by a passing fishing boat and delivered to the island of Yushan in the archipelago city of Zhushan in China's Zhejiang Province. The cargo ship's captain had died, and two of the pilots had fallen ill, so after the wreck, the Ryukyuan pilot who had been hired in Naha quickly ordered the Ryukyuan crew to use cooking knives to shave their heads in the Japanese style and to tell the Chinese authorities their names were Kinsaemon and Gosaemon. To maintain the policy of hiding Satsuma's relationship with Ryukyu, they were to stress that their ship had come from Satsuma, not from a Ryukyuan port.[25]

In Ryukyu, Chinese envoys visiting from the Qing court to present investiture patents meant that the concealment policy operated there, too. When the Chinese envoys were in residence, no one was allowed to mention any subject related to Japan, and an order went out forbidding the display of public notices written in Japanese. Japanese language, dates according to the Japanese calendar, Japanese-style names, and Japanese poetry all were forbidden. Even the use of the common Japanese Kan'ei coins was forbidden; the Ryukyuan *hatome* coins were substituted for them. In addition, Japanese books, tools, votive tablets offered to temples and shrines, votive plaques painted with horses in the Japanese style—these and other Japanese items were to be hidden away from the Chinese visitors. These instructions were given not only to residents of Naha and Tomari, but to government officials and village heads on outlying islands as well.

Guard stations were set up in three locations in Naha and were charged with watching street traffic, to limit direct contact with the Chinese visitors. Satsuma's local representatives and other staff stationed in Ryukyu moved to Gusukuma Village, in the Urasoe district north of Naha. Careful watch was kept to make sure the Chinese visitors did not go beyond the city limits, and any groups or individuals likely to come into contact with the visitors were given scripted answers to any possible questions they might be asked by the Chinese. When dealing with the Chinese, Amami was treated as if it were still part of the kingdom, while in fact it was firmly under Satsuma's direct control, so the royal government even put procedures in place to deal with the possibility of one of the Chinese mission ships running aground or sinking in the Amami islands. On top of this, all visits by Japanese ships to Naha's harbor were stopped for the duration of the Chinese investiture envoys' visits.

### China Does Not Meddle with the Policy of Concealment

The Chinese were not unaware of the existence of the concealment policy. The investiture envoys knew about the Satsuma invasion, and they were aware of Ryukyu's direct exchanges with the Japanese mainland. Many Japanese editions of classic Chinese texts circulated in the kingdom, and the envoys knew the royal government used Japanese Kan'ei coins, which were supposed to have been taken out of circulation, in the markets at Shuri and Naha. They could also tell that their interlocutors were under a state-ordered prohibition, because they would not talk openly about the conditions of their home country and were hiding something—but the Chinese envoys did not bother to look more deeply into the mystery, and there is no indication they had any problem with it. Even if they could detect the reality of Japan's rule over the kingdom, as long as they did not seek any real explanations, neither did they have to report this deception on the part of the Shuri royal government to the Chinese imperial court. The only thing they had to report was the allegiance that the Ryukyu king had to the Chinese emperor, to whom he had pledged his loyalty.

Despite widespread worry that the Chinese would bring out into the open the real relationship between the Shimazu and the royal government, in fact, as long as Ryukyu continued to observe proper form in the matters of required tribute and the investiture patent ceremonies, China did not interfere in the kingdom's internal affairs. It, too, did not wish to provoke any hostility in its relations with Japan. Additionally, the Qing court continued to regard Ryukyu as a member of the "barbarian horde" in the Chinese sphere, and as such, it provided a politically stable buffer zone between China and Japan. Consequently, though China sensed to some degree the true state of affairs in Ryukyu, it did not officially claim any rights of exclusive suzerainty over the kingdom.

The overwhelming authority of China, the greatest political and military power of Asia, provided the motivation for the royal government's policy of sinification. For preserving its good relations with China, nothing was more important than the system of ceremonial diplomacy exemplified by "offering tribute" and "investiture patent." Its relationship with China as a vassal became the means by which the kingdom preserved itself, and the royal government invested heavily in the tribute and investiture missions. Therefore, the next chapters explore exactly how Ryukyu's offering tribute and investiture patent played out in the context of the *bakuhan* system.

CHAPTER SIX

# The Ryukyu Kingdom's Tribute Trade

## PREPARATIONS AND LEGATION LEADERS FOR MISSIONS TO CHINA

### The Forty-Seven-Hundred-Mile Round-Trip Journey to China

The Ryukyu Kingdom continued to send tribute to China for more than five hundred years after the first mission sent by King Sattō in 1372.[1] During this period, the political circumstances surrounding the kingdom underwent many changes even as it continued offering tribute. Ryukyu's political organization altered after the Sanzan period when it came under the rule of the First and Second Shō dynasties, and China saw its ruling dynasty change from the Ming to the Qing. In addition, the Satsuma invasion of 1609 profoundly affected the political environment yet again. In the midst of these transformations, the frequency of tribute missions to China changed from era to era. In general, the missions may be classed either as the regular tribute missions or as missions made with special purposes, such as congratulating a new emperor upon his assumption of the throne or carrying thanks for the bestowal of a patent of investiture upon a Ryukyuan king. The regular tribute missions may be separated into the following seven periods, showing the frequency limits as imposed by China:

| | |
|---|---|
| First | 1372–1474 (No limit on frequency) |
| Second | 1475–1506 (Once in two years) |
| Third | 1507–1521 (One per year) |
| Fourth | 1522–1611 (Once in two years) |
| Fifth | 1612–1622 (Once in ten years) |

Sixth 1623–1632 (Once in five years)
Seventh 1633–1875 (Once in two years)

After 1667, a second ship, the mission retrieval ship [*sekkōsen*], made the journey to China to collect the returning envoys. Because it, too, carried trade cargo to sell, in effect the tribute trade missions became an annual event.

In 1421, Emperor Yongle moved his capital from Nanjing to Beijing, meaning the Ryukyuan envoys had to travel to the new capital from Fuzhou. After setting sail from Naha to make the 800-kilometer crossing over the great expanse of the East China Sea to Fuzhou, the envoys traveled an additional 3,000 kilometers to Beijing, making the round-trip distance a total of 7,600 kilometers [4,720 miles]. A variety of ceremonies and events were held in the Ryukyu Kingdom before the envoys embarked on this journey. There is no single document remaining from the royal government that describes the entire process in detail, from appointing the envoys and their crossing to China to their eventual return. However, a relatively complete set of records remains regarding the tribute legation dispatched in 1844 (Daoguang 24), and from them we may see what a tribute mission looked like.[2]

Besides tribute envoys, the tribute ships of the Qing dynasty carried envoys bearing thanks for the grant of a patent of investiture, envoys charged with congratulating a new emperor upon his ascension to the throne, those bearing news of the death of a Ryukyuan king, and finally envoys with messages of sympathy on the death of an emperor. The ships were also dispatched to meet the imperial investiture envoys and bring them to the kingdom. The 1844 mission, however, was just a regular tribute mission.

### Formation of a Tribute Legation

Government business in China was called *tabiyaku* [travel duty]; personnel sent on travel duty were called *totō yakunin* [China-crossing officials]. In years in which tribute was sent, these officials were usually selected in February from a pool of applicants hoping to do travel duty who had submitted a travel application to the relevant upper-level government office.

According to the travel credentials that the officials of the 1844 mission presented to the Chinese authorities, they included the senior envoy, the vice envoy, the ship's envoy, the royal interpreter, the ship's interpreter, the resident interpreter, and a general functionary. The senior envoy's title of *jimoku kan* indicated a court rank in the royal government; the vice envoy's title of *seigi taifu* was a Kumemura rank indicating an official of upper or lower third rank. The royal interpreter served the envoys who would travel to Beijing; the ship's interpreter handled the trade business to be conducted out of the Ryukyu House in Fuzhou; and the resident interpreter remained stationed in Fuzhou even after the tribute mission had been completed, to handle official matters. China interpreters from Nagasaki learned Chinese mainly from contact with merchants from Jiangsu, Zhejiang, and Fujian, and thus they spoke those local southern dialects rather than Mandarin Chinese, the common language used by officials throughout China. In contrast, the Ryukyuan interpreters did not speak the local dialects, but used only Mandarin.

The ship's envoy was responsible for the purchase of Chinese goods. He remained in Fuzhou for about half a year, trading the ship's cargo and buying the goods desired by Satsuma (the primary goods) or the royal government (the secondary goods).

The duties of the general functionary originally included overseeing the various matters pertaining to the ship itself, but by the early modern period, his responsibilities included performing the ritual observances to the Bōsa, or Maso, the sea deity, to ensure her protection for the ocean crossing; he also saw to the incense kept burning in her shrine on board the ship. Others in the tribute group included the low-ranking crew and the ship captain. During the Qing period, crews were frequently recruited from the communities of Naha, Tomari, the Kerama islands, and Kudaka Island. Finally, also on board and listed as "sailors" or "subordinates," were the students on their way to study in China. The word used for the sailors on the ships, *suishō,* was an abbreviation for *kansui ishō,* literally "barbarians familiar with water."

### Forming Legation Groups and Work Teams

Of official legation members in the 1844 tribute mission, the flagship carried 118, and its smaller companion ship carried 82. Those on board could be divided into three separate groups: (1) the legation party that would continue to Beijing to present tribute; (2) the team that would remain in Fuzhou to engage in trade; and (3) the ships' crews. The members of a China crossing were sorted into small *kumi,* or "lord-and-retainer" teams, according to their assigned duties; several teams together made up a single *ōyado,* a "great lodge." The tribute trade took place under the organization of these great lodges. Led by legation officials, who in China were called *guānyuán* [J. *kan'in,* government officials], these groups lodged together, sharing meals and accommodations. Before their departure, they engaged in elaborate preparations and role-playing to prepare for all possible situations they might encounter in China, conducting any number of rehearsals for the all-important tribute ceremony. The tribute legation that traveled in 1844 began their training on the 1st Day of the Fifth Month.

According to the *Shinkōsen shidashi nikki* [Journal of the Tribute Ship Cargo], which chronicled the 1844 trip, by the time the ships commissioned to carry the tribute envoys sailed out of Naha's harbor, a full program of ceremonial rituals and official events had been observed. These included, in the Fifth Month, the Journey Blessing, the Ritual Prayer to Bōsa, a Pilgrimage, and Firearms Training. The Sixth Month saw the Prayers of the Three Districts, Oaths, the China Ship Naming, Embarkation of the Bodhisattva, and the Tea Rice Banquet. Finally, in the Seventh Month came the Transfer of the Declaration to the Emperor, the Transfer of Silver, Loading the Great Cargo, and Embarkation.

## CHINA-CROSSING RITUALS AND TRIBUTE EVENTS

### Journey Blessing and Ritual Prayer to Bōsa

In the Journey Blessing ceremony, all the members of a China mission gathered at Shuri Castle for an audience, first with the king, and then with the queen, to receive their blessings. This ceremony was the first of a whole series of observances and related events connected with the tribute mission.[3]

The Ritual Prayer to Bōsa was a religious ceremony showing strong influence from Chinese Daoism. It offered respect to Bōsa [known as Maso in Japanese and Mazu in Chinese], a virgin goddess who protected sailors and fishermen, and asked for a safe journey. Maso, accompanied by Junpūji and Senrigan, was a protective sea deity, also known as the Heavenly Concubine [Tenpi], the Heavenly Empress [Tenkō], or the Holy Mother of Heaven [Tenjō seibo]. Lore says she was born in Song China in 960 as Lin Mo, a daughter of the Lin family of Meizhou in Putian County, Fujian Province. At the age of thirteen she was initiated into the mysteries of Daoism, and when she was sixteen, a Daoist immortal appeared to her out of a well and gave her a magical talisman. Thereafter, the story goes, she was able to foresee good and bad fortunes, and her divine power protected many people from calamity and shipwreck. Even after her death and ascension to heaven at the age of twenty-eight, signs of her power continued to appear, and people enshrined her as the "departed saint." After this she became known as Mazu [Maso in Japan, as noted earlier]. Mazu's cult had its origins in the miracles attributed to Lin Mo and the massive following that grew around her among the common people.

Even today, in China, in Taiwan, and among overseas Chinese communities, Mazu has a large following as a Daoist deity, and many others believe her to be an incarnation of Guanyin [J. Kannon]. In Ryukyu, she was known as Būsa-ganashi (that is, Great Boddhisattva [J. Bosatsu-sama]).[4] Out at sea, in the face of any raging storm or pirate attack, a prayer to Maso was believed to provide protection and deliverance from danger. In that age when it was impossible to get accurate weather forecasts for the ocean conditions before setting sail, there was no way to know when a storm from the Pacific Ocean would hit a ship crossing the East China Sea, and sea travel always carried the risk of death. Maso brought comfort to those hazarding their lives to travel across the ocean. She was a powerful protectress who would hear their prayers and shelter them from disaster on the high seas. In Ryukyu, temples dedicated to Maso included the Shimo Tenpi-gū in Naha; the Kami Tenpi-gū in Kumemura; and the Tenkō-gū on Kume Island. The religious ceremony of Ritual Prayer to Bōsa, asking for the safety of the ships carrying the tribute legation of 1844, took place at the Kami Tenpi-gū in Kumemura.

### Pilgrimage and Firearms Training

The pilgrimage ritual was a procession to the temples and shrines in Kumemura, Naha, and Naha's outlying areas to pray for safe passage. Besides Maso, the pilgrims appealed to other deities of the Chinese Daoist tradition, such as Lóngwáng [J. Ryūō, the Dragon King], Tiānzūn [J. Tenson, Venerable God, Ch. Tàiyǐ tiānzūn], and Guāndì [J. Kantei, Daoist God of War]. They also visited the temples at Naminoue Gokokuji and Rinkaiji to perform dance and music rituals to request the protection of the deities enshrined there.

In firearms training [J. *teppō keiko*], the travelers practiced their fighting skills. Rampant piracy made the seas off the coasts of Fujian and Zhejiang Provinces very dangerous, so the tribute ships were provisioned with weapons and built with narrow openings along the sides through which weapons could be fired. The legation members had to practice using weapons such as bows, lances, and guns in case of a confrontation with pirates during the voyage. So-called *hiki* guards, named for the military organizations responsible for the defense of castles and harbors during Ryukyu's classical period, were used on board the tribute ships to guard them. After the Satsuma invasion, however, weapons were under the control of Satsuma's administrator, and the firearms training was conducted under the administrator's supervision and with weapons lent by his office. Generally, the training lasted a week and took place to the north of Naha in what today is the north side of Tomari Harbor. In their written vows, the officials joining the tribute mission wrote, "If pirates attack as we are making our journey to and from China, I will work with the others on the ship as we have practiced, and I will not give way to cowardice."[5] An entry in the *Kyūyō*, the kingdom's official history, dated in the seventh year of King Shō On's reign (1801), notes that "when attacked by pirates, [those aboard ship] lined up in their assigned positions and without pause opened fire, protecting [the ship] by shooting their weapons."[6] We may understand from this that everyone on board the China ships was included in the prepared battle plans. Contemporary illustrations of the ships show areas for everyone, including students, officials, and interpreters, as well as the ship crew, marked according to their occupations, but nowhere on the ship do we see space reserved for any guardsmen. Thus it is clear that when necessary, all the members of the tribute legation venture joined in the fight.

### Prayers of the Three Districts and the Oath

The highest-ranking religious title in the Ryukyu Kingdom was that of Kikoe Ō-gimi, a hereditary position held by either a royal princess or the queen. This priestess lived in special quarters at Shuri Castle, and her duties included praying for the king's longevity, the well-being of the royal family, and abundant crops. The royal capital city of Shuri was divided into the so-called three *hira,* or districts, of Mawashinohira, Haenohira, and Nishinohira; each district was the domain of a priestess of the cult of the earth mother, Ō-amushirare [Great Mother Ruler]. In a ritual called Prayer of the Three Districts, the priestesses, known as Makabe Ō-amushirare, Shuri Ō-amushirare, and Gibo Ō-amushirare, would take the China legation members into Kikoe Ō-gimi's palace to pray to the deity enshrined there. The legation received a ritual cup of sake from Kikoe Ō-gimi in a religious ceremony unique to the kingdom. It was another ritual of blessing and prayer for a safe journey.

In the oath, all the members of the tribute legation made a pledge always to honor Satsuma's will, an oath sealed with blood. They promised not to engage in smuggling or to bring in books related to Christianity, reflecting Japan's policy of closed borders, or *sakoku.* The ceremony, usually held in the main hall of the Naminoue Gokokuji, a Shingon Buddhist temple, was attended by the officials from Satsuma, the chief priest of the temple, and very high officials of the royal government.

### China Ship Naming and Embarkation of the Bōsa

The China Ship Naming was a christening ceremony for the ships chosen to carry the tribute envoys to China. The group of people bound for China visited Shuri Castle, and the priestesses provided ship names appended with the beautifying term *-tomi* [wealth], such as *Sejiara-tomi* (power-rule-fierce-wealth), *Seiyari-tomi* (power-send-wealth), *Sedaka-tomi* (world-high-wealth), and *Ukitoyomi* (float-prosperity-see), that conferred divine protection on the ships.

The Embarkation of the Bōsa took place just before the tribute ships departed for China. This was a ritual for the ceremonial transfer of Bōsa (also known as Maso or Mazu, as noted earlier) into a shrine on board ship. A statue of Bōsa, or Maso, from Tenpi-gū was carried in procession through the streets on a palanquin, accompanied by music, and finally placed in the Bōsa *u-dun* [palace of the Bodhisattva], a shrine for her in the ship's stern. According to the *Shinkōsen shidashi nikki,* an auspicious day had to be chosen for this transfer of the Bōsa into the shipboard shrine. On the 4th Day of the Seventh Month, the legation officials presented the *Hiyorigaki* [Book of Date Selection] to be used in determining a plan for embarking the Bōsa. After careful scrutiny, the ninth was chosen. However, the day before the chosen date, the ceremony was delayed due to bad weather. On the twelfth, the process for selecting a date was repeated, and a new date of Seventh Month, 19th Day was set. Finally, on a date ten days later than initially planned, the ceremony to enshrine the Bōsa on board ship took place. Thus, the statue of the Bōsa was embarked only after the right day had been determined with the utmost care. While the ship was at sea, the official responsible for religious services performed ceremonies, burning incense as he prayed; meanwhile, back at the home shrine, Tenpi-gū, rituals were performed every day until the tribute ship had returned safely home.

### The Tea Rice Banquet and Transfer of the Declaration to the Emperor

The king and the three royal councilors [Sanshikan] attended the Tea Rice Banquet, also called the Tea Rice Banquet for the China Legates, or the Journey Gala, to observe the ceremonies for a safe sea passage and to celebrate the imminent departure of the China mission. The legation group went up early in the morning to the *u-nā,* the great courtyard in front of the Seiden at Shuri Castle, and on a signal, the ship crew braided a rope. As they worked, singers titled Omoro Pēchin and Omoro Seitō performed *omoro,* religious songs. The rope they braided was stretched straight out from the Seiden along the sacred *ukimichi* [floating road], a path that only the king could tread. The legation officials dined and drank liquor in the Officials' Hall;[7] lower-ranking officials were also banqueted in other locations. At the conclusion of the banquet, the king appeared at the front of the Seiden dressed in Chinese court robes, and the tribute envoys unfurled banners and sang the "Travel Song." When these rituals were finished, the members of the tribute legation processed out of the castle to the steady beat of a gong, following the lead of those carrying the rope.

The Transfer of the Declaration to the Emperor [J. Jōhyōto] took place in the Seventh Month. In this ceremony, a group of the China-crossing officials received the king's ritual declaration of loyalty to be offered to the Chinese emperor. In addition, the tribute ships also carried *zīwén* (official communiqués) addressed to other foreign legations stationed in Fujian. The task of composing the declaration and the official communiqués was entrusted to Kumemura officials, but they were not necessarily handed directly to the Chinese as is. They could get wet during the voyage, for example, or a need for revision might arise after arrival in Fujian, or some political event could create the need to amend the contents of these documents as the legation was under way. In anticipation of such situations, the envoys were dispatched on their mission equipped with blank scrolls stamped only with the royal seal, so-called *kōdō* (lit. empty roads). When needed, the envoys could write new declarations and communiqués that fit altered circumstances. The "empty roads" were important documents for the tribute legation; any that remained unused were returned to the royal government once the legation had returned home.

### Transfer of the Silver and Loading the Great Cargo

In the Transfer of the Silver ceremony, the tribute legation was provided with the funds to purchase items on behalf of Satsuma or the royal government, as well as to finance any expenses encountered in China. The journal for the 1844 mission relates that the first silver transfer was on the 17th Day of the Seventh Month; the second silver transfer took place on the eighteenth, and finally on the nineteenth, the transfer of the officials' trade silver. The officials' trade silver was intended for use by the legation officials to conduct their own private business in China.

Next came Loading the Great Cargo. This "great cargo" included all the cargo loaded onto the tribute ships, but it was common practice on the tribute ships to divide the cargo bound for China into goods intended to be offered to the court as true tribute, and goods intended to be ancillary cargo, to be used in trade and bartering. In the period stretching from the collapse of the Ming dynasty to the establishment of its successor, the Qing dynasty, mother-of-pearl conch was included in the tribute cargo, but during the Ming dynasty, the most important offerings were horses and sulfur. After 1692, tribute offered to the Qing emperor included 12,600 *kin* (about 7,560 kilograms) of purified sulfur, 3,000 *kin* (1,800 kilograms) of copper, and 1,000 *kin* (600 kilograms) of refined tin. These three products were always included as tribute goods.

The sulfur was mined in Iōtori-jima, a small island with a surface area of about 2.5 square kilometers, located roughly 25 kilometers [about 15 miles] west of Tokunoshima. A tempering process refined the sulfur, after which it was shaped in small, round cakes. Iōtori-jima, as the source for the all-important tribute sulfur, remained under the control of the royal government even after the Satsuma invasion. The copper was in the shape of rods, obtained through the Satsuma *han* from Osaka; the tin also came from Satsuma.

During the Ming dynasty, important ancillary cargo included sappanwood, pepper, and tin. When trade with Siam (Thailand) ended in the 1570s, high-quality ramie linen cloth, used for summer clothing, gained in importance. Beginning in the reign of the Qing emperor Kangxi (r. 1662–1722), ramie linen was replaced by banana-fiber cloth [J. *shōfu*] and banana-fiber cloth embroidered with crests [J. *monshōfu*], as well as *saidon* [J. *saidon shōfu,* soft banana cloth] and *donjuku* [J. *donjuku shōfu,* soft boiled banana-fiber cloth], banana-fiber cloth of differing textures. Later, the ancillary cargo came to consist largely of products harvested from the sea, including items like shellfish, which were wrapped in straw (*tawara-mono*), and other things, like kelp. During the loading of the great cargo, in addition to the regular tribute goods, this ancillary cargo was also inspected and loaded.

The holds of the tribute ships were partitioned into sections; each section was further divided into small compartments. These small cargo holds were called *funama,* or "ship rooms." Each member of the tribute legation filled his allotted ship rooms with his "personal luggage," and each was permitted to sell for profit any portion of this luggage after landing in Fujian. However, this system was compromised by the frequency of smuggled goods being included in the load. Such smuggling is alluded to with the 1844 legation. The legation members were required to make a written vow, stamped with a seal of blood, in what was in fact a completely meaningless pledging ceremony, before boarding ship.

### Embarkation and Setting Sail

Once the long series of events and ceremonies had been completed, finally the company could board ship. In the Tondō, a building looking out over Naha's harbor, all the lower-ranked Satsuma officials met with representatives of the *sessei* and the Council of Three to observe the legation officials boarding, a process that began with a formal roll call (*ninzū aratame*). Usually, the tribute legation members were not allowed to disembark once they had finally stepped on board ship, in order to ensure the security of the loaded cargo. Without a favorable wind, this shipboard confinement could last for up to two months as they waited for the wind to turn.

A sand bar near the mouth of Naha Harbor meant that sailing out of the harbor required negotiating one of three channels, known as the China Ship Channel [J. Tōsen-guchi], the Yamato Channel [J. Yamato-guchi], and the Miyako-Yaeyama Channel [J. Miyako-guchi]. The tribute ships exited the harbor by way of the China Ship Channel. If the winds were not favorable even after setting sail, the ships might wait at a special mooring at Ago Harbor on Zamami Island; sometimes they moored at Kanegusuku Tomari on Kume Island to await the winds. As they waited, the whole ship's company focused its attention on China. The tribute ship of 1844 lay moored for a while offshore of Naha. Its scheduled departure date for China was for Ninth Month, 13th Day, but the wind changed its direction and the ship was unable to set out to sea until the twentieth.

### Tribute Ship Design Based on Fujianese "Bird Ships"

The tribute ships were modeled after the "bird ships" of Fujian, so named because their sails resembled birds' wings. One section of Naha Harbor, the *suradokoro,* was dedicated to shipbuilding and repairs. In the language of Old Ryukyu, shipyards were called *suraba*. The word *sura* originally meant "treetop" or "branch tip"; it came to have the extended meaning of a site where ships were built and launched, boats being likened to young birds flying from their nests in the treetops. The word *suradokoro* comes from comparing a shipyard, and the ships that depart from it, to a nest in which a bird's eggs lie warm and safe, until finally they hatch, the chicks grow, and then they set out on their life work and journeys.

The vivid imagery of birds leaving the nest may be readily applied to the tribute ships. While the ship crew braided the great rope in the *u-nā* in front of the Seiden at Shuri Castle, as part of the Tea Rice ritual asking for safety during the sea crossing (see earlier), they would sing the following *omoro:*

| | |
|---|---|
| *Shuri owaru tedako-ga* | Child of the Sun [i.e., the King] who dwells at Shuri |
| *Hajiya-no saiku atowete* | Gather together the carpenters who build ships |
| *Hane-uchi suru ko-haibusa* | And hatch |
| *Sudachife* | The young falcons that beat their wings |
| *Gusuku owaru tedako-ga* | Child of the Sun who dwells in the Precinct[8] |

Comparing a tribute ship to a bird, the song is a prayer asking that the ship fly before the wind like a falcon, majestic in flight.

### Tribute Ships' Magical Talismans

Any tribute ship sailing out of harbor flew a flag reading 進貢 (*shinkō,* bearing tribute; see Figure 6.1). It also bore a variety of magical talismans to help ensure safe passage across the sea. The ship's prow was painted with

*Figure 6.1.* A Ryukyuan tribute ship (*shinkōsen*) prominently flying the "centipede flag." Shinkōsen no zu, from *Zusetsu Ryūkyū Ōkoku*.

the face of a *shīsā,* a lion dog, marked with the character 王, "king." Giant eyes were painted on both sides of the ship, and triangular flags, five-colored flags, and the *hinomaru* [a red circle on a white background] flew from all three masts. The mainmast carried a weather-vane flag, as well as a splendid "centipede flag" [*mukadebata*] more than ten meters in length. On the rear mast fluttered a smaller centipede flag, and the "seven stars flag" [J. *shichisei-hata*], representing the North Star.

The *hinomaru* represented a wish for clear weather; the five-colored flags called on the five elements in yin-yang cosmology [metal, wood, water, fire, and earth] to fend off evil spirits. The centipede flag was flown because a traditional story told how the great centipede could intimidate malicious sea deities and ensure good weather. The North Star flag showed the seven stars of the Great Dipper (Ursa Major), believed to be the chariot carrying the Great Emperor of the North, who provided protection against disaster. In addition, the *shīsā* marked with the character for "king," painted on the front end of the ship, had the magical power to keep away the evil deities and magical monsters living in the sea. The custom of setting the head of a *shīsā* at the ship's prow was copied from the bird ships of Fujian. A Bōsahata, a religious banner, flew near the location of the Bōsa's shrine at the stern of the ship. Alongside it flew a flag for Kanteiō [Ch. Guān dì wáng]. The Ryukyu Kingdom took Kantei as its guardian demon; with his military prowess, Kantei's name symbolized strength and intimidation. Thus the tribute ships were provided with a variety of magical protective charms; in addition, the ships were brightly painted with blue, red, black, and yellow, primary colors that could easily be distinguished from afar.

### Tribute Ships' Round-Trip Route

In 1709, the Ryukyu House in Fuzhou published a woodblock print book, the *Shinan kōgi* [lit. General Instructions Pointing South], to be used as a voyage instructional manual by the tribute ships as they traveled between Naha and Fuzhou.[9] The *Shinan kōgi* contained instructions on the use of a compass, for the modern compass had been introduced to Ryukyu by the ship crew that brought the Chinese investiture envoys in 1683. This book was based on the compass techniques taught by the Thirty-Six Families of Kumemura. Filled with masses of vital information, it contains the first maps of Ryukyu's thirty-six islands and other ocean islands; records the compass bearings for sea routes; gives instructions for using a compass; includes a copy of the *Tenpi reiōki* [Records of Tenpi's Efficacy], which gives examples of Maso's divine protection from ocean hazards; tells how to track the distance traveled; provides a table recording the seasonal direction and periods of the winds; and gives a list of auspicious days for sea travel. In short, the *Shinan kōgi* was an indispensible piece of equipment when embarking on a sea voyage.

According to the *Shinan kōgi,* once a tribute ship had left port and set out across the ocean, its route was first to head directly for Nanqishan, an island offshore of Wenzhou in Zhejiang. Once there, ships were directed to turn south along the coastline, and once past Dinghai, they would finally reach Wuhumen [the Gate of Five Tigers], guarding the mouth of the Min River at Fuzhou (see Figure 6.2). There were so many islands off the coast of Zhejiang and Fujian, however, that it could be difficult to determine a ship's exact location based only on the information in the *Shinan kōgi.* In fact, the ship crews probably also used more detailed maps, such as the sea chart preserved in the archives of Kume Island's Yosenaga family, which shows in great detail the ocean geography of the Chinese coast with its many islands.

## THE RYUKYU HOUSE IN FUZHOU

### The Gate of Five Tigers or the Gate of Demons

The tribute ships took advantage of the northeasterly winds as they followed the Zhejiang coast south to Wuhumen, the Gate of Five Tigers. Fuzhou, where the Ryukyu House had been established, is the capital city of Fujian Province, on the lower reaches of Fujian's great Min River, which

*Figure 6.2.* Ryukyuan tribute ships arriving at Wuhumen Harbor. From *Ryūkaku Danki,* a 1797 account of conversations with visitors from Ryukyu. University of Hawai'i Library Sakamaki/Hawley Collection.

has its source in the Wuyi Mountains. To reach the city from the Min River's mouth, however, the tribute ships had to go upstream from Wuhumen. The Min is famous for its fast current, but if the ships waited for the tide to rise, they could ride the reverse flow upriver to the city. When tribute ships were expected, the security officer stationed at Wuhumen at the mouth of the Min River sent out sentry boats to patrol the area, and usually these boats would provide a convoy to escort the arriving ship into port. However, the Fujian coast was a hotbed of piracy, and it was a common occurrence that ordinary merchant ships would be beset and taken by pirates within sight of Wuhumen, at the very entrance to the harbor at Fuzhou.[10]

### Inspection by the Min Guard Station and the Harbor Master

Its passengers having been confirmed by their licensing papers that they were indeed tribute envoys from the Ryukyu Kingdom, the tribute ship made its way to the Min River security station and the officials there for a personnel and cargo inspection. The inspectors reported their findings to the official in Fuzhou responsible for the direct control of the tribute trade, the magistrate of coastal defense [Ch. *hǎifáng tóngzhī*, J. *kaibō dōchi*]. The tribute ship sent in 1844 arrived at Wuhumen on Ninth Month, 27th Day, escorted by patrol boats, and it was inspected by the Min security officials on Tenth Month, 1st Day. When this was complete, the ship made its way up the Min River, once again escorted by the military vessels, and anchored in Fuzhou three days later.

During the Qing dynasty, Fuzhou's ocean trade market was regulated by the Maritime Trade Office, but when a tribute ship moored in the harbor, it was the coastal defense prefect who came on board to conduct a thorough check of licensing papers, the official letter listing the members of the tribute legation who would be continuing to the capital, the tribute cargo, the ancillary cargo, the quantity of silver, weapons, and the number of people aboard ship. This was a customs control inspection, but the cargo on board was exempt from duty.

The inspection over, the cargo was transferred to a canal barge to be carried to the Wanshou Bridge and unloaded at the Ryukyu House, known to the Chinese as Rou Yuanyi.[11] Everyone on board spent the next five days at the Fuzhou Ryukyu House. The cargo, under the sharp-eyed supervision of the Chinese authorities to ensure there was no impropriety in its handling along the way, was also moved into the compound.

### The Ryukyu House in Fuzhou

Fujian Province was also known as Min; the capital, Fuzhou, was often called Rongcheng [Banyan City], for the banyan trees that grow there. During the Ming dynasty, the Maritime Trade Office moved from Quanzhou to Fuzhou. Fuzhou, rather than Quanzhou, had long been the preferred land ing city for the Ryukyuan envoys and had been the focal point for trade activities involving a long stream of people and goods.

The Ryukyu House stood outside the city walls to the southeast, near the Shuibumen [Waterworks Gate]. For a very long time, foreign tribute legations were not allowed quarters within the city itself, and it was the custom for the various tributary nations to build their embassies outside the city walls. In the Ming dynasty *Record of the Fujian Maritime Trade Office* [J. *Fukken shihaku teikyo shishi*], by Gāo Qí, a description tells that the Ryukyu House had three front and five back rooms used as public areas; six sleeping rooms for the China-crossing officials, twenty-seven for ships' crews; and two more that served as quarters and offices for the Chinese guards.[12] The Ryukyuans resided in the Fuzhou Ryukyu House under orders that allowed them to go out during the day, but at night they had to remain inside. All expenses were borne by the Chinese government, with each legation member, according to his rank, allotted the basic cost of living for such items as food for the duration of their stay in China.

The Ryukyu House also had shrines, such as the altar for Maso, an altar to the dead, and an altar to local gods. At the altar to the dead, mortuary tablets commemorated those who had died during their sojourn in China; the altar to local gods was dedicated to local earth deities of the Daoist tradition. Finally, once a tribute ship had arrived safely in China, the ship's shrine to Bōsa was placed in the altar at the Ryukyu House until it was time for the return trip.

### Three Teams: Capital Bound, Returning, and Remaining at Fuzhou

Once at the Ryukyu House in Fuzhou, the tribute party split into three groups. The first group consisted of the envoys who would continue to Beijing for the tribute ceremony at court with the emperor, returning home two years later with the off-year tribute ship that came to collect them. The second group would stay in Fuzhou for a shorter time to conduct business transactions, returning home the following year on the same ship that had brought them. Finally, the members of the third group would stay on for three years, returning home with the off-year tribute ship that came to collect the next tribute legation. The Chinese supervised these groups, labeling them the "capital bound," the "returning," and the "posted" groups, respectively. The tribute legation included a chief envoy and a vice envoy, 3 court interpreters, and their attendants, for a total of about 20 people. The returning group counted about 160 members, including a chief ship interpreter, a junior ship interpreter, the ship's master-at-arms, the cargo master, their attendants, and the ship's crew. The group that would remain posted at Fuzhou, about 16 people, included 1 resident interpreter and his staff.

### Ten Families of the Ryukyu Trade

The arrival of an envoy legation brought a period of intense activity to the Ryukyu House, because it meant the start of the open house trade period (the tribute trade).[13] Usually, the resident interpreter would make a request for permission to begin the trade period to the magistrate of coastal defense, the official responsible for supervising the tribute trade. The magistrate, following precedent, would then submit a trade petition to the provincial administrative commissioner [Ch. *bùzhèngshǐ*, J. *fuseishi*], a senior government official. In this petition, the magistrate assured his superiors that the cargo to be traded did not include any prohibited items such as weapons or gunpowder, or history books or political tracts that contained strictly prohibited news of the outside world. The commissioner would then forward the request to the governor and governor-general of Fujian, the two top ministers in charge of military and government matters. Trade could begin only after the governor and the governor-general had given their nods to the petition.

Those members of the envoy legation who were responsible for trade activities were diligent in their work; the goods they were interested in acquiring included many items, such as raw silk thread and silk fabrics, various medicinal products, dyes, and woolen cloth. During the trade period, traffic in and out of the Ryukyu House was strictly controlled, and the list of trade goods was also reported to Beijing. In order to prevent any illegal trading when goods were in transit from the Ryukyu House to be loaded onto the returning tribute ship, the cargo was carefully checked against this master list. All the goods acquired during the trade period were exempt from customs duties.

The trade in Fujian during the Ming dynasty was conducted under the auspices of government-backed brokers [Ch. *yáháng*, J. *gakō*, see the section "Trade Brokers in Quanzhou" in Chapter Three]. During the Qing dynasty, however, trade was conducted under the supervision of the "Ten Families of the Ryukyu Trade" [Ch. Shíjiā Qiúshāng, J. Jikka Kyūshō], a group of ten families, such as the Zhao, Zheng, and Li families, who had formed into an organization of trading brokers. Their organization was based near the Ryukyu House. The Ryukyu House's system was to provide a list of requirements as to the price and quantity of the Chinese goods to be acquired, and the Ten Families would then send out buyers to Suzhou and Guangzhou [Canton] to procure the desired goods.

### Local Interpreters and Resident Interpreters

During the Qing dynasty, the practice of stationing in Fujian three local Chinese interpreters, proficient in Ryukyuan, continued as before. In 1843, the year before the Daoguang 24 tribute ships set sail, the interpreters relocated into the Ryukyu House, establishing official stations at the front gate and at one of the side entrances. These local interpreters were required for any transactions at the various government offices; they accompanied the tribute envoys when they made their journey to the capital; and they provided their services for testimony on behalf of shipwreck victims in or outside the borders of Fujian Province.

Fundamentally, employment as a local interpreter was hereditary. These interpreters played a large role during negotiations between Ryukyuans and Chinese, and any outcome favorable to the Ryukyuans was dependent on their cooperation. In order to reward their efforts and ensure their continued goodwill, the Shuri royal government sent them a yearly honorarium as a formal gesture of thanks.

Because they spoke Mandarin Chinese, indispensible when dealing with government officials, and because they were familiar with the forms and rituals surrounding the tribute ceremonies, these local interpreters accompanied the chief envoy and the vice envoy on their journey to Beijing. They also acted as guides and interpreters for the entire round-trip. Their great understanding of Ryukyuan concerns meant that they also served as adjuncts when the Chinese government sent envoys to Shuri.

The Ryukyuan interpreters posted in-country resided in Fuzhou until their replacements arrived on board the off-year tribute ship. Their work was central to the trade transactions conducted out of the Ryukyu House, handling the requests for permission to begin the open house trade period. These posted Ryukyuan interpreters, the Ten Families, and the local interpreters from China all cooperated closely in running the Ryukyu House trade affairs, with each group striving to fulfill their duties smoothly and in accordance with the law.

Besides trade matters, the interpreters posted at the Ryukyu House engaged in negotiations and business formalities with the public authorities, taking on considerable responsibilities. The Okinawa Prefectural Museum collection includes a manual for handling such matters, the *Chéngbǐng wénjí* [J. *Teihin bunshū,* Collection of Petitions], used by the interpreter Liáng Bìdá [J. Ryō Hitsutatsu], who accompanied tribute legations during the Daoguang era (1820–1850). The phrase "for use in government business in China" is written below the index on the front cover. The manual has entries explaining how to deal with matters not directly related to the tribute missions, such as maintenance of the Ryukyu House and helping shipwreck survivors to return home again. As the title implies, it was also an important reference manual for correctly drafting letters and documents to be sent the Chinese government and officials. It seems likely that all the Ryukyuan interpreters kept a copy of the manual nearby, as an essential resource in completing their duties.[14]

## THE LEGATION'S JOURNEY TO THE CAPITAL

### Twelfth Month, 20th Day, Arrival Deadline

As the "returning" and "posted" groups went about their various tasks after arriving at Fuzhou, the group of twenty persons continuing to Beijing, from the chief envoy on down, prepared for the trip. Throughout the Qing period, tributary envoys as a rule attended the New Year's ceremonies held at the Qing court in January, and to do so, they had to be in the capital city by the 20th Day of the Twelfth Month. Generally, the Ryukyuan missions were on the road to the capital by the end of the Ninth Month or the beginning of the Tenth Month, accompanied by a Chinese escort that served as both guidance and protection.

The sulfur brought as part of the tribute offering was placed into a government warehouse in Fuzhou; the envoys carried the rest of the tribute, such as copper and tin, with them to the capital. Chinese officials accompanied the legation on the round-trip between Beijing and Fuzhou as imperial escorts. Many of the officials accompanying the tribute legation of 1844 were aides or clerks reporting to the provincial governor; additionally, military officers were assigned as escorts. Their responsibilities included issuing the supply tallies that specified the contributions, such as men, horses, and provisions to be delivered by the way stations along the road. The main route from Fuzhou to Beijing had long been set, but it could change due to circumstances such as local fighting and natural disasters. As Map 3 shows, the route went over both land and water, and the Chinese government provided the men and horses necessary to make the land segments, as well as the boats needed to navigate the rivers and canals.

A report to Satsuma known as the *Ryūkyaku danki* [Record of Conversations with Visitors from Ryukyu] contains a description of the journey (see Figure 6.3):

> Each province along the way provided escorts to accompany the envoys, as well as five or six junior attendants to carry parasols. They welcomed the envoys with music, and when the legation travelled by boat, a master musician rode on the chief envoy's vessel and played for him. When the envoys travelled by road, all the senior and junior officials were carried in sedan chairs, and their attendants rode on horses or carts. When the legation had to pass through a guard barrier, they beat gongs and fired off guns. The officials of the various provinces paid the legation's tolls for the round trip journey; and they lodged at night at the government hostels.[15]

As the tribute envoys passed from one province to the next on their road to the capital, their escorts were also responsible for reporting their progress to the emperor in Beijing.

### Journey of More Than Sixty Days

The envoys traveling with the tribute mission of 1844 left Fuzhou for Beijing on the 14th Day of the Tenth Month, rather later than usual. They boarded their barge docked near the Ryukyu House outside the city walls and floated downstream to arrive the next day on the Min River proper. By the eighteenth, they had completed the one-hundred-kilometer upstream

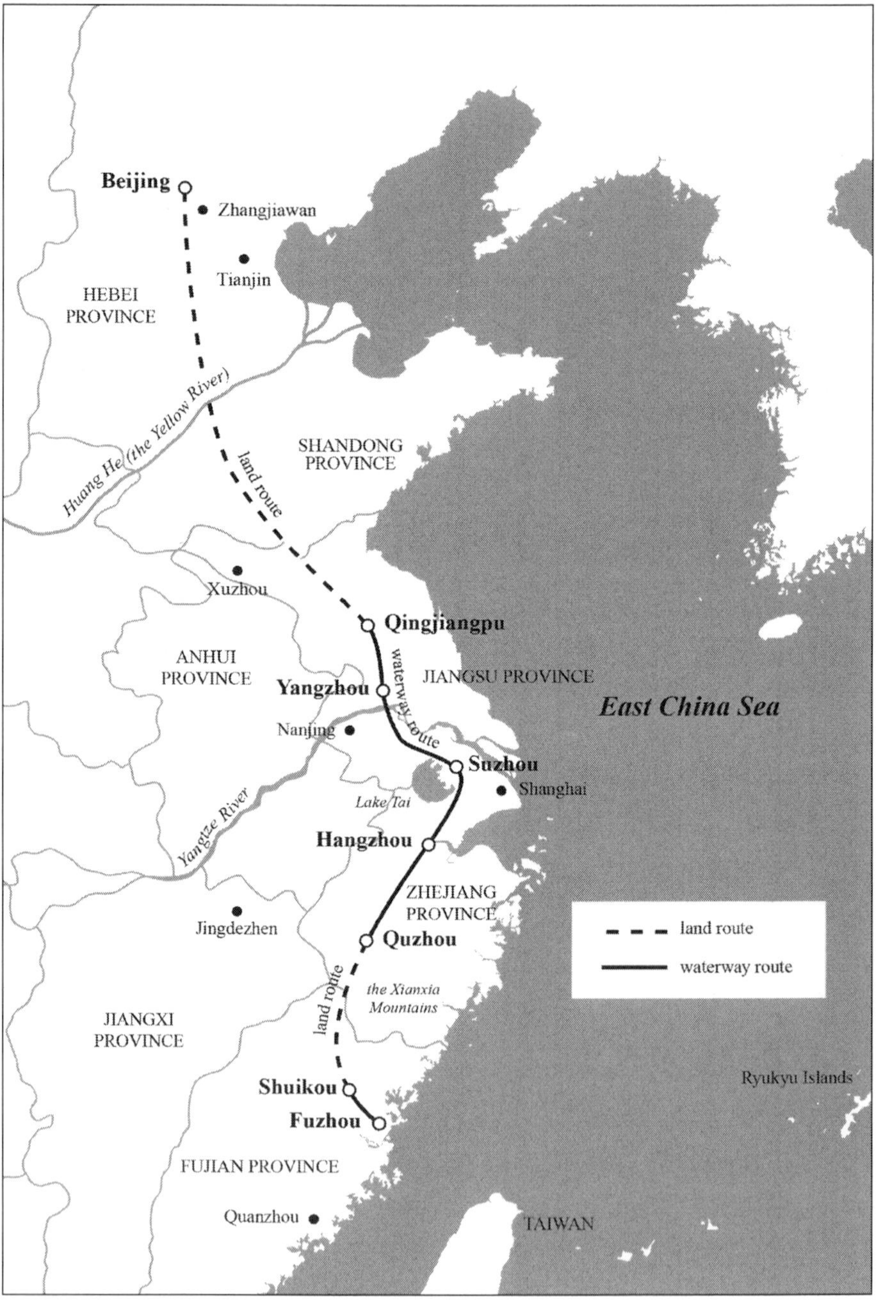


*Map 3.* The route taken by Ryukyuan envoys between Fujian and Beijing. Waterway portions followed canals and estuaries not visible on the map.

*Figure 6.3.* A procession of Ryukyuan envoys through Shandong Province, bound for Beijing. From *Ryūkaku Danki*, a 1797 account of conversations with visitors from Ryukyu. University of Hawai'i Library Sakamaki/Hawley Collection.

journey to Shuikou. Riverboats that simply floated downstream to the river mouth at Fuzhou had to be pulled upstream for the return trip. Boat crews tied ropes around their bodies and, trudging sometimes in white water up to their waists, sometimes along a rock path on the side of the river, hauled the boat upriver against the rushing water.[16]

On the nineteenth, the party set out overland from Shuikou. Following a rugged road, they cleared the steep pass at Xianxialing in the mountains that straddled the border between Fujian and Zhejiang Provinces and arrived at the city of Quzhou in southwestern Zhejiang Province on the 6th Day of the Eleventh Month. The next day, they boarded barges once again, coming to Hangzhou on the twelfth.

The tribute mission of 1832 (Daoguang 12) had arrived in Beijing on the 23rd Day of the Twelfth Month. Because they were three days late, the escorting officials' ranks had been each reduced by one level as punishment. Though the emperor had later issued a special order pardoning them, their records still showed the demotion, which they must have regarded with great shame. So in order to avoid such a punishment themselves, or perhaps in response to the recent humiliation suffered by China at the treaty signing after its defeat in the Opium War of 1839–1842, the escorts of the 1844 mission hurried the group along its road without the usual banquets and entertainments in the various provinces along the way.

The day after their arrival in Hangzhou, they set out along the canal to Suzhou, arriving on the sixteenth. They continued without stopping, making Qingjiangpu in northern Jiangsu Province on the twenty-fifth. The next day, they were back on the land route through Shandong Province, moving toward Changxindian in the southwest corner of Beijing. Finally, on the Twelfth Month, 17th Day, they arrived in Beijing. As planned, the legation sent its Chinese interpreter inside to announce their arrival and was put under the care of the officials who came to greet them on behalf of the government's Bureau of Rites, responsible for foreign tributary missions to the capital. The long journey from Fuzhou across China's interior had taken them sixty days.

## ACTIVITIES IN BEIJING

### Audience with the Emperor

Once in Beijing, the legation was installed in quarters at the *huì tóng guǎn,* a guest residence for use by foreign tributary missions. The residence commissioner, appointed by the Bureau of Rites, was responsible for them as their host; his numerous staff saw to the immediate needs and care of the legation group. The Qing court covered all their daily expenses and living costs, but no one in the group was permitted to wander freely through the city, and there were many restrictions on the legation members' movements. They were not permitted to stay anywhere else, but had to remain quartered at the *huì tóng guǎn* for their entire stay in Beijing. On the twenty-fourth, they presented themselves to the emperor at the Zhonghua Palace inside the Forbidden City, receiving from him the inquiry of "Is there peace for the Ryukyuan king?" Afterward, they were provided with a banquet, followed by a dramatic performance, after which they returned on the same day to the *huì tóng guǎn.*[17]

Of all the official ceremonies scheduled for the legation, the main event was the *chōga* ceremony, the New Year's Day audience with the emperor, a grand ceremony that took place in the courtyard in front of the Taihe Hall [Tàihédiàn, Hall of Supreme Harmony], the main hall of the Forbidden City. Since many of the foreign envoys did not know the protocol for the ceremony, it was established practice for palace officials to conduct early morning rehearsals called "practice ceremonies" several days before the audience itself. The envoys of 1844, together with their attendants, participated in these "practice ceremonies" on the twenty-sixth. On the same day, the court bestowed half a sturgeon on them from its kitchens. The custom of such a gift grew out of the fact that the words for "sturgeon," known also as "scarlet carp," were written in Chinese characters that included elements meaning "visit" and "emperor." Sturgeon are rare fish found in large rivers and deep inshore waters and may reach lengths of over three meters. Thus even half a fish was a considerable gift. An official scribe with a Korean tributary embassy described the taste of the sturgeon broth that he sipped in the kitchens as "very simple and mild."[18]

To the east of the Gate of Heavenly Peace [Ch. Tiānānmén] stood the Imperial Ancestral Hall [Ch. Tàimiào], enshrining emperors of both the Ming and the Qing dynasties. At the end of every year, the sitting emperor visited this shrine to perform ceremonies in worship of his ancestors, and when he processed through the Meridian Gate [Ch. Wǔmén] at the main entrance to the Forbidden City, officials were required to line up before dawn to kowtow to him as he went by. This ceremony was held on the twenty-ninth. The Ryukyuan legation also joined the crowd kneeling at the Meridian Gate. On the thirtieth, there was a banquet and a feast ceremony, during which the Cup of Heaven ritual was conducted. This consisted of passing down a cup of wine from the emperor to the assemblage.

The emperor came out from the Taihe Hall on the three most important national holidays, New Year's Day, the winter solstice, and the emperor's birthday, to receive the congratulations of the gathered officials. The Ryukyuan envoys, along with all the Chinese officials, both military and civil, and all the other foreign tributary embassies, gathered on New Year's Day in the Forbidden City to greet the emperor in the courtyard in front of the Taihe Hall and to have an audience with him. Korea, Ryukyu, Annam (Vietnam), Miandian (Burma), and others sent envoys who participated in the New Year's Day ceremonies at the Forbidden City. Each made their obeisance to the emperor in order of precedence; the Ryukyuan envoy was treated as holding the third court rank, making his place in the order after the Korean ambassador's and before those from Annam and Miandian.

On the 4th Day, a banquet was held in the imperial palace, during which the ritual of the Cup of Heaven was performed again, followed by musical entertainment. On the eighth, the emperor observed the festival of the God of Heaven, performing ceremonial prayers for abundant crops, and once again, all officials had to be outside the gate, kneeling and bowing as he passed. They were there again the next day, on the ninth, when the emperor departed the imperial palace to visit his villa Yuán míng yuán [the Old Summer Palace], a European palace built in the baroque style, located northwest of the Forbidden City. On the fifteenth, the Ryukyuan envoys were invited to attend a banquet at Yuán míng yuán, where again they were given the Cup of Heaven and entertained with a variety of artistic performances. They returned a final time to Yuán míng yuán on the nineteenth to hear the emperor's prayer for peace. They were told they had met their tributary obligations and could now return to their country. On this occasion, the emperor addressed to them the words, "May your king have peace."

On Second Month, 4th Day, gifts of silk goods for the king and the envoys were bestowed on the legation in a special ceremony. These imperial gifts were splendidly arranged on a dais, and the envoys faced the Taihe Hall to perform once again the three kneelings and nine bows before receiving them. With this last obligation fulfilled, the formal ceremonies in Beijing were over.

### Trade at the Guest Residence

During their stay in Beijing, the duties of the royal envoys, besides presenting their nation's tribute and paying their respects to the emperor, included the important task of purchasing Chinese goods from the merchants who visited the guest residence. The trade conducted by tribute legations during their stay at the residence was called the "open market" [Ch. *kāishì*, J. *kaishi*]. For most legations, the open market lasted for three to five days, but in the cases of Korea and Ryukyu, no time limit had been imposed. The market operated every day until about sunset, always under the supervision of officials from the Bureau of Rites. Chinese merchants who bargained in bad faith, and thus delayed the departure of the legation on its return trip, were punished, as were those who made secret deals during the market period. Legation members who entered private residences with the intention of conducting business had their goods confiscated, and the imperial gifts bestowed on them at the end of their visit were sharply reduced in quality. All business between legations and merchants was conducted with silver cash; as a rule, there were no purchases made on credit. In Beijing, the Ryukyuans sought items difficult to obtain in Fujian, such as medicines, or the expensive paintings, scrolls, and Chinese ceramics so eagerly sought after by Japan's wealthy classes.

### Return to Fuzhou

The tribute legation of 1844 stayed in Beijing for about fifty days. On its return trip, the group also included four royal scholarship students who had completed their studies. They started out on their return journey on the 9th Day of the Second Month. Though it was possible to travel by barge to Dezhou in Shandong Province, in the Second Month the region was mired in the depths of winter. This meant there was little water flowing in the waterways, and such as there was would likely be frozen solid, so the tribute legations of this era of the Qing dynasty usually chose to travel overland. The return journey was a reprise in reverse of the earlier route. The first stage ended on the 1st Day of the Third Month, when they arrived in Qingjiangpu in northern Jiangsu Province; from there they went by barge, arriving in Suzhou on the eleventh, Hangzhou on the nineteenth, Quzhou on the twenty-ninth, and traversing the Xianxialing mountain road to arrive in Shuikou on the 18th Day, Third Month. On the twenty-first, they arrived once again at the Ryukyu House in Fuzhou.

During the Qing dynasty, tribute legations in Fuzhou were bestowed with the official imperial almanac, the *Almanac of Standard Time* [Ch. *Shíxiànshū*, J. *Jikensho*].[19] Distribution of this almanac was known as "establishing the first day," and with it the emperor set the imperial calendar for the following year. The Chinese dynasties regarded "establishing the first day" as a matter of great importance, and the almanac's distribution had a political purpose of giving both suzerain China and her vassal states the same standard measure for time. All matters concerning the heavens were under the jurisdiction of the emperor as the Son of Heaven. All heavenly matters were his sacred responsibility, on behalf of Heaven, and none but the emperor was permitted authority over them.

By royal order in 1678, Sai Chōkō was sent from Ryukyu to Fuzhou to study calendar making.[20] After four years of study, he returned home and distributed his new almanac, the *Daisei jiken reki* [Great Qing Time Principle Calendar], through the whole country. In turn, the later *Senjitsu tsūsho* [Guide for Selecting Days], based on Sai's original almanac, came into wide use. The Chinese-made almanac never arrived before May or June of each year, when the returning tribute ships came into Naha. For this reason, the *Senjitsu tsūsho* was, in effect, used to set dates for both public and private events throughout the entire year, though officially any decisions based on it were only provisional until the official almanac arrived.

### Tribute Missions as Death Journeys

Fuzhou lies about three thousand kilometers from Beijing, making the round-trip a journey of six thousand kilometers, and there were no few deaths among the tribute legations along this long road. Those who died far from home in Beijing were entombed in Zhangjiawan; those who died en route were buried in tombs along the way. Even today, in Huaiyin County of Jiangsu Province may be found the tomb of the royal legate Zhèng Wényīng [J. Tei Bun'ei], and there are several such tombs of visiting officials in every part of China. While the legation of 1844 was in China, one of the officials hosting the legation, Xiàng Kèxiù, died at the Ryukyu House on the 3rd Day of the Twelfth Month and was buried in the Ryukyuan cemetery in the city's suburbs.[21]

One corner of the Fuzhou Ryukyu House was dedicated to prayers for those Ryukyuans who had come to the end of their lives in a strange land. A shrine, the Sūhōshi, was built in 1791. The shrine was called Sūhō as a way of soothing the spirits of the deceased, for *sūhō* means "to proclaim the sublime [achievements]" of those who died away from home on their legation journey. In January 1937, Kobata Atsushi found about five hundred mortuary tablets in the old Ryukyu House while doing research there.[22] Around the same time, Higashionna Kanjun, another researcher interested in the Ryukyu House, found evidence for 578 entombed persons in the death registries of the Ryukyu House.[23] Cemeteries with Ryukyuan tombs, holding the remains of those who died, may be found in both the southern and eastern parts of Fuzhou. Besides those who succumbed to local hazards and endemic diseases to die in China, these death registries also include many who fell victim to shipwreck or pirate attack. It is no wonder that China voyages were also known as "death voyages."

## THE ROAD HOME

### Wrapping Up Business at the Open House

The group of officials who had remained in Fuzhou to conduct their business during the envoys' absence finished their last transactions by Second Month, 5th Day, but they were still there awaiting the change of winds when the tribute legation of 1844 returned to the city on the 21st Day of the Fourth Month. The newly returned envoys did not, however, board the same ship as the business officials; instead they had to wait for the arrival in the Ninth Month of a second ship sent to collect them, and did not get home until early summer of the following year.[24]

Both ships usually followed the same route on the return trip. According to the above-mentioned navigation guide *Shinan kōgi,* the ships rode the southwestern winds that blew in the Fifth Month, and taking a southeasterly heading, they passed the northern tip of Taiwan, made their way past Chōgyodai, Kume Island, and the Kerama island group, to finally arrive in Naha Harbor. The route differed for the journey in the other direction, to China, because the return ships took advantage of the winds out of the south. With good winds, the journey took seven days and nights.

In the case of the two ships sent on the tribute mission of 1844, the one boarded on Fifth Month, 5th Day, 1845, by the returning group entered the high seas outside of Wuhumen on the 23rd Day of that month, and the announcement of their return to Ryukyu was made on the 28th Day. The ship carrying the envoys and the resident interpreters was scheduled to return the following year, in 1846; however, because the mission retrieval ship arrived late in Fuzhou, the legation did not return home until the Fifth Month, 21st Day, 1847.

### Tribute Ships' Return and Overseeing the Unloading of Cargo

Until such matters as determining the nature and quantity of the Chinese goods designated for the Shimazu clan, establishing the value of the China-voyage silver, and the resale of the remaining imported goods had been completed, all was held under tight control. The returning tribute ships and everyone aboard were subjected to strict inspections designed to minimize smuggling.

On sighting a returning tribute ship, the sentinels at the beacon stations on Kume Island sent up a smoke signal. At this signal, the stations on the islands of Tonaki, Zamami, and Tokashiki, successively, sent signals to Oroku on Okinawa Island. From there, word was sent immediately to Shuri Castle. One signal meant one ship; two meant two ships had been sighted. In the meantime, inspection officials at Kume and Kerama islands conducted stringent checks for any hidden Chinese goods intended for personal gain, as these islands had been known to hide goods in the past. When the tribute ship finally entered the harbor at Naha, the royal government prohibited any unauthorized vessels from approaching it. Satsuma's agents and government officials boarded immediately to conduct the official ship inspection. In addition to sending ashore the ship's captain and navigator, they made a general inspection of the cargo. Once this inspection was complete, four or five officers were stationed on board the ship day and night in rotation, in another precaution to prevent smuggling. A temple in the Nishimura area of Naha, the Rinkaiji, functioned as a base of operations for officials from both Satsuma and the royal government as they managed the ship inspection and the roll call of those on board the tribute ship. They issued a bill of lading for the entire cargo brought from China, and no Ryukyuans, Satsuma merchants, ship captains, or crew members were permitted to handle any of it without permission.

Once ashore, the returning legation officials visited Shuri Castle to report the tribute ship's return and to burn the license and talismans they had carried with them. The weapons kept on board during the mission to China had to be returned to Satsuma's administrator; similarly, the statue enshrining Bōsa/Maso had to be transferred to its special palanquin and processed through the streets, accompanied by music and ceremony, to be reinstalled safely at Tenpi-gū. Though this ended the tribute legation's long and arduous journey to China, a high-ranking government official, with adjunct scribes, was appointed as "presentation supervisor" [*henjōbutsu sairyōnin*], and had to accompany the goods destined for the Shimazu lord on the journey from Ryukyu to Satsuma.

### Ceremony to Receive the Imperial Rescript

For the most part, the tribute ship carrying the envoys was met with the same procedures and precautions, with one additional ceremony that was not necessary for the first ship. In this ceremony, the Reception of the Imperial Rescript, the tribute envoys presented the reply from the Chinese emperor, to whom the king had declared his loyalty.

After the tribute ship had landed at Naha, the rescript was mounted on the *ryūtei* [dragon dais], a display platform for the rescripts kept at Tondōsaki on the bank of the harbor. Then three cannons were fired, followed by the beating of three drums. Next, the legation group moved toward Shuri Castle, accompanied by music, and the dragon dais was carried in and set down in front of the stone steps of the Seiden. There the king sat, dressed in Chinese court robes, waiting for the dais. Following the commands issued in Chinese by an interpreter from Kumemura, the gathered officials burned incense and performed the ritual of three kneelings and nine prostrations as required by the solemn ceremony to receive the imperial rescript. After the chief envoy had presented the report of his return, the *mi-oya tairi onsōshi,* next he had to travel to Satsuma in his role of China source envoy, to report on the entire tribute mission, as well as on conditions and events in China. Only then had he fulfilled the requirements of his long travel duty.

In the following chapter, we consider the patents of investiture that conferred authority on the Ryukyuan king.

CHAPTER SEVEN

# The Imperial Investiture System and the Ryukyu Kingdom

## THE INVESTITURE OF THE RYUKYUAN KING

### The Symbols of Investiture: Crown of Leather, Robes of Leather, and Royal Seal

During the Ming dynasty, a system of sumptuary laws ensured that any person's rank was obvious at a single glance; thus, crown robes identified members of the imperial family, and court dress identified government officials. These laws applied to the rulers of the nations around China's borders as well. The *Míng shǐ* has an entry on "crown robes for foreign rulers and subjects" that reads, "During the Yongle Era [1402–1424], the Ryukyuan King of Chūzan was granted the leather cap, the jade tablet, the *lín páo* emblem robes, the rhinoceros horn belt, and Second Rank at Court."[1] The entry refers to the investiture of King Bunei in the second year of the Yongle era [1403], when the king was granted second rank in the Chinese system of ranking its own noble government officials with ranks that ranged from first to ninth.

During the Ming dynasty, the royal regalia included the king's crown (the crown of leather), his robes (the robes of leather), and finally the royal seal. The person who bore the crown and the royal robes, and who controlled the royal seal, displayed his power as king to the world at large and reigned over all the nobles and commoners below him.

The "crown of leather" [J. *hibenkan*, Ch. *píbiànguān*], gifted by the Ming court, so named because originally such crowns had been made from white deer leather, was a type of headwear traditional to the Han Chinese. Only members of the emperor's immediate family, such as the crown prince and the emperor himself, were permitted to wear it. The Ming-period crown given to the Ryukyuan king was made of silk, and the *Rekidai hōan* describes it as a "seven-striped, beaded, folded-silk gauze crown-of-leather."[2] The "seven stripes" referred to the seven rows of crystal, coral, and jade beads sewn from the front to the back of the crown; the number of rows was determined by the rank of the person who wore it. In this orderly system, the Ming Chinese emperor's crown bore twelve rows, and the Chinese crown prince's nine. Local rulers were permitted seven rows. The "folded-silk gauze" was a fine silk woven with narrow black stripes.

Besides the crown of leather, there was the "great crimson plain robe of leather" and the "five-symbol silk gauze robe of leather."[3] The "robes of leather" were the round-necked robes worn at the imperial court, with long, hanging sleeves, high standing collars, and green trim along the cuffs, collar, and bottom hem. The "great crimson" robe was a plain, unfigured garment. The "five-symbol" robe was adorned with five of the twelve imperial symbols of authority, in this case, the grains of millet, the water weed, the sacrificial cup (in the shape of a wine cup), the sacrificial axe, and the abstract symbol *fu,* symbolizing good and evil. The remaining seven symbols were the sun, the moon, the constellation of the Big Dipper, the mountain, the dragon, the pheasant, and fire; only the robe of leather worn by the Chinese emperor bore all twelve. The crown prince and his brothers wore nine of these symbols; local rulers were permitted five. As a side note, the Japanese Muromachi shogun and the Korean king of the same time period had been granted permission to wear nine-symbol robes.

The king's seal (see Figure 7.1) was called the "camel-back silver-gilt seal" because the grip was humped like a camel's back, and it was made of silver decorated with gold plate.[4] Japan and Korea had been granted golden seals with grips shaped like turtle shells, but Ryukyu, Annam (Vietnam), Java, and Siam (Thailand), among others, were granted the camel-back seal. Based on the symbols and details of the crown of leather, the robes of leather, and the royal seal, the Ryukyuan crown carried with it the rank of local ruler within the Chinese imperial system, and the Ryukyuan king was granted standing as a nominal member of the imperial clan. In the eyes of the investiture envoys, these facts made the king an official of the second rank (in the ruler-and-subject relationship) in the Chinese bureaucracy, and at the same time gave him standing as a local ruler related to the imperial clan.

The Manchurian conquerors who founded the Qing dynasty continued to grant the use of royal seals. However, they abolished the Han Chinese styles of headwear and court dress, and as the crown of leather and the

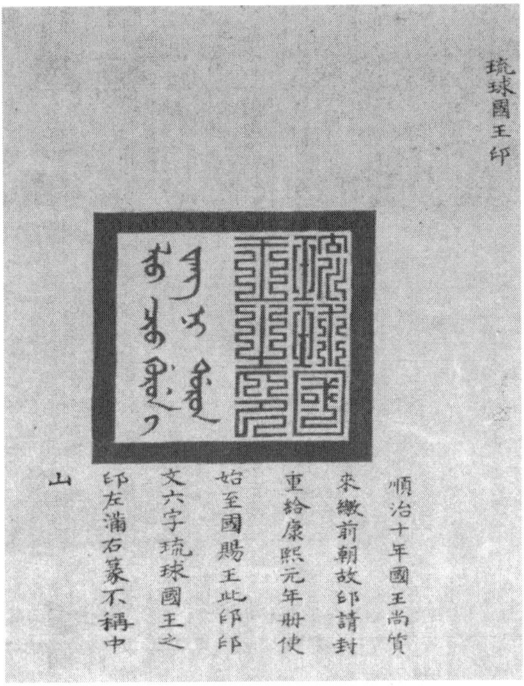


*Figure 7.1.* The royal seal of the Ryukyu Kingdom. From *Ryūkyū kokuō sakuhō no zu*, date unknown, University of Hawai'i Library Sakamaki/Hawley Collection.

robes of leather lost their earlier meaning, they were no longer granted by the court. All the same, the Ryukyuan kings continued to follow the court fashions of the Ming period and styled their own robes of leather of fabric woven with the dragon emblems granted by the Qing dynasty for use in ceremonial robes. In addition, in 1754, the royal government added five more rows of beads to the seven formerly on the crown of leather, to bring the total up to the imperial twelve.

## The Title "King of Chūzan" and the Second Shō Dynasty's Stratagem

More than 460 years passed between Ryukyu's first investiture, for King Bunei, son of Chūzan's King Satto, in 1404, and that of the kingdom's last monarch, King Shō Tai, in 1866. Shō Hashi unified the three domains of Sanzan in the first half of the fifteenth century, and he is still remembered as the main protagonist in establishing the kingdom's international trade and diplomacy through its tributary and investiture relationship with China. Nevertheless, the Chinese rescripts for the occasion of investiture continued to say that the emperor "grants thee investiture as the Chūzan

King of the Ryukyu Kingdom." The title of "the Chūzan king" was the orthodox address to the successors of the Ryukyu Kingdom, and it remained so, unchanged, until Ryukyu's last king, Shō Tai.

A coup d'état toppled the First Shō dynasty in 1469, and the Second Shō dynasty (of no blood relation to the first, despite the similarity in names), led by Shō En, came to reign over the Ryukyu Kingdom. The dramatic regime change had involved wresting authority from a king whose position had been sanctioned by China, but Shō En said nothing of this to the Chinese court. Disregarding the fact that he was older than Shō Toku, last king of the First Shō dynasty, Shō En, claiming himself as *seishi,* the legitimate heir to the throne, reported the death of his "father king" to China and received his investiture. The Chinese acted as if they knew nothing of the events surrounding the regime change and, without hesitation, invested the new monarch in a ceremony held at Shuri Castle, as required by the Confucian worldview.

### Requiring a Guarantee for Patents of Investiture

Upon the investiture of the fourth king of the Shō dynasty, Shō Sei, in 1534, for the first time the ministers from the rank of the royal councilors [Sanshikan] on down jointly signed a written guarantee that they recognized the new monarch's claim to the throne.[5] Subsequently, this document became a prerequisite; the investiture ceremony could take place only after the approval and cooperation of the lower bureaucrats whose work supported the Shuri royal government had been obtained.

Originally, there were two ways to convey a "patent of investiture": either China would dispatch an envoy with the patent, or the kingdom receiving the patent would send an envoy to China to formally accept it. In the case of the Ryukyu Kingdom, from the very beginning, the practice was for China to dispatch its envoy to Ryukyu.

The system of investiture functioned against the background of the immense authority of the Chinese Empire, Asia's largest autocracy. A patent of investiture conferred legitimacy on the Ryukyu Kingdom's royal succession, and this political formality, by confirming the Chinese emperor's recognition of the "new king" as ruler, formed a central foundation of the king's authority and political control. The ceremony of investiture, as a proxy for the Chinese emperor's sublime authority, augmented the Ryukyuan king's own royal power. The patent also included the all-important recognition of Ryukyu as a tributary state of China. China conferred a total of twenty-three patents of investiture on the kings of Chūzan, granting fifteen during the Ming and eight during the Qing dynasty.

## DISPATCH OF THE IMPERIAL INVESTITURE ENVOY

### Official Appointment of the Investiture Envoy

Records of events during the investiture envoys' sojourns in Ryukyu still remain: the memorial service of the late king; the investiture ceremony of his heir; and the envoy legation's observations of local customs, manners, geography, history, and language are all recorded in texts generically known as *Records of the Investiture Envoys* [J. *Sappō-shi roku*, Ch. *Cèfēngshǐ lù*].[6] The envoys were not actually required to keep formal records, but in fact many did. Of the records kept for the nations around China, most concern only the Ryukyu Kingdom; only a few of the remaining cover other nations such as Korea or Annam (Vietnam). Using the accounts found in these records, let us consider what it meant to be dispatched as an investiture envoy, and what an investiture ceremony involved.

After the death of a king, his successor dispatched an envoy to carry notification to China. Once all preparations to receive an investiture embassy had been completed, the royal government sent an envoy bearing a formal request for a patent of investiture to the Chinese court. Immediately upon the emperor's acceptance of such a request, the prospective envoys were selected. During the Qing dynasty, envoys sent to Korea were rather highly placed government officials holding between lower first and upper third ranks; in contrast, those sent to the Ryukyu Kingdom were low-ranking officials of the upper fifth to upper seventh ranks. Similarly, Annam (Vietnam), which like Ryukyu held second tier in the Chinese system, was also sent only officials holding lower ranks.

As an example of the process: when Zhao Wenjie and Li Dingyuan were named as chief and vice envoy to King Shō On's investiture in 1799, they had been selected from among a group of fourteen candidates. The two men went to the Palace of Heavenly Purity in the Forbidden City in the early morning hours of Eighth Month, 19th Day, for an audience with Emperor Jiaqing [r. 1796–1820], where they received the orders formalizing their appointments as envoys.[7] The persons selected for such tasks were deemed competent to discharge their duties in a manner that would not compromise the authority of the suzerain nation's emperor; however, those dispatched on these missions did not, as a rule, regard this duty as an unalloyed honor.

When Zhao Wenjie was on his return journey as investiture envoy, his ship met first with rough seas, and then pirate attack. He suffered a nervous breakdown and died several years after returning home, without ever fully recovering.[8] The tribute legations sent across the stormy stretch of the vast ocean traveled at great risk of death, to the extent that, as mentioned in Chapter Six, the Ryukyuans referred to the tribute missions as "death journeys." When even seafaring people who were accustomed to the hardships of the seas found such journeys fraught with danger, then surely words cannot describe the fear felt by the Chinese envoys themselves. They were scholarly men, with no experience of ocean crossings, sent out from China on a journey undertaken only once every several decades. When a request for investiture arrived from the Ryukyu Kingdom, Chinese government officials feared to be chosen as members of the embassy, and there are no few cases of officials striving to avoid being selected. Though appointment as an investiture envoy ensured one's future advancement within the government service, those named to these positions could not have regarded their orders with pleasure.

### Dispatch of the Crown Ship

Government officials appointed to the positions of chief and vice envoys were granted the right to wear the robes of officials of the first rank. Though in fact the investiture envoys sent to Ryukyu were fairly low-ranking officials within the Chinese government, historical documents show that the Ryukyuans referred to them as "imperial messengers" [J. *chokushi*]. They were regarded as ambassadors plenipotentiary on special duty; thus, for the duration of the investiture missions, the Chinese envoys' official status was temporarily elevated to first rank so that they would outrank the Ryukyuan king.

Once the envoys were appointed as investiture envoys, the cabinet provided them with the necessary documents, which included the imperial edict, the imperial rescript, a eulogy for the late king, and a prayer addressed to Mazu that would be performed in Fujian. In addition, they received a banner depicting an oxtail and a bird's wing, proclaiming them as emissaries of the emperor. The chief envoy had a staff of twenty persons; the vice envoy had fifteen. They were permitted up to eight palanquin bearers; several artists, such as poets and skilled painters, were also part of the embassy.

Upon appointment, the vice envoy was the first to make his way to Fujian. During the Ming dynasty, two ships, a flagship and a companion ship, were built for the voyage, at a shipyard on the banks of Fuzhou's great Min River.[9] However, during the Qing dynasty, beginning with the investiture of Shō Kei in 1719, merchant ships regularly served as the envoy's vessels. The ships bearing the investiture embassies were known in China as "ships of the seal" [Ch. *fēngzhōu*, J. *hōbune*, seal ship]; in the Ryukyu Kingdom, they were called "crown ships" [J. *kansen/okansen;* Ok. *kwanshin/ukwanshin*] for the crowns of leather they once carried to the old kings of Chūzan. The ships that carried the envoys Hai Yu and Xu Baoguang in 1719 were fairly large: about 33 meters [108.2 feet] long, 9 meters [29.5 feet] wide, and 5 meters [16.4 feet] high. They were partitioned into four holds from bow to stern; each hold had three levels from top to bottom. Usually on such voyages, besides the members of the investiture embassy from Beijing, were the ships' crews and others including guards, interpreters, doctors, chefs, bakers, picture framers, blacksmiths, musicians, Daoist priests, and tailors, for a total of four or five hundred persons on board.

A prayer ceremony to ask Mazu (Maso) for a safe voyage was held just before setting sail for Ryukyu. The prayer ceremony was ordered by the emperor, and because the address to Mazu was also read, it came to be called the "address ceremony." During the Ming dynasty, the envoys performed this ceremony at a shrine to Mazu located downstream in Guangshi, near the mouth of the Min River; during the Qing, the prayers for a safe journey were offered up in an "address ceremony" held at the Yí shān yuàn in Fuzhou.

### Various Investiture Ceremonies

By the time the Chinese envoys arrived in Fuzhou, the emissaries sent from Ryukyu to serve as their escorts and interpreters were already waiting for them. In about the Fifth or Sixth Month of the old lunar calendar, the investiture embassy, accompanied by their Ryukyuan hosts, would sail down the Min River from Fuzhou, and taking advantage of the seasonal winds out of the southwest, would set off across the ocean. Once the watchers waiting in Ryukyu spotted the crown ships, signal fires would be set, first on Kume Island. The message would pass from one island to the next, until finally Shuri Castle was notified of the crown ships' arrival.

The ships moored in the China Ship Channel, just off of Miegusuku in Naha Harbor (see Figure 7.2). Senior officials, ferried out two at a time in small boats, gave their formal welcome in the Rite of Three Greetings to Welcome the Imperial Edict. Until King Shō Boku's investiture in 1756, a senior minister would go down to the harbor to greet the envoys on behalf of the heir; however, in response to a request from the Chinese envoys, beginning that year the heir himself waited at the Geion-tei [Ok. Giun-ti, Pavilion of Warm Welcome] in Tondōsaki to greet them at their arrival. With the heir's invitation to disembark, first the imperial edict, followed by other

*Figure 7.2.* Chinese ships carrying envoys for the investiture (*sakuhō* or *sappō*) of the Ryukyuan king arrive at Naha. From *Ryūkyū kokuō sakuhō no zu*, date unknown, University of Hawai'i Library Sakamaki/Hawley Collection.

items, and finally the envoys themselves, were ferried to land in small boats. The group assembled at the Geion-tei held a ceremony centered on the formal rite of welcome [J. *geishō gichū*, Chi. *yíngzhào yízhù*]. They performed the ritual of three genuflections and nine kowtows to the imperial decree and the imperial rescript, displayed on the portable Dragon Shrine, embellished with the dragon medallion, the symbol of the emperor.

During the Ming dynasty, the ceremony for the imperial decree and the imperial rescript included only five bows and three kowtows, but this was changed to three genuflections and nine kowtows in the Qing. This was a ceremonial bow in which one knelt three times on both knees, and each time one knelt, one laid oneself down and touched one's forehead to the floor three times. In China, it was, without question, the highest gesture of respect that could be made.

After this ceremony, the envoys proceeded formally through the streets, accompanied by music, to their lodgings at the Tenshikan [Heavenly Embassy; see Figure 7.3]. In honor of these emissaries of the Son of Heaven, this building had been constructed in the style of a Chinese government office; a large, yellow banner emblazoned with the word *sappō* ["patent of

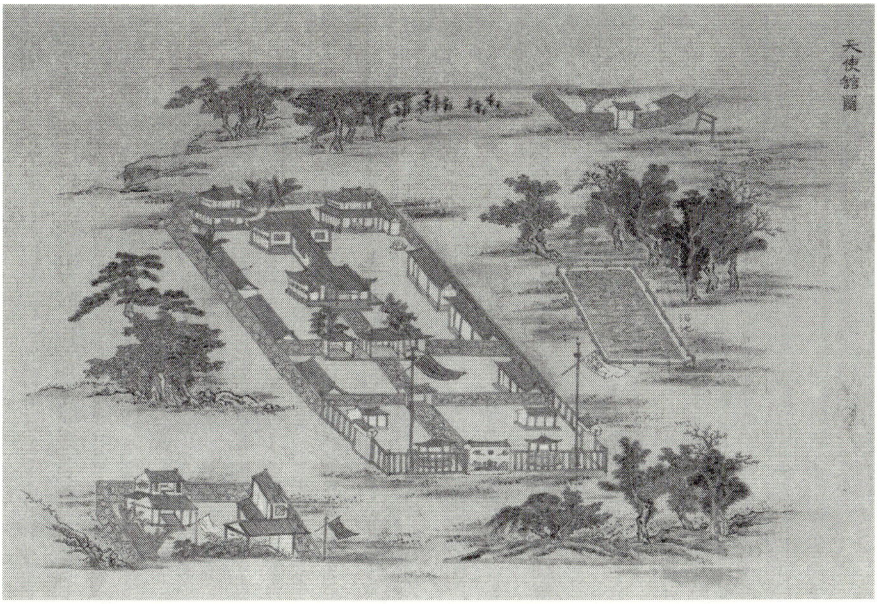


*Figure 7.3.* The Tenshikan, a special compound by Naha Harbor where Chinese envoys stayed when visiting Ryukyu for the investiture of the Ryukyu king. From *Ryūkyū kokuō sakuhō no zu*, date unknown, University of Hawai'i Library Sakamaki/Hawley Collection.

investiture"] flew high above it. The portable Dragon Shrine and the investiture gifts from the emperor, carried in a portable shrine known as the Saitei, or Painted Shrine were placed in the Tenshikan.

### Ceremony of the Patent of Investiture

Before the official investiture at Shuri Castle could take place, the spirit of the late king had first to be enshrined at the royal family's shrine, Sōgenji, in a ceremony called the "rite of guidance" [J. *yusai no rei*]. At the conclusion of this observance, preparations could begin at Shuri for the investiture ceremony. The important points along the route followed by the envoys were decorated, and the town itself took on a festival atmosphere. The investiture was a kind of rite-of-passage ceremony that acknowledged the successor's transition from crown prince to king. The patent of investiture with which the Chinese emperor formally granted authority to the Ryukyuan king also made clear to all the world that he was king not only in name, but also in fact. On the day of the ceremony, a guard formed along the route from the Tenshikan to the royal palace (see Figure 7.4), and the festival mood was heightened by the banners and rosettes of crimson cloth that

*Figure 7.4.* A Chinese investiture envoy proceeds to Shuri Castle along a route lined by royal guards of the Ryukyu Kingdom. From *Ryūkyū kokuō sakuhō no zu,* date unknown, University of Hawai'i Library Sakamaki/Hawley Collection.

festooned the buildings and gates along the way. That day, a procession of officials called on the envoys at the Tenshikan. Once the imperial edict and the investiture gifts sent to by the emperor had been installed on the portable Dragon Shrine and the Painted Shrine, these accompanied the investiture envoys in a procession to Shuri Castle.

According to the *Chūzan denshin roku* [Report of an Envoy to Chuzan], on the occasion of Shō Kei's investiture, the crown prince met the envoy legation in front of the Shureimon, the iconic second gate leading into Shuri Castle. When the Dragon Shrine arrived, he performed the obeisance of three genuflections and nine kowtows, after which he guided them to the Kankaimon, the Gate of Welcome (see Figure 7.5). From there, the crown prince led the procession to the great courtyard in front of the Seiden, Shuri's Main Hall, where the investiture ceremony itself would take place (see Figure 7.6). The imperial edict and the imperial gifts were arrayed in a specially constructed shelter, called the Kettei, standing in front of the Seiden; the ceremony was conducted to the accompaniment of ritual music. To the left and right of a dais in the altar, called the *u-an* [great table], stood the chief and vice envoys. A "ritual officer" [J. *inrei-kan*] served as the master of ceremonies for the solemnities.

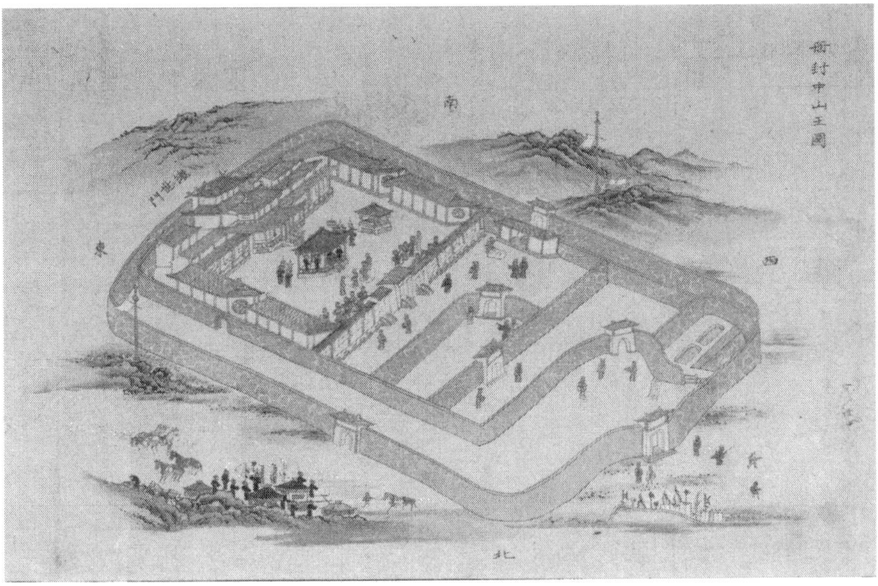


*Figure 7.5.* Chinese envoys arrive at Shuri Castle to perform the investiture ceremony for the Ryukyu king. From *Ryūkyū kokuō sakuhō no zu,* date unknown, University of Hawai'i Library Sakamaki/Hawley Collection.

*Figure 7.6.* Chinese guests (in the foreground, sporting pigtails) attend an autumn ceremony in the courtyard of Shuri Castle. From *Ryūkyū kokuō sakuhō no zu,* date unknown, University of Hawai'i Library Sakamaki/Hawley Collection.

First, the ritual officer led the crown prince to the Kettei and seated him. Next, the imperial edict that had been brought over by the chief envoy was read. This was the high point of the ceremony, as the official reader [*sendōkan*] declaimed: "[The emperor] grants thee investiture, and recognizes the Chūzan King of the Ryukyu Kingdom." From this moment, the heir to the throne, heretofore referred to by the Chinese only as "crown prince" and "heir," was officially recognized by China as holding royal rank and was admitted to the use of the title of king.

Usually, after the conclusion of an investiture ceremony, the imperial edict was to be returned to China. However, in the case of Ryukyu, the edict granting the Ryukyuan patent of investiture was permitted to remain as a "treasure transmitted to the kingdom" [J. *denkoku no takara*], and it was stored at Shuri Castle.

## ASSESSMENT NEGOTIATIONS

### Imperial Investiture Envoys as Trade Representatives

Because the members of the investiture embassies were permitted to carry goods as ships' ballast, many of those who joined the embassies brought merchandise for the express purpose of selling it for profit. There were many individuals among the private attendants of the envoys, the soldiers, and others from Fujian who made contracts with Fuzhou merchants to carry merchandise in addition to their own personal baggage, to sell at the highest possible price. About two years before the arrival of an investiture embassy, the Ryukyuans would establish a temporary Office of Assessment in the Bureau of Trade. The director of assessment was someone familiar with Chinese trade products and was responsible for setting prices for individual products. Setting prices was referred to as an "assessment" of the goods,[10] but the Chinese side and the Ryukyu side did not always see eye to eye. Because the items were sometimes very expensive, or products for which the Ryukyuans had no need, the two sides could not agree on the prices, and frequent conflicts arose.

On occasions when imports exceeded exports, the royal government was short of silver to purchase the Chinese products, especially since these expenses were in addition to the cost of hosting the investiture embassy. Thus, trading took the form of a series of negotiations between the Chinese and the Ryukyuans, beginning with the captain of the crown ship submitting a list of the trade goods, and the Ryukyuan officials responsible for assessing the valuations using this list to set their prices. If the Chinese did not accept these prices, the negotiations would continue until a compromise was reached. Money changed hands only once the two sides had reached an agreement.

### Disagreements over Assessments

The assessment negotiations began at the Tenshikan shortly after the crown ships' arrival in port. The start of trade was called "open house," as it was at the Ryukyu House in Fuzhou. The investiture embassy of 1719 included more than six hundred persons, and a serious fight developed over the valuation of the goods the Chinese had brought with them. A large portion of these goods remained unsold, delaying the ships' return to China. That year, instead of remaining for about five months, and sailing as usual during the Tenth Month of the lunar calendar, the ships stayed in port for eight and a half months. Though a compromise was struck with a somewhat higher value allowed on their goods, the Chinese crown ships finally had to return home carrying many of the goods they had brought.[11]

Normally, those aboard the crown ships were permitted to bring personal cargo weighing no more than 100 *kin* [about 60 kilograms, or 132 pounds], but this limit was not strictly enforced. There were even cases of military officers with official responsibilities openly carrying goods on board, though they were expressly forbidden from doing so by the Chinese authorities.

As a very small nation, the kingdom did not have ready resources of silver, and it could be a problem for shippers when for some reason the royal government could not buy expensive goods. The government's repeated requests that the investiture embassies not bring such a large quantity of goods, or that they at least refrain from bringing such expensive luxury goods, were to no avail, and the high-priced items that caused such trouble for the Ryukyuans continued to be brought in for assessment. Representative of such were tortoiseshell, tortoise claws, musk, camphor, and cinnamon; when visiting Chinese brought such items, the Ryukyuan government assessed and purchased them.

The members of the embassies while in Ryukyu invariably bought large quantities of things like kelp, sea cucumber, and abalone to bring home with them, for which they offered prices below the market prices in Fuzhou. The Ryukyuans were willing to negotiate better prices for such items, but the so-called straw-wrapped goods such as sea cucumber, abalone, and others were among the commercial products strictly regulated by the Japanese *bakufu* and were not available in the quantities desired by the Chinese. Thus, the assessment negotiations conducted on the occasion of a royal investiture were an unending source of problems.

Though the length of an investiture embassy's stay was not set, a departure date was determined after the conclusion of the assessment negotiations and subsequent trade. Only then could the government give a farewell banquet for the ships, and finally the ships could set sail. The embassy ships, having selected a propitious day between the Ninth and Eleventh Months of the old lunar calendar for departure, rode the seasonal northeast winds out of Naha Harbor. After arriving in Fujian, and after first making a pilgrimage to Mazu's shrine to give thanks for a safe journey, those who lived in Fuzhou separated from the embassy group, and the chief and vice envoys and their attendants continued on to Beijing to make their reports to the emperor. For its part, Ryukyu sent an emissary to the court bearing thanks for the grant of the patent of investiture. With this, the public ceremonies and rituals of the investiture were complete.

### The Royal Government's "Great Challenge" Diplomacy

From a historical perspective, one might take the view that the Ryukyu Kingdom's tribute legations and its investiture rites are little more than diplomatic ritual. However, this would not be entirely accurate. As it labored under the *bakufu* system to adopt an ever more Chinese-style government, the small kingdom was forced to bear the heavy economic burden of hosting investiture embassies for four or five months, with the costs of providing banquets and other amenities during their residency, plus the obligations incurred through the assessment negotiations, and repayment of the silver borrowed from Satsuma to cover these expenses. As for the tribute legations, the China-crossing officials permitted to engage in trade on their own and Satsuma's behalf did achieve some handsome profits; however, the royal government was still forced to stand for multiple costs, including gathering the tribute cargo; predeparture ceremonies and events; the building, repair, and maintenance of the tribute ships; the silver allotment that the kingdom was secretly holding on behalf of Satsuma to use for private trade during the missions; remuneration for the Chinese interpreters; gifts for Chinese officials and contacts; and all the expenses of maintaining the Ryukyu House in Fuzhou. Its only recourse for repaying the silver borrowed from Satsuma was by the cultivation and sale of ever more sugar.

So why, we must ask, did the royal government continue nurturing its suzerain-vassal relationship with China through the political rituals of tribute and patents of investiture in the context of the greater East Asian international community? And why did it continue to pursue sinicization? It was not simply that the tribute legations and granting of patents of investiture were appropriate diplomatic niceties; rather, it was a necessary defense measure taken to ensure the continued existence of the kingdom, which might otherwise be completely subsumed under the *bakufu*'s "nation."

The term "great challenge" [J. *go-toriai*] appears frequently in the old documents of the royal government. The challenge, besides its modern meaning of "rivalry" or "dispute," referred to the agreements and mediations that formed the basis of alliances and diplomacy. For the royal government, struggling to find its balance between its two looming and powerful neighbors, diplomacy was most definitely a great challenge.

The kingdom could not ignore the fact that it was, in effect, ruled by Satsuma, backed by the authority of the shogun and the Edo *bakufu;* but sinicization continued all the same, in parallel to the growing power and influence of Satsuma and the *bakufu.* Ryukyu's sense of sovereignty was born from this great challenge diplomacy, which itself stemmed from the dual-identity polity, which held Ryukyu to be a vassal of China and a vassal of Japan. And because any slipup in the execution of this great challenge diplomacy would greatly impact the kingdom's continued existence, the ruling members of the royal government always imbued the challenge with great meaning.[12]

However, amidst the chaos at the end of the Tokugawa period, as Japan began to open up, a radical change was about to occur that would no longer permit Ryukyu to pursue its risky dual-identity great challenge diplomacy, and would transform the destiny of the kingdom.

CHAPTER EIGHT

# The End of the Kingdom

## THE IMPACT OF THE MEIJI RESTORATION

### The Upheaval of Modernization

The agitation to overthrow the Japanese shogunate reached its peak in the Tenth Month of 1867 (Keiō 3). Shōgun Tokugawa Yoshinobu, no longer able to resist pressure from the powerful feudal clans of Satsuma and Chōshū, relinquished political power to the imperial court. This restoration of imperial rule signaled the end of the *bakuhan* system of government that had endured for more than 260 years.

Beginning with the voluntary return of their lands and people to the emperor's control [J. *hanseki hōkan*] by the feudal lords of Satsuma, Chōshū, Hizen, and Tōsa in the First Month of 1869, the new government succeeded in restoring to the emperor 274 domains throughout the whole country. Further, in the Seventh Month of 1871, the government issued an imperial decree abolishing the feudal domains and establishing the prefectures [J. *haihan chiken*]. With this, in a single stroke, the government demolished what had been a decentralized system of feudal domains and established in its place a centralized power structure that transformed Japan into a modern and unified sovereign nation.

As this series of monumental and historic changes were sweeping over Japan, Ryukyu remained as before under the jurisdiction of what was now called Kagoshima Prefecture, and the waves of change did not immediately reach the kingdom. The year after the establishment of the prefectures, Kagoshima followed long-established routine and appointed Fukuzaki Kiren as its resident agent in Ryukyu. Later, two prefectural officials, Ijichi Sadaka and Narahara Shigeru, were sent to Ryukyu to serve as government liaisons. They explained the restoration movement to the royal government and announced that the reform of the national government would not bring any great changes to the existing governance of Ryukyu.

### Establishment of Ryukyu *Han*

After the abolition of the feudal domains [*han*] and the establishment of the prefectures, Japan set aside for the time being the issue of Ryukyu and how it fit into Japan's relations with China. When it signed the Sino-Japanese Friendship and Trade Treaty in 1871, the Japanese government made sure it included a provision to the effect that "territory owing allegiance to both signatories shall not be encroached upon by either, and its security must be preserved in perpetuity." This clause left undefined the limits of the modern nation's territorial jurisdiction. The border between Japan and China in the early modern period had not been a clearly drawn line, but a zone; and the kingdom, though for all intents and purposes under the rule of Japan, had long survived in that zone as a nation recognizing the jurisdiction of both China and Japan. However, as long as the kingdom was permitted to continue without a clarification of its ambiguous existence as vassal to two nations, it was inevitable that the Japanese government, with its objective of establishing a modern, sovereign state, would become involved in territorial disputes with China over the region. In a strategic move to resolve the matter of Ryukyu's double allegiance, Japan renamed the Ryukyu Kingdom as the Ryukyu *han*, or the Ryukyu feudal domain; King Shō Tai was designated as *han'ō*, or king of the Ryukyu *han*, subordinate to the Meiji emperor. This strategy meant that, like all of Japan's feudal domains, the kingdom fell under domestic administration and in the future would be subject to the policy of *hanseki hōkan*, the return of feudal lands and population to the emperor, as well as that of *haihan chiken*, the replacement of the feudal domains with prefectures.

In the Seventh Month of 1872, the royal government received an order from Kagoshima's vice governor, Ōyama Tsunayoshi, to send an emissary to congratulate the emperor on his restoration to power. The royal government took the matter as equivalent to the Tokugawa-era tradition of dispatching emissaries to the capital with congratulatory messages on the appointment of a new *shōgun*. It drew up a formal document of congratulations from the king and then submitted it to Kagoshima Prefecture's provisional secretary of protocol, Migimatsu Gosuke, for inspection. This inspector changed the original "Ryukyu-koku Chūzan-ō" [the Chūzan King of the Land of Ryukyu], referring to King Shō Tai, to simply read "Ryukyu Shō Tai" [Shō Tai of Ryukyu]; deleted the Ryukyuan titles of *ōji* [prince] for the chief envoy and *uēkata* [minister] for the vice envoy; and added the Japanese date of Meiji 5 above the Chinese-style date of the original letter. His changing of "Ryukyu-koku" [Land of Ryukyu] to "Ryukyu-han" [feudal domain of Ryukyu] and referring to the king as "king of the feudal domain" reflected the Meiji government's agenda, of which the royal government remained at that point unaware.[1]

The royal government named Shō Ken (Prince Ie) as chief envoy, accompanied by Shō Yūkō (Giwan Uēkata Chōho) as vice envoy. The embassy traveled to the capital via Kagoshima, attending a ceremony in the Foreign Ministry's reception rooms at the Imperial Palace on September 14. As decided by the Meiji government, they were given an imperial decree granting a "patent of investiture." Besides confirming Shō Tai's authority, this document redesignated "Ryukyu" as the "Ryukyu *han*," and the king was appointed as the new "king of the feudal domain."[2]

### Control of Ryukyu *Han* Transferred to the Ministry of Foreign Affairs

With the establishment of the Ryukyu *han*, the administration of Ryukyu's foreign diplomacy was transferred to the Ministry of Foreign Affairs, and the government furnished the Ryukyuans with an official residence in the Mochinokizaka area of Iidamachi such as those once kept by the daimyo. Then Ijichi Sadaka, who had earlier been posted to the Ryukyu *han*, was ordered to close down the old Satsuma magistrate's office and establish in its place a branch office of the Foreign Ministry. The magistrate, Fukuzaki Kiren, was ordered to continue in his position in the Ryukyu *han*. Because the old governance relationship with Satsuma had come to an end, in November the Ryukyuan officials residing at the Ryukyu House in Kagoshima were recalled home. Along with the establishment in Ryukyu of a branch office of the Foreign Ministry, in March of the following year, the Japanese government ordered that personnel be posted to the Ryukyu residence in Tokyo on a rotating basis. The Ryukyu *han* dispatched as its resident director the Japanese-language-proficient Ba Kensai (Yonabaru Uēkata Ryōketsu).[3]

Others sent to serve at the Ryukyu *han* residence in Tokyo included upper- and lower-level officials; they remained for one year. Three times a year, on the feast days of New Year's Day, Kigen [the anniversary of Emperor Jinmu's ascension to the throne], and the Meiji emperor's birthday, the resident director followed established custom and visited the Imperial Palace bearing the congratulations of Ryukyu's king. In the eyes of the royal government, this *han* representative's duty in Tokyo was equivalent to the duties performed by the personnel posted to the Ryukyu House in

Satsuma under the *bakufu*. Because the kingdom retained tacit consent to conduct the tribute trade with China, and so preserved even under the new government its old double status as a tributary to both China and Japan, the royal government believed it would be able to maintain sovereignty.

### The Miyako Shipwreck Massacre

However, the situation changed completely on the Tenth Month, 18th Day, 1871, when a tribute ship out of Miyako Island, on its return trip after carrying a cargo loaded in Naha in the spring, ran into a terrible storm. The ship was wrecked off Bayaowan [modern Taidong] on the southeastern coast of Taiwan; fifty-four of the sixty-six surviving crew members under the command of Nakasone Gen'an were massacred by Taiwanese aboriginals when they managed to reach shore. The fallout from this shipwreck disaster developed into a crisis that shook the Ryukyu Kingdom to its foundations.

When Ijichi Sadaka, working in Naha, heard the details of this shipwreck, he immediately reported them to Ōyama Tsuneyoshi, the governor of Kagoshima. Ōyama responded to his urgent message by drafting a proposal calling for the subjugation of Taiwan. Ijichi, who by then had gone to Tokyo as part of a congratulatory embassy, presented this document to Foreign Minister Soejima Taneomi on the Eighth Month, 14th Day, 1872. Imperial Army major Kabayama Sukenori, commander of the Kumamoto Chinzai Second Detached Garrison, had hurried to the capital earlier and reported on the matter to the general of the army and Imperial Councilor Saigo Takamori on the Eighth Month, 9th Day. He also submitted a written opinion on the incident to Saigo Takamori's younger brother, Lieutenant General Saigo Tsugumichi, recommending a strong response to the incident.

The Ryukyu *han* became embroiled in the matter as Ōyama, Ijichi, and Kabayama, all former retainers of what had been the Satsuma *han*, spoke aggressively for dispatching troops to Taiwan. The policy of concealment toward China was in fact still being followed, but as the Ryukyu *han*'s imminent loss of self-rule became more obvious, Governor Ōyama and the others rapidly abandoned any pretense at concealment and, as part of their reprisal and to affirm Japan's imperial authority abroad, began considering measures for incorporating the kingdom into the Japanese polity.[4]

### Engineering the Taiwan Expedition

The U.S. minister to Japan, Charles E. DeLong, argued that Japan had the right to mount an expedition in retaliation after the shipwreck incident in Taiwan, because China did not effectively control the aboriginal territories in Taiwan; these areas were, under international law, "unclaimed territory."

He brought in Charles W. LeGendre as an expert on conditions in Taiwan, having been until shortly before the American consul stationed in Amoy (modern Xiamen). LeGendre also held that because southeastern Taiwan was "unclaimed territory," Japan was within its rights to be first in colonizing the area. This support caused Foreign Minister Soejima Taneomi to believe that the international community would recognize as legitimate a military expedition to occupy aboriginal territory.

The proposal to invade made by Ōyama, Ijichi, and Kabayama was accepted, and the Meiji government began preparing to send a punitive expedition to Taiwan. Two political objectives motivated the expedition: first, though ostensibly a reprisal for the massacre of the ship's crew from Miyako Island, the expedition was to "occupy aboriginal territory" in an aggressive expansion of the territory under Japan's national sovereignty; and second, it served notice to China that Ryukyu was a possession of Japan and under its jurisdiction.

In March of 1873, the government sent Foreign Minister Soejima as a special ambassador to China. He was to present the ratification papers for the Sino-Japanese Friendship and Trade Treaty (1871) and attend an audience with the Tongzhi emperor [r. 1861–1875]. His mission objectives included ascertaining the Chinese position on the massacre of the Ryukyuan shipwreck victims and seeking out a pretext under which troops could be sent to Taiwan. On June 21, Soejima sent Yanagihara Sakimitsu and Tei Eiei to the Qing government Foreign Affairs Office, to sound out the Chinese about the shipwreck incident. Máo Chǎngxī, a minister at the Foreign Affairs Office, responded by noting that twelve of the Ryukyuans had been rescued from massacre and safely returned home, and adding that since they were from Ryukyu, a tributary state of China, surely the matter had nothing to do with Japan. Máo went on to explain that Taiwan's aboriginal tribes could be divided into either "wild tribes" [J. *seiban,* Ch. *shēngfān*] or "cultivated tribes" [J. *jukuban,* Ch. *shúfān*]. The latter had submitted to Chinese rule and been incorporated into Chinese territory. The Miyako shipwreck massacre, however, had been committed by "wild tribespeople," uncivilized savages outside Chinese jurisdiction.[5]

Although Máo's characterization of the uncultivated "uncivilized savages" as outside the norm did not really exclude them from Chinese rule, for Yanagihara, intent on identifying a legal justification for invading Taiwan, Máo Chǎngxī's exposition on "uncivilized tribes" provided sufficient grounds for his purpose. Yanagihara announced that if measures were not taken by China to look into the matter of the "wild tribes," Japan was prepared to take punitive measures, and this brought his discussions with the Foreign Affairs Office to an end for the day.

### Saigō Tsugumichi's Expeditionary Force

The expeditionary forces consisted mainly of troops from the Kumamoto garrison, and with the addition of about 300 recruits with *samurai* background from Kagoshima, a force totaling 3,650 men departed from Nagasaki on May 17, 1874. They landed at Sheliao (in modern Pingtung County) on the twenty-second, and the military movements were over by early June after the subjugation of several dozen "aboriginal villages." The Japanese Army held to its plan of "occupying aboriginal territory" by remaining in place once the conquest was complete, ignoring Chinese demands for withdrawal.

The Japanese government ordered Yanagihara Sakimitsu, its ambassador to the Qing court, to enter into discussions with China. On July 12, in order to transform the issue of Ryukyu into a domestic one, management of the Ryukyu *han* was transferred from the Ministry of Foreign Affairs to the Ministry of the Interior; what had been a branch office of the Foreign Ministry in Naha became instead a branch office of the Interior Ministry. Next Ambassador Yanagihara was ordered to use the recent expedition as a basis for severing Ryukyu's tributary relationship with China. The negotiations regarding the Taiwan expedition did not focus on the issue of Ryukyu; instead, the government intentionally magnified the issue of jurisdiction over Taiwan in its face-off with China. China insisted that Japan's incursion into Taiwan violated the provisions of the Sino-Japanese Friendship and Trade Treaty, infringing on China's sovereignty, and demanded the immediate withdrawal of the expeditionary forces. However, Yanagihara asserted Japan's right of jurisdiction as the occupiers of "savage territory without rulers," over which the Chinese held no authority. The negotiations engendered a hard fight, with neither side yielding to the other.[6]

### The Ambiguous Notion of "People Belonging to the Nation of Japan"

In order to break this deadlock, the Japanese government decided to send to China its minister of the interior, Ōkubo Toshimichi, with a brevet as ambassador extraordinary and plenipotentiary that gave him the authority to decide for war or peace. As a way of bolstering Japan's justifications for the incursion, Ōkubo wished to hold a memorial service for the massacre victims from Miyako Island before he left for China; however, the royal government would not cooperate, and plans for a ceremony came to nothing. Additionally, after his arrival in China, negotiations met with complications concerning jurisdiction over Taiwan just as they had for

Yanagihara. No resolution seemed forthcoming, and Ōkubo threatened to call off the talks. Finally, with the arbitration of Sir Thomas Wade, the British ambassador to the Qing court, the matter of jurisdiction over Taiwan was laid aside and a possible resolution to the matter of Ryukyu's double allegiance appeared. The mutual agreement, concluded on October 31, 1874, that finally brought the matter to a peaceful close included a line saying that "China finds Japan's Taiwan Expedition justified for the protection of its citizens."[7]

This agreement did not specifically refer to the victims of the massacre as "citizens of the Ryukyu *han* of Japan" but used the more general term "people belonging to the nation of Japan." There were others among China's tributary nations that also paid double tribute; thus to China the wording of the mutual agreement did not mean that China had released Ryukyu from its status as tributary. The Japanese government, however, pushed its own understanding of the agreement by holding that when China had allowed that the Taiwan expedition had been a justifiable reprisal on behalf of the Miyako victims of the massacre, it thereby recognized Japan's right of jurisdiction over Ryukyu, because of course, "people belonging to the nation of Japan" included the citizens of the Ryukyu *han.*

## FORCED ANNEXATION

### Termination of the Dual Allegiance

After his return to Japan, Ōkubo took steps to end Ryukyu's dual allegiance, terminating Ryukyu's authority to engage independently with the Qing government. On July 14, Matsuda Michiyuki met with Shō Hitsu (Prince Nakijin), the representative of the king, and delivered the government's directive [J. *tasshi*]:

1. Offering tribute to China or sending congratulations on the ascension of a new emperor is forbidden.
2. Receiving patents of investiture from China will cease.
3. Dates will be given according to the Meiji calendar, and all festivals will be observed as it proclaims.
4. Two or three officials will be selected and posted to Tokyo for instruction in, and later will administer, Japanese criminal law codes.
5. Ten youths will be sent to Tokyo for education and to become familiar with the modern world.
6. The Ryukyu House in Fuzhou will cease operations.
7. The king will visit Tokyo to express gratitude to the emperor for the feudal domain's establishment.
8. A military garrison will be established in the domain.[8]

The directive did not have as its only purpose the termination of Ryukyu's right to conduct its own international relations, such as continuing its tributary relationship with China; it was also intended to begin the incorporation of the territory into the Japanese polity by legally stationing Japanese troops there. Certainly, this came as a complete shock to the royal government, which had believed Foreign Minister Soejima's promise that "the Ryukyu *han*'s government and national polity will be left intact indefinitely," made to Ryukyu's representative in Tokyo, Ba Kensai. He had visited the private residence of Foreign Minister Soejima Taneomi after Ryukyu's change of status to feudal domain, to make a direct appeal for the preservation of Ryukyu's dual allegiance to both China and Japan.[9]

**Dispatch of Secret Envoys**

Ryukyu's tributary relationship with China, with its features of tribute and royal authority bestowed through the grant of patents of investiture, was the foundation upon which the Ryukyu Kingdom relied for its existence. The directive by which the Japanese government was forcing Ryukyu to terminate its tributary relationship with China seemed to the Ryukyuans to spell the collapse of their kingdom. Faced with this crisis of life or death for the kingdom, the leaders of the royal government strongly resisted the terms of the directive and repeated their request to continue operating under the system of dual allegiance.

Even so, after receiving the directive, the tribute missions to China were called off. The ship that should have departed to bring home the most recent tribute legation from 1874 was not allowed to sail, and the tribute legation scheduled for 1876 was canceled at the same time. At about this same time, as the royal government was making its repeated requests to maintain the status quo, a ship that had been rescued while adrift at sea returned from Fujian. It carried from the authorities there, first, a query as to why no ship had come to carry home the tribute legation of 1874; and second, a *zīwén,* an official communiqué, demanding an explanation for the kingdom's failure to send an emissary congratulating the Guangxu emperor [r. 1875–1908] on his ascension to the throne. The royal government petitioned the Japanese that it must respond to the *zīwén* because the ceremonial observances around an enthronement were rituals of national importance that reflected on China's dignity as a suzerain state, but the Meiji government refused permission. In response, Shō Tai secretly sent his brother-in-law Shō Tokukō (Kōchi Uēkata Chōjō), a senior government official of the magistrate class, to China in December of 1876, to appeal to the Chinese by explaining the Japanese government's interdiction on sending tribute. Shō Tokukō slipped into China with the help of a group of men knowledgeable about China, including Sai Taitei, a former tribute envoy, and Rin Seikō, who had been a government-sponsored scholar in Beijing.

However, Shō Tai's secret message concerned only the order to cease sending tribute; it said nothing of the measures the Japanese government had taken to enforce the order. At this point, the royal government was still invested in the "policy of concealment," that is, concealing from China Ryukyu's true relationship to the Japanese government. When Shō Tokukō presented his secret missive to the emperor, it was immediately turned over to the Foreign Affairs Office, in charge of handling international negotiations. From there, the matter went to Hé Rúzhāng, slated to be China's first ambassador to Japan, with an edict ordering him to take up the tribute interdiction with the Japanese Ministry of Foreign Affairs.[10]

### The First Chinese Ambassador to Japan Protests

Hé Rúzhāng departed from Shanghai in November of 1877.[11] After his arrival in Tokyo, he was visited at the embassy by officials from the Ryukyuan residence in Tokyo who wished to speak out about conditions in Ryukyu. They gave him the details of the entire matter by showing him the correspondence between the royal government and Tokyo, and, for the first time, revealed the truth of the royal government's policy of concealment. Hé Rúzhāng sent a letter to Lǐ Hóngzhāng, the Chinese general who had acted alone in handling the negotiations with Japan over the Sino-Japanese Friendship and Trade Treaty and the problems in Taiwan, and who continued to wield great power over Chinese international affairs from behind the scenes. In the letter, Ambassador Hé refers to the royal government's policy of concealment, which it had adhered to all along, as "Ryukyu's folly." In fact, other lands with which China held diplomatic relations had sworn double fealty; the Kazan khanate in Central Asia had also sent tribute to two masters, Russia and China. Thus there was nothing in Ryukyu's double allegiance to make it unique, and no inconsistency in China's protesting to the Japanese government over the logical validity of double allegiances.

In September 1878, Hé Rúzhāng visited Foreign Minister Terashima Munenori at the Ministry of Foreign Affairs to ask for an explanation for the cessation of tribute and to strongly protest the actions of the Japanese government. Following this visit, Ambassador Hé continued to insist on raising the matter of Ryukyu's double allegiance at more than ten negotiation sessions, in an attempt to reinstitute the tribute trade and the bestowal of patents of investiture. Terashima, however, refused to discuss the matter, insisting from start to finish that the Ryukyus were exclusively under the sovereignty of Japan and their governance a matter of Japanese internal affairs. The Ryukyu issue became the hidden reef upon which negotiations between the two nations foundered.

The Meiji government gave orders on December 27 for Matsuda Michiyuki, now chief secretary of the Home Affairs Ministry, to return Ryukyu. Other orders abolished the Tokyo office of the Ryukyu *han* established in March 1873 and sent home the Ryukyu *han* officials who had met with Hé Rúzhāng and other foreign representatives in search of support. Matsuda arrived in Naha in January of the following year, along with the *han* officials who had been stationed at the capital. He brought with him further orders that any travel to Tokyo or outside the territory of the *han* must first be approved by the branch office of the Ministry of Home Affairs and its minister and he once again pressed the Ryukyu government to submit to the directive. The royal government had refused to do so, bolstered by Hé Rúzhāng's vehement protests to the Ministry of Foreign Affairs and China's support behind the scenes to continue as always in seeking to preserve its traditional government based on the policy of double allegiance.

After his return to Tokyo, Matsuda presented on February 13 his "Report on the Second Mission to Ryukyu" [J. Dainikai Bushi Ryūkyū Fukumeisho], in which he called for Chancellor Sanjō Sanetomi to abolish Ryukyu as a *han* and make it a prefecture instead. Given the royal government's refusal to submit to the directive, the development of the diplomatic dispute with China, and the difficulties in accomplishing its plans as expected, the Japanese government acted swiftly to handle the situation.[12]

### Restoration of the Land and People to the Emperor, and the Abolition of the Feudal Domains and Establishment of the Prefectural System

The Japanese government appointed Matsuda Michiyuki as head of the disciplinary action. Backed by a police force and half a battalion of infantry, he went to Shuri Castle on March 27 and delivered a new set of peremptory directives to the Ryukyu *han*, including orders for the "surrender and evacuation of Shuri Castle," "removal of the king to Tokyo," and "the handing-over of the various registries of property, persons, and officials." Kinashi Seiichirō was authorized to develop prefectural ordinances, and what had been the branch office of the Ministry of Home Affairs was converted into the provisional prefectural government offices.

March 31 saw the first stage of King Shō Tai's departure from Shuri; that night the king and his wife and consorts left the castle. Shuri Castle was subsequently confiscated by the Japanese government and converted to quarters for the Kumamoto Garrison's troops stationed in Okinawa. Then, on April 4, the Ryukyu *han* was officially abolished and, under the *hanseki hōkan* policy that returned people and land to the emperor, incorporated into Japan's centralized authoritarian structure as Okinawa Prefecture. Because of the royal government's opposition to the conversion of the Ryukyu *han* to a prefecture, the Meiji government simultaneously forced through the abolition of the *han* when it returned the lands and people to the emperor, unlike on the Japanese mainland, where the two actions had been taken at different times. Under this series of political measures, collectively known as the "Disposition of Ryukyu" [琉球処分, J. Ryūkyū Shobun], the Ryukyu Kingdom was finally annexed to Japan and completely detached from China.[13]

At the same time the disposition was announced, Matsuda Michiyuki, who had been sent with a group of police to oversee the process, ordered a ban on all private communications. When the *han* had been collectively abolished and the prefectures established in the Japanese mainland, the *han* leaders had been removed from office and ordered to move to Tokyo; similarly, the government ordered King Shō Tai to move to the capital. His retainers, however, sought somehow to delay his removal to the capital by insisting that he was too ill to go. On April 27, Matsuda sent the king's son and heir, Crown Prince Shō Ten, ahead to Tokyo so that he might himself make an appeal to postpone the king's removal. On May 27 orders came compelling the king to the capital, there to settle on a property of 2,000 *tsubo* [about 1.6 acres] granted to him in the Fujimichō neighborhood of Kōjimachi District [in modern Chiyoda].

After the establishment of Okinawa Prefecture, to avoid social turmoil brought on by precipitous changes to a social system such as Ryukyu's, which was different from that of mainland Japan, the Meiji government implemented a policy based on preserving traditional customs and political mores, taking the line that it would avoid reforming land ownership, the tax system, or regional organization. This policy of preserving traditional institutions was a diplomatic maneuver to appease the Chinese, who had so vehemently opposed the Disposition of Ryukyu. It served also to quiet the leaders of the former royal government, out of power after the dismantling of their administration, and to allow the elite [*shi*] class to continue collecting their hereditary stipends.[14]

## The Resistance Campaign Turns to China for Help

Nabeshima Naoyoshi, upon taking up his position as Okinawa's first governor, issued an order that the officials working in Shuri, Naha, Kumemura, Tomari, and the various regional and village offices should continue in their positions.[15] However, the officials who had served in the royal government refused to work as commanded by the Japanese officials handling the annexation or to follow the new prefectural ordinances. They shuttered all the government tax offices and refused to accept tax collection documents. The officials of the royal government swore not to cooperate with the prefectural government, signing their pledges in blood and fomenting a resistance movement of disobedience and boycott in every region. The prefectural authorities, however, proved thorough in their suppression of such resistance, arresting and treating harshly any suspected participants. Finally, the leaders of the royal government were forced to call off their campaign. After this, the resistance changed tactics, sending secret missions to beg for China's intervention as suzerain to restore the Ryukyu Kingdom to its previous status.

Around this time, Shō Tokukō, Sai Taitei, and Rin Seikō had stayed on in Fuzhou, hoping to make a direct petition for help to Beijing. As foreign ministers, they had the right to express their views or report to the king, but as lower-ranked retainers (that is, retainers of a retainer), they were not permitted to make direct appeals. In the end, they were not permitted to make their appeal to Beijing, and they received an edict from the emperor, ordering them to return home. Shō, Sai, and Rin disregarded this order, instead remaining at the Ryukyu House in Fuzhou, along with Mō Seichō, who had been chief envoy for the Ryukyu Kingdom's last tribute legation sent to China in 1874. Ryukyuans in Fuzhou were required to reside at the Ryukyu House, and they were not permitted to move freely outside its walls. Thus, they monitored the developments of the Chinese ambassador Hé Rúzhāng's negotiations with the Japanese government in Tokyo without ever leaving the Ryukyu House in Fuzhou.

With the establishment of Okinawa Prefecture, the community of Kumemura, source of the government officials who had directed the royal government's policy of sinicization, was dissolved and ceased functioning effectively. Interest in resisting the changes seethed among the Kumemura gentry, and messages concerning the prefecture's establishment were sent secretly to Shō Tokukō's party in Fuzhou. On June 6, Fujianese merchants delivered a message entrusted to them by Crown Prince Shō Ten, then in Tokyo, informing in detail on the circumstances of the annexation.[16] Shō Tokukō and his associates, having awaited news of Hé Rúzhāng's negotiations with great anticipation, were shocked to hear of the kingdom's collapse. In Shō Tokukō's eyes, Shō Tai's forced residence in Tokyo reflected the status of the kingdom itself, held under house arrest. Shō Ten's secret missive instructed Shō Tokukō to leave Fuzhou immediately and head north to make an appeal to the central government. Shō Tokukō promptly disguised himself as a Chinese by shaving his head and arranging his hair in a pigtail and traveled to Tianjin. There he found Lǐ Hóngzhāng, then serving simultaneously as viceroy of the metropolitan province of Zhili and superintendent of trade. On July 3, Shō Tokukō submitted to Lǐ a written petition asking for assistance for the Ryukyu Kingdom.[17]

This document was an unmistakable protest against Japan, and marked a change from earlier petitions regarding the Japanese government, which had been consistent in pressing for the restoration of the system of dual allegiance. The forced annexation had brought home to Shō Tokukō the impossibility of restoring Ryukyu's autonomy by preserving its status as a *han* under double allegiance, as hitherto petitioned by the royal government. Shō Tokukō's petition clearly outlined his hope for the kingdom's restoration, pressing China to act on its prerogative, as the suzerain state in East Asia's traditional international tributary system of tribute offerings and patents of investiture, to make an armed intervention to protect one of its tributary nations, freeing the kingdom from Japanese rule and returning it to the Chinese sphere, its sovereignty restored. Police authorities in Okinawa Prefecture named such protest activities in China the "Ryukyu Restoration Movement." They remained vigilant and referred to those who slipped away to China in order to generate support for a restoration as "Qing deserters" (*dasshinjin*).

## FAILURE OF THE MOVEMENT TO RESTORE THE KINGDOM

### The Proposal to Divide the Islands

In both Tokyo and Beijing, China had difficulties finding a solution for the Ryukyu issue,[18] but former U.S. president Ulysses S. Grant's visit to China seemed like a golden opportunity. In May 1879, Prince Gong asked Grant to mediate discussions over Ryukyu's sovereignty issues, as did Lǐ Hóngzhāng when Grant visited Lǐ's offices in Tianjin. Grant went on to Japan in June, and with his mediation, the already foundering negotiations over Ryukyu became further entangled with Japan's treaty revision negotiations with the Great Powers of Europe and the United States. In the meantime, negotiations over the status of Ryukyu continued between Japan's ambassador in Beijing, Shishido Tamaki, and the officials at the Office of Foreign Affairs.[19]

With its goal of forging Japan into a modern, sovereign nation, the Meiji government during this period regarded as its first priority the renegotiation of the unequal treaties, concerning matters such as extraterritoriality, tariff agreements, and most-favored-nation status, imposed by the nations of Europe and the United States during the last years of the Tokugawa shogunate. Instead of the difficult approach taken by his predecessors Soejima Taneomi and Terashima Munenori, of dealing with each Western nation individually, the newly appointed foreign minister, Inoue Kaoru, swept aside precedent and began negotiating with the Western powers as a combined group. His greatest fear was that they might refuse Japan's request to enter into treaty negotiations, using as an excuse the notion that they couldn't renegotiate such things as tariffs and extraterritoriality as long as the terms of the Sino-Japanese Friendship and Trade Treaty, which covered those matters and which was set to expire in 1883, still remained in effect.

Given Inoue's concern that these discussions with the Western powers should go well, he realized the need to first modify the agreements with China. With this in mind, he initiated overtures to make changes to the Sino-Japanese Friendship and Trade Treaty, aggressively exploiting the issue of Ryukyu and its complicated relationship with China. In September 1880, the Japanese government proposed to divide the Ryukyuan islands, ceding the southern island groups of Miyako and Yaeyama to China. In exchange, China would agree to modify the terms of the treaty to allow Japan to pursue commercial interests within China, which had earlier been restricted. Given how often the Meiji government had decried Chinese involvement in the Ryukyu issue as interference in Japan's national sovereignty, the offer to cede islands was the height of absurdity. The government, however, pursued its own national interests, even if it meant exposing such contradictions.

### Obstructions to Reaching an Agreement

At this same time, China was in the middle of difficult negotiations with Russia over the status of the Ili river basin region in Xinjiang. By threatening the Chinese with the possibility of a Japanese-Russian pact, the Japanese government managed to gain the advantage in its own discussions with China. On October 28, Japan won an agreement from China's Foreign Affairs Office for a special treaty over Ryukyu, including "additional conventions" and "guarantees."[20] It was signed ten days later, with an agreement that ratification would occur within three months. China's acceptance of the cession of Miyako and Yaeyama, in order to restore the Ryukyu Kingdom there and so preserve the age-old tributary-suzerain relationship, grew out of its desire to reassert China's position as suzerain ruling over its tributaries in the traditional East Asian system encompassing China and its barbarian satellites. This treaty seemed to offer the possibility of a settlement over the issue of Ryukyuan sovereignty, which had been so disordered by Japan's handling of the Disposition of Ryukyu.

The Japanese government conducted these negotiations in secret and did not inform the Ryukyuans of the plan to divide the islands. However, the Ryukyuans in self-imposed exile in China, as well as officials of the former royal government, were kept informed by Lǐ Hóngzhāng and other Chinese emissaries in Tokyo. The Qing exiles persisted in submitting petitions to the Foreign Affairs Office protesting the treaty to divide the islands. They could not accept breaking up the kingdom, and they protested that Miyako and Yaeyama, poor and remote, were too unproductive to serve as bases to establish an independent nation.

In the 1870s and 1880s, a group of officials in China popularly known as the Qīngliú [J. Seiryū, Purification], or the Qīngliúdǎng [J. Seiryū-tō, Purification Party], were actively trying to align policy making with their traditional Confucian moral principles. One of these, a native of Fuzhou named Chén Bǎochēn, supported the petitions brought by the Ryukyuan Qing exiles and made a report to the emperor opposing the Foreign Affairs Office's treaty for the division of the Ryukyuan islands. The petitioners had tried to recruit many officials and civilians with the power to affect policy, but Chén Bǎochēn's action on the eve of the ratification of the disastrous treaty raised him, in the eyes of the Qing exiles, to the level of savior of the Fuzhou lobby.[21]

Subsequently, Lǐ Hóngzhāng took Shō Tokukō's objections to the treaty as a reason to energetically oppose it. When he, too, submitted a report to the emperor, in which he included a letter from Hé Rúzhāng telling of the Ryukyuan king's own objections to the treaty, debate over whether to ratify the treaty collapsed.

### Negotiations Break Down

The Chinese government frequently made policy, especially concerning its national affairs, only after consulting with high-ranking regional administrators such as provincial governors or inspectors general. The process of sending out inquiries and awaiting the officials' reports concerning the treaty to divide the Ryukyus delayed any final policy decision. On December 1, Japanese foreign minister Inoue Kaoru sent an internal memo of instruction to Ambassador Shishido saying that it was a gross insult to the Japanese envoy and to the Japanese government for the Chinese to sign a statement of intent without having any intention of ratifying the treaty. Shishido was to continue demanding that the Foreign Affairs Office ratify the treaty, and if China continued to disregard Japan's demands, then he should cut off negotiations and return home.[22] On January 17, 1881, after repeated demands to the Foreign Affairs Office had yielded no response, Shishido sent a final communiqué laying the responsibility for the treaty's failure on the Chinese government. He left Beijing on the twentieth and returned to Japan from Shanghai on the warship *Kongo*. Shishido's departure from the capital signaled the final breakdown of all negotiations for the treaty to divide the islands.

China reached a settlement with Russia for the return of the Ili river basin when it signed the Treaty of St. Petersburg on February 24, 1881. On March 5, the Guangxu emperor issued an edict to the Foreign Affairs Office to once more take up negotiations over the Ryukyu issue. After August, the Japanese government revisited its plan to divide the islands, and in extreme secrecy asked the British governor of Hong Kong, Sir John Pope Hennessy, to mediate in discussions with Lǐ Hóngzhāng, who wielded great influence both in the Foreign Affairs Office and over China's efforts to modernize. Inoue Kaoru, revealing his wish to conduct talks with Lǐ Hóngzhāng through Hennessy's secret diplomacy, ordered his consul in Tienjin, Takezoe Shin'ichirō, to open informal negotiations.[23]

Meanwhile, the Qing exiles, fearing that the treaty to divide the islands would again become an issue, were tenacious and repetitive in protesting such a treaty and sought whatever means they could find to prevent it. The protests of these exiles influenced Lǐ Hóngzhāng. He took up the heart of their objections and tried to negotiate the inclusion of the island of Okinawa in the territory that would be the kingdom's domain. However, even in these informal discussions, the Japanese government was adamant in limiting the cession to the Miyako and Yaeyama island groups and could find no common ground with Lǐ Hóngzhāng in his aim of widening the boundaries of the Ryukyu Kingdom. The ten-year moratorium on revisions to the Sino-Japanese Friendship and Trade Treaty ended in April of 1883. Inoue, without calling off the difficult negotiations over the division of the islands, asked to open talks limited to revising the treaty. This request was refused by the Chinese, who wished to solve the Ryukyu issue at the same time. In the end, the search for a resolution to the question of Ryukyu's sovereignty came to nothing, and the issue continued to cast a shadow over relations between China and Japan, without ever being reopened as a topic for official negotiations.[24]

### The Movement to Restore the Kingdom and the Suzerain-Tributary Issue

Contemporaneously to the movement to restore the Ryukyu Kingdom, conflicts arose in Korea and Annam (Vietnam), tributary nations under the jurisdiction of China's Ministry of Rites, just as Ryukyu had been. In Korea, the antigovernment and anti-Japanese Imo Mutiny [J. Jingo Jihen, K. Imo Gullan] broke out on July 23, 1882, when soldiers and some city residents rose in the capital city of Hanseong [now Seoul]. China responded by sending troops and the Qing Northern Fleet, under the command of Admiral Dīng Rǔchāng. In 1884, Chinese troops stationed in Korea under the command of Wú Zhàoyǒu and Yuán Shìkǎi suppressed the Gapsin Coup [J. Kōshin Jihen, K. Gapsin Jeongbyeon], a coup d'état in which Korea's pro-Japanese independent faction attempted to overthrow its pro-Chinese conservative faction. France was maneuvering to add Annam (Vietnam) to its colonial empire; China, as its suzerain nation, sought with increasing force to prevent that from happening. When the French began showing force in Tonkin in what is now northern Vietnam, China dispatched troops to fend them off and the Sino-French War [1884–1885] burst out. China's tactics of armed intervention were not solely for the protection of its tributary satellites, but also for the promotion of its own national defense and strategic interests. The question of whether China would be able to preserve the East Asian system of exchanging tribute and patents of authority had great impact on the movement to restore the Ryukyu Kingdom.

The leaders of the former royal government made frequent secret journeys to make petitions to the Chinese, asking continually for armed intervention, such as in Korea and Annam (Vietnam), to settle the question of Ryukyuan sovereignty. They had concluded that the kingdom could not otherwise be restored. Their petitions were aimed at hard-liners in the Qing government who advocated military intervention, as well as at those officials most closely involved in shaping policy toward, and handling events involving, the tributary nations of Ryukyu, Korea, and Annam (Vietnam).

### The Restoration Movement Loses Cohesiveness

During the period in which the restoration movement was developing, China, even as it was still surrounded by its tributary subject nations, was undergoing a historical process of transformation, the dissolution of the Chinese Empire. Korea in the east, Annam (Vietnam) and Burma to the south, and tributary nations in Central Asia were falling away. At the same time, the Western powers were moving in to gain protectorates and even colonies in the areas around China. In the Treaty of Tianjin, after the Sino-French War of 1884–1885, France secured Annam (Vietnam) as a protectorate, and China relinquished its suzerain rights to exercise any authority over Vietnam's military or diplomatic affairs. Similarly, one by one, China's former tributaries slipped away, such as when Burma became a British colony in 1886. Of the tributary lands in East Asia that had once been under the jurisdiction of China's Ministry of Rites, only in Korea was there a strong movement to preserve China's suzerain status. The traditional East

Asian order based on the exchange of tribute and patents of investiture was on the brink of complete collapse.

In Ryukyu, with the establishment of a Japanese governing bureaucracy headquartered at the prefectural offices, the former royal government officials saw the loss of all their ruling authority. After 1887, as the central figures of the restoration movement, such as Mō Seichō, Shō Tokukō, and Mō Hōrai, died in exile in China, the restoration movement gradually lost its momentum. However, as long as China continued to maintain its age-old suzerain-tributary relationship with Korea, thereby keeping alive East Asia's system of tribute and patents of investiture, hope remained for a restoration of the kingdom. This conviction on the part of former royal officials kept the restoration movement alive.

### Fateful Turning Point: The First Sino-Japanese War

As the Chinese hegemony collapsed and China's international standing fell, the ideology of the Ryukyuan resistance movement also showed signs of changing. Younger scions of noble Shuri families, such as Takamine Chōkyō, Goeku Chōi, and Ōta Chōfu, sent to Tokyo to receive a modern education, came to accept the Disposition of Ryukyu as a fait accompli. They began searching for a way to forge a modern identity for Okinawa that would resuscitate Okinawan society even as it remained a part of Japan. Later these young intellectuals, choosing to refer to themselves as citizens of Japan, became active opinion leaders in Okinawa. They were the center of a movement that sowed the seeds of a sense of prefectural identity, setting off the first stirrings of a new, modern Okinawa.

In September 1893, they launched the *Ryūkyū shinpō* with the aim of promoting "assimilation" into Japanese society. By educating the general public, the *Ryūkyū shinpō* was also meant to improve the low esteem in which Okinawans were held by the numerous mainland Japanese merchants resident in Okinawa, who controlled both its government and its economy. The newspaper reflected the political and ideological views of the young Shuri upper-class intellectuals who had founded it. Included among them were the fourth son of King Shō Tai, that symbol of the restoration movement; Shō Jun, a close family member, later became involved as well, showing that even part of the royal family had distanced itself from the restoration movement. In the pages of their newspaper, these young intellectuals harshly criticized as feudal and anachronistic the movement to restore the kingdom, with its traditional system of paying tribute in exchange for the patents of investiture. Thus, the solidarity of the ruling families upon which the restoration movement had relied was compromised from within. Gradually, support grew for the modernization advocated in the *Ryūkyū shinpō,* and Okinawa's society became split between distinctly opposing views.

Sometime after this, the Japanese government sought to increase the reach of Japan's sovereign rights by objecting to China's suzerainty over Korea, resulting in a dispute that developed into the First Sino-Japanese War (1894–1895). The ideological positions enunciated by the young intellectuals in their *Ryūkyū shinpō* had thrown the Ryukyu restoration movement into a crisis period, but now, fifteen years after the dissolution of the royal government, the royalists found themselves with the best chance they had ever held of reviving the kingdom. The Qing exiles, who had long been calling for an armed intervention on their behalf, knew that Korea was China's last remaining tributary nation in East Asia. If suzerain China were to successfully defend its relationship with Korea by achieving a victory in a military conflict with Japan, the exiles believed that the restoration of the Ryukyu Kingdom must directly follow. The Sino-Japanese War was fought not only over Korea, but also to settle the future of Ryukyu. The war was truly a fateful turning point in determining whether Ryukyu would continue to be ruled by a prefectural government as a part of Japan, or the Ryukyu kingdom would finally be restored.

### The Southern Fleet to Recapture Ryukyu

After the start of the war, a rumor of unverifiable origins spread to the effect that the Chinese Southern Fleet, based in Fujian's port of Mawai, was going to recapture Ryukyu, and from there to attack Kyushu. The fleet was known as the "Yellow Fleet" from the golden dragons painted on the ships' hulls and depicted on flags flying from their masts. Because the possibility of such an invasion was also reported in the newspapers of the Japanese mainland, it was not dismissed as being mere rumor, and in fact, the more bellicose Chinese factions had indeed proposed launching an invasion of Ryukyu from Fujian Province.

On the first and fifteenth day of each month, supporters of the restoration movement observed the ceremony of *momoso o-mono mairi* [one hundred people shrine visit], in which they wore the ceremonial robes of Old Ryukyu and made pilgrimage visits to ceremonial sites and Buddhist temples in Shuri, praying for a Chinese victory as well as the health of Shō Tai, the former king. In contrast, the *Ryūkyū shinpō* vehemently criticized these supporters, naming them the "Obstinacy Party" [Ganko-tō] and reported assiduously on Japan's successive triumphs in the war.[25]

In this environment, the rumors of the Southern Fleet's plan to attack Okinawa spread rapidly, stirring great anxiety throughout the prefecture. Kodama Kihachi, serving simultaneously as principal of Okinawa Ordinary Middle School and the Okinawa Normal School, called for the formation of a volunteer group called the "Patriots Brigade" [J. Giyūdan], made up mainly of students and faculty from his schools. For as long as the emergency lasted, they were sent into military training that included staging mock maneuvers replicating real battle conditions, including live ammunition, under the guidance of the Kumamoto Garrison's Okinawa Detached Corps [Kumamoto Chindai Okinawa Bun'itai]. In addition, Japanese mainlanders resident in Okinawa, under the leadership of Fumoto Sumiyoshi, formed the Alliance Justice Association [Dōmeigikai], with a membership roll of about 370 men. Having sent their wives and children back to mainland Japan, they met every day at the Nanyōkan in Naha for arms practice. Okinawa roiled in an atmosphere of uncertainty, and threatened by the possibility of attack, many of Naha's residents fled into the countryside carrying their furniture and household goods. Until the end of the war, the people of Okinawa trembled, swinging between the extremes of sorrow and joy at the rumor of invasion by the "Yellow Fleet."[26]

### Becoming "Okinawa" in Japan

The First Sino-Japanese War ended in victory for the Japanese. In the first clause of the peace treaty signed at Shimonoseki on April 17, 1895, the Chinese renounced the suzerain authority over Korea that was exemplified by the exchange of tribute and patents of investiture. The Ryukyu issue was nowhere mentioned, and though China did not explicitly surrender its suzerain rights over Ryukyu, it was understood given its defeat in the war, which resulted in the humiliating loss of its own territory in the cession of Taiwan. Of course, China's defeat determined the fate of the Ryukyuan restoration movement and marked the final collapse of China's tributary system in East Asia. The Chinese cabinet minister sent to Shimonoseki to conclude the peace treaty talks was Lǐ Hóngzhāng, to whom for so long the Qing exiles had been sending their petitions with high expectations for help in restoring the Ryukyu Kingdom.

The possibility of restoration of the kingdom disappeared with the defeat of suzerain China, and the restoration movement was left without any recourse for action. As the Qing exiles abandoned their cause and made their way home, the calls to "rebuild the kingdom" [J. *fukkoku*] and "restore the king" [J. *fukkimi* or *fukukimi*] faded away. Even Shō Yūtoku (Urasoe Anji Chōchū), who had played a central leadership role in the movement, left the Ryukyu House in Fuzhou after the deaths of Mō Seichō, Mō Hōrai, and Shō Tokukō.

The dissolution of the Ryukyuan restoration movement removed the region's last real ties with China. The Japanese government instituted reforms of land tenure, taxation, and districting, reorganizing Okinawa Prefecture on the same lines as the prefectures of mainland Japan. In an imperial edict promulgated on March 5, 1896, the prefecture's administrative districts were redrawn, establishing the two wards of Shuri and Naha and the five counties of Shimajiri, Nakagami, Kunigami (southern, central, and northern Okinawa Island, respectively), the Miyako island group, and the Yaeyama island group.[27] The "Regulations for Okinawa's Districts and Island Officials" [Okinawaken Magiri Shima Ri-in Kitei] promulgated on March 29 of the following year retitled the kingdom period district and island magistrates' offices as town halls and abolished the positions held by the former local officials.[28] Though military conscription had been postponed because of the link between local civil unrest and China, conscription was enforced after 1898. On March 10, 1899, the Okinawa land distribution laws were announced; they were put into effect starting on April 1, and after this, the laws of mainland Japan were also increasingly applied to Okinawa.[29] The people of the Ryukyu Kingdom found themselves completely cut off from the social system in the early modern period over which the old royal system had still cast its shadow. Now, as Japanese citizens in the greater Japanese culture, they set about living in a changing world, carving out a new history for themselves.

# Afterword

## *Traces of the Ryukyu Kingdom*

Okinawa has traveled a different historical path from that of mainland Japan's cities and prefectures and occupies its own unique position in the modern world. If you look carefully at the events of history, you'll notice that the wider your perspective, the more you'll see connections among those events. And that's exactly the way it is with the history of the Ryukyu Kingdom. From the birth of the kingdom until its demise, the significant turning points in its history echoed the structural changes East Asia itself was going through.

Formed in the midst of transformations in East Asia, the kingdom could not avoid making adjustments when East Asia itself underwent further revolutionary changes. After the kingdom lost its status as an independent nation with its conquest by the Shimazu clan at the beginning of the seventeenth century, its continued existence as a kingdom was deeply influenced by its relations with China and Japan, its fate entirely at the mercy of the national characters and stability of both. The royal government adopted an unusual national identity in its dual policy of "Ryukyu, vassal of Japan" and "Ryukyu, vassal of China," struggling to balance the political power of its two great neighbors, and to somehow create a neutral buffer zone separating the two nations, as the key to the survival of the kingdom.

As Japan underwent its modern-era transformation into a centralized nation exerting exclusive authority within its territory, it could no longer accept the Ryukyu Kingdom's dual allegiance and began incorporating the region into the modern Japanese nation as Okinawa Prefecture. Standing on its rights as suzerain, China objected strongly; the subsequent upheavals surrounding the Disposition of Ryukyu and the severance of its tributary relationship with China were life-changing events for the kingdom's people. Today there are surely few Okinawans who do not accept their status as "Japanese." All the same, the kingdom's history was different from Japan's, and its people accordingly had their own worldview as well. As the phrase the "Disposition of Ryukyu" indicates, the Japanese government forced integration on the region, "disposing" of the matter as it would of any routine action. The manner of integration may have warped things to some degree, so the current sense of unity with Japan held by most Okinawans took a very long time to achieve.

The people of the little kingdom that burst like a comet upon the stage of history in the fourteenth century share a history similar to that of many other countries and have a variety of Asian experiences. From this, they accumulated an assortment of cultural elements and fused them to create their own unique culture. This melding and stratification of diverse elements in its position as the "Cornerstone of Asia" displays the true strength of Okinawan culture. Though Okinawa's presence in Asia as an independent polity ended with the extinction of the kingdom, readers should realize that the Asian traditions and ideas blended into Okinawan culture, and that distinguish it from the culture of the Japanese mainland, are its heritage from the Ryukyu Kingdom and its "Asian experience." The historical backdrop is especially colored by the influence of Chinese culture. This was not simply the natural result of the ceaseless exchange of people and ideas that began with the start of Okinawa's tributary relationship with China, but also the inevitable consequence of the kingdom's grand strategy of sinification in order to ensure its own continued survival.

In the period following the fall of the kingdom, the worldview of the prefecture's inhabitants changed greatly. Still, the cultural and psychological heritage fostered by its historical experience as East Asia's cornerstone, different from the Japanese mainland, continued unbroken, and there is much that continues to live even today. Without a doubt, the Japanese cultural landscape is greatly diversified by the brilliant streak of color added to it by the unique people and culture that form the basis of "Okinawan-ness."

The Disposition of Ryukyu, the forced annexation of Okinawa by the Japanese government, ended the suzerain-tributary relationship between China and the Ryukyu Kingdom. I have described how, even as the Japanese moved to integrate the kingdom, China's claim to suzerain rights over Ryukyu made the Chinese object furiously to the annexation. The issue of Ryukyu's return to tributary status is usually understood to have been settled with Japan's victory in the Sino-Japanese War. However, such was not the case. When U.S. president Franklin D. Roosevelt, British prime minister Winston Churchill, and chairman of the Republic of China Generalissimo

Chiang Kaishek met in Cairo in 1943 to discuss how they would deal with Japan after the end of the Second World War, the Ryukyu issue was closely reviewed and discussed with some energy. The diplomatic papers and the conference memoirs of his counterparts clearly report that Chiang Kaishek proposed that Ryukyu, just like Korea, be restored to independence after the conclusion of the war.[1] The government of the Republic of China (Taiwan) still maintains this policy disregarding Japan's territorial sovereignty, and officially the question of Ryukyu's return to tributary status remains unresolved in their eyes. And now, official government documents in Beijing's First Historical Archives, including late–Qing dynasty foreign policy *tōan* addressing the issue of Ryukyu's sovereignty, like the *tōan* mentioned in the introduction, are cautiously being opened to the public.

The Disposition of Ryukyu was a series of political measures that forced Okinawa's integration into Japan. Today, it may be regarded as a necessary step in Japan's formation as a sovereign territory and a nation-state, and acknowledged as the spark that began the modernization of Okinawan society. Even so, it does not follow that the Chinese view of an integration made without regard to Chinese objections, made with neither the understanding nor the consent of a China standing on its authority as suzerain, would change with a war settlement. The embers of the Ryukyu Kingdom still glow to this day, casting light on all of us.

# Notes

*Introduction*

1. For an in-depth archeological view of the Ryukyu Islands, see Richard Pearson, *Ancient Ryukyu: An Archaeological Study of Island Communities* (Honolulu: University of Hawai'i Press, 2013).

2. Wèi Zhēng, *Suí shū,* vol. 81 (vol. 46 of the "Biographies" section). A typeset version can be found in Wèi Zhēng, *Suí shū,* vol. 6 (Beijing: Zhōnghuá shūjú, 1973), pp. 1822–1825.

3. Despite the name ("Wa" was another name for Japan), as will be seen in this discussion, these pirates were by no means all Japanese. In this book we use the Japanese term *wakō* or simply "pirates."

4. Older histories refer to the northern and southern kingdoms as "Sanhoku" and "Sannan," respectively. Sai On (1682–1761) began the practice of referring to them as Hokuzan and Nanzan, and many works use those terms today. The translators follow Akamine's wording here.

5. The characters for Ryūkyū Shobun are 琉球処分. The term is highly charged and continues to rankle Okinawans to this day, as *shobun* suggests "getting rid or disposing of (something)," or "punishing (someone)."

6. See the notes and bibliography for more information on various texts of the *Rekidai hōan.* Note that Okinawan historian George Kerr has translated the title as "Treasury of the Royal Succession." As will be seen in many of the notes, the "revised edition" (*kōteibon*) includes section numbers, which further subdivide the text in a three-part classification (eg.,"Section 1-22-3").

7. Urasoe-shi Kyōiku Iinkai, eds., *Ryūkyū ōkoku hyōjōsho monjo,* 19 vols. (Urasoe: Urasoe City Library, 1988–2002). A comprehensive index was also compiled: Urasoe-shi Kyōiku Iinkai, eds., *Ryūkyū ōkoku hyōjōsho monjo sōsaku-in* (Urasoe: Urasoe City Library, 2011), available through the Urasoe Shiritsu Toshokan Okinawagaku Kenkyūshitsu, and through Gajumaru Books (http://gajumarubook.jp).

*Chapter One: The Gusuku Period*

1. Kunaichō Shoryōbu, ed., *Hyōtō Ryūkyūkoku ki* (Tokyo: Kunaichō shoryōbu, 1962). A reproduction of the picture can be found at http://manwe.lib.u-ryukyu.ac.jp/library/itoman/12.htm.

2. Fujiwara no Akihira, *Shin sarugakuki,* in *Tōyō bunkō* vol. 424, ed. Kawaguchi Hisao (Tokyo: Heibonsha, 1983), pp. 279–293.

3. Translator's note: In 1151, the widow of Sung merchant Wáng Shēng was named in an arrest warrant and rounded up along with many others in a raid on Sung merchants ordered by Dazaifu deputy governor Muneyori. See Kawazoe Shōji, *Chūsei Kyūshū no seiji to bunka* (Tokyo: Bunken shuppan, 1981), p. 64. Some historians believe she was Japanese, though Kawazoe's account does not say so.

4. Asato Susumu, *Kōkogaku kara mita Ryūkyūshi,* vol. 1, *Ko-Ryūkyū sekai no keisei* (Naha: Hirugisha, 1990), pp. 66–68.

5. Cài Xiāng, *Lìzhi pǔ* (Shanghai: Shāngwù yìnshùguǎn, 1936), p. 2.

6. For a facsimile text, see the Chinese Text project, http://ctext.org/library.pl?if=en&file=3006&page=40. For a printed text, see Ibid., http://ctext.org/wiki.pl?if=en&chapter=909015. The Chinese characters used to write "Liúqiú" in this document (流求) were commonly encountered in earlier records.

7. *Ganxi,* "Moved by Memories of the Past," in *Jiànnán shīgǎo,* vol. 59. An English translation of the full poem appears in Burton Watson, trans., *The Old Man Who Does as He Pleases* (New York: Columbia University Press, 1973), p. 60. Watson believes that Liúqiú "probably refers to Taiwan, which at that time was considered part of Ryukyu."

8. *Sìbù cóngkān chūbiān suōběn,* vol. 107 (Taipei: Taíwān shāngwù yìnshùguǎn, 1967), p. 61.

9. See Ota Yukio, "Futatsu no 'Ryūkyū': Jūsan jūyon seiki no Higashi Ajia ni okeru 'Ryūkyū' ninshiki," Kumamoto University Repository System, March 31, 2009, p. 215n7, http://reposit.lib.kumamoto-u.ac.jp/bitstream/2298/16119/1/kaA17251007_201–218.pdf.

### *Chapter Two: Founding of the Ming Dynasty and the Rise of the Ryukyu Kingdom*

1. 海禁, Ch. *hǎijìn,* J. *kaikin.*

2. Elsewhere, Akamine refers to the northern and southern domains as Sanhoku and Sannan, respectively.

3. A digital copy of this work can be found at: http://www.wul.waseda.ac.jp/kotenseki/html/ru04/ru04_04709/index.html.

4. Hokama Shūzen and Saigō Nobutsuna, eds., *Omoro sōshi, Nihon shisō taikei 18* (Tokyo: Iwanami shoten, 1972), p. 368.

5. The character 鑑 is often used for written histories in China and was adopted by Ryukyu and Japan, as well. It has frequently been translated as "mirror of " but its connotation when used in a title is that what is written therein should be seen as exemplary. The translators here prefer a less literal and more evocative "reflections on" since these historical narratives tend to be highly literary.

6. Ifa Fuyu, Higashionna Kanjun, and Yokoyama Shigeru, eds., *Ryūkyū shiryō sōsho,* vol. 5 (Tokyo: Inoue shobō, 1962), pp. 9–10 of *Chūzan seikan* section. (Each section of this volume has discreet pagination. The *Chūzan seikan* section is the first one in the volume.)

7. Tei Heitetsu (Kuwae Katsuhide, ed.), *Kyūyō* (Tokyo: San'ichi shobō, 1971), p. 21.

8. *Ming tàizǔ shílù* (1), vol. 76, entry for 1372 (Hongwu 5), Tenth Month, 21st Day, Jia-Yin, (Taipei: Institute of History and Philology, Academia Sinica, 1968), pp. 3–4.

9. Akiyama Kenzō, *Nisshi kōshōshi kenkyū* (Tokyo: Iwanami shoten, 1939), p. 552.

10. Kobata Atsushi, *Zōho chūsei nantō tsūkōbōekishi no kenkyū* (Kyoto: Rinsen shoten, 1993, pp. 204–206). For more information on the Ming court's preferential treatment of Ryukyu, see Okamoto Hiromichi, *Ryūkyū ōkoku kaijō kōshōshi kenkyū* (Ginowan: Yōju shorin, 2010).

11. Okamoto Hiromichi, "Minchō ni okeru chōkōkoku Ryūkyū no ichizuke to sono henka: Jūyon jūgo seiki o chūshin ni," *Tōyōshi kenkyū,* 57:4 (1999): 10–12.

12. *Kōraishi*, book 3, vol. 137 (Tokyo: Kokusho kankōkai, 1909), p. 762, and book 1, vol. 45 (Tokyo: Kokusho kankōkai, 1908), p. 677.

13. *Richō jitsuroku* [*K. Yijo sillok*], book 5, vol. 31, entry for 1416 (Taizong 16), First Month, 27th Day, p. 10, and book 5, vol. 32, entry for 1416, Seventh Month, 23rd Day, p. 7 (Tokyo: Gakushūin Daigaku tōyō bunka kenkyūjo, 1955).

14. *Míng tàizŭ shílù* (1), vol. 232, entry for 1394 (Hongwu 27), Third Month, 10th Day, p. 3.

## *Chapter Three: Ryukyu in the East Asian Trade Sphere*

1. Wada Hisanori et al., eds., *Rekidai hōan* (revised edition), book 2, vol. 40, section 1-40-01 (Okinawa Kenritsu Toshokan Shiryō Henshūshitsu, 1992), pp. 535–536. The *Rekidai hōan* is a collection of diplomatic records, in Chinese, for the Ryukyu Kingdom, covering the years 1424 through 1867. There were two copies compiled. One (the Royal Copy) was kept on the premises of Shuri Castle; the other (the Kumemura [or Kuninda] Copy) was kept in the Tenpi-gū Shrine in Kumemura. However, the Royal Copy, which had been taken to Tokyo, was destroyed in the Great Kantō Earthquake of 1923, while the Kumemura Copy was destroyed in the Battle of Okinawa in World War II. All that remains today are blueprinted copies and handwritten copies of the originals. For a partial English translation, see Atsushi Kobata and Mitsugu Matsuda, trans., *Ryukyuan Relations with Korea and South Sea Countries; an Annotated Translation of Documents in the Rekidai Hōan* (Kyoto: self-published, 1969).

2. Walter de Gray Birch, trans., *Commentaries of the Great Alfonso Dalboquerque*, vol. 3 (London: Hakluyt Society, 1880), p. 89. This excerpt is reproduced with permission from the Hakluyt Society.

3. Cited in Akiyama Kenzō, *Nisshi kōshō shiwa* (Tokyo: Naigai shoseki, 1936), pp. 256–257. Chapters 16–18 of Akiyama's book (pp. 254–303) discuss Ryukyuan traders in Southeast Asia in some detail.

4. Armando Cortesão, trans. and ed., *The Suma Oriental of Tomé Pires: An Account of the East, from the Red Sea to Japan, Written in Malacca and India in 1512–1515; and, The Book of Francisco Rodrigues: Rutter of a Voyage in the Red Sea, Nautical Rules, Almanack and, Maps, Written and Drawn in the East before 1515*, Hakluyt Society; 2nd ser., nos. 89–90 (Nendeln, Liechtenstein: Kraus Reprint, 1967), p. 130.

5. For scholars, the relevant Chinese characters are: *seishi* 正使, *fukushi* 副使, *tsūji* 通事, *kachō* 火長, *kansen chokko* 管船直庫, *jimuchō* 事務長, and *shōsui* 梢水.

6. This time and route are deduced from a series of entries in the *Xīngchá shèngrăn*, a digital copy of which can be found at: http://ctext.org/library.pl?if=en&res=81929. See esp. pp. 7, 17, and 32.

7. Hokama Shūzen and Saigō Nobutsuna, eds. *Omoro sōshi, Nihon shisō taikei 18* (Tokyo: Iwanami shoten, 1972, 2000), p. 281.

8. *Kōraishi*, book 3, vol. 137 (Tokyo: Kokusho kankōkai, 1908–1909; reprinted 1977), p. 762.

9. *Richō jitsuroku*, book 8, vol. 52, entry for 1431 (Sejong [J. Sesō] 13), Ninth Month, 6th Day, (Gakushūin Daigaku tōyō bunka kenkyūjo, 1956), p. 24. The characters for *Sejong sillok* are 世宋実録.

10. Yasuda Akira et al., eds., *Unpoi irohashū* (Kyoto: Rinsen shoten, 1977), p. 95.

11. *Richō jitsuroku*, book 12, vol. 6, entry for 1441 (Danjong [J. Tansō] 1), Fifth Month, 11th Day (Gakushūin Daigaku tōyō bunka kenkyūjo, 1957), p. 23.

12. For contemporary maps of East Asia, Japan, Tsushima, Kyushu, and Ryukyu, see Chōsenshi Henshūkai, ed., *Sin Suk-chu's Kaitō shokokuki* (Keijō: Chōsen sōtokufu, 1933).

13. *Kyūyō, Okinawa bunka shiryō shūsei* 5 (Tokyo: Kadokawa shoten, 1974), pp. 177–178.

14. Takara Kurayoshi, "Ryūkyūshi ni okeru 'kodai,'" in Tsuboi Kiyotari and Hirano Kunio, eds., *Shinpan kodai Nihon, 3: Kyūshū, Okinawa* (Tokyo: Kadokawa shoten, 1991), pp. 428–430.

15. For more on Buddhism in the Ryukyu Kingdom, see Nakō Hōshō, *Okinawa bukkyōshi* (Naha: Gokokuji, 1968); and China Sadahiro, *Okinawa shūkyōshi no kenkyū* (Ginowan: Yōjusha, 1994).

16. Hokama Shūzen and Saigō Nobutsuna, eds. *Omoro sōshi, Nihon shisō taikei 18* (Tokyo: Iwanami shoten, 1972), p. 273.

17. Chōsenshi Henshūkai, *Kaitō shokokuki.*

18. *Richō jitsuroku,* book 13, vol. 27, entry for 1462 (Sejo [J. Seiso] 8), Second Month, 16th Day, (Gakushūin Daigaku tōyō bunka kenkyūjo, 1957), p. 20.

19. *Ryūkyūkoku yuraiki,* vol. 2, in *Ryūkyū shiryō sōsho,* vol. 1, ed. Ifa Fuyu and Higashionna Kanjun (Tokyo: Tokyo bijutsu, 1972), p. 61.

20. Chōsenshi Henshūkai, *Kaitō shokokuki,* pp. 109–110. The "*Ryūkyūkoku ki*" section also contains subsections on the Ryukyuan line of kings, the cities in the kingdom, the manners and mores of the kingdom, roads and highways, and so on.

21. *Richō jitsuroku,* book 16, vol. 105, entry for 1478 (Seongjong [J. Seisō] 10), Sixth Month, 10th Day (Gakushūin Daigaku tōyō bunka kenkyūjo, 1958), p. 18.

22. The characters are 王府 and 王相府, respectively.

23. *Míng tàizōng shílù* (2), entry for 1418 (Yongle [J. Eiraku] 16), Second Month, 14th Day, in *Ryūkyū kinsekibun takuhon shūsei,* ed. Okinawa Kenritsu Toshokan (Okinawa Prefectural Library, 1981), p. 1. The "stele at the Ankokuzan Garden" is kept in the Okinawa Prefectural Museum.

24. The characters for "Old Port Pacification Superintendency" are 旧港宣慰使. It was a system used briefly under the Ming to invest Chinese diasporic populations with tribute nation status. The translators here have followed the translation for this term used by Columbia University graduate student Nolan Benson.

25. *Rekidai hōan* (revised edition), book 2, section 1-43-18, p. 644.

26. Abu Abdullah Muhammad Ibn Abdullah Al Lawati Al Tanji Ibn Battuta, or simply Ibn Battuta (1304–1368 or 1369) was a Moroccan Berber Muslim scholar and traveler who is known for the account of his travels and excursions, called the *Rihla* (Voyage) in Arabic.

27. For a discussion of the relationship between Quanzhou and Ryukyu, see Wang Lianmo, "Urasoeshi, senshūshi—Sōhō no kankeishi ni kansuru jakkan no mondai ni tsuite no chōsa kōshō," in *Ryūkyū/chūgoku kōryūsho o saguru: Urasoeshi, senshūshi yūkō toshi teiketsu kinen gakujutsu/bunka tōron hōkokusho* (Urasoe City: Urasoeshi kyōiku iinkai, 1988), pp. 40–72.

28. *Míng xiànzōng shílù (Min kensō jitsuroku),* book V, vol. 89, entry for 1471 (Chenghua [J. Seika] 7), Third Month, 25th Day, p. 10 (Taipei: Institute of History and Philology, Academia Sinica, 1966).

29. Ibid., vol. 103, entry for 1472 (Chenghua [J. Seika] 8), Fourth Month, 21st Day, p. 8.

30. Ibid., vol. 140, entry for 1475 (Chenghua [J. Seika] 11), Fourth Month, 10th Day, p. 3.

31. Ibid., vol. 177, entry for 1478 (Chenghua [J. Seika] 14), Fourth Month, 18th Day, p. 6.

32. *Míng yīngzōng shílù (Min eisō jitsuroku),* book I.3, vol. 3, entry for 1435 (Xuande [J. Sentoku] 10), Third Month, 25th Day, p. 8.

33. Ibid., book I.3, vol. 58, entry for 1439 (Zhengtong [J. Seitō] 4), Eighth Month, 15th Day, pp. 5–6.

34. Ibid., book II.4, vol. 192, entry for 1450 (Jingtai [J. Keitai] 1), Fifth Month, 24th Day, pp. 19–20.

35. Kagoshima-ken Ishin Shiryō Hensanjo, ed., *Kagoshima-ken shiryō, kyūki zatsuroku,* book 1, part 2, vol. 39, section 1470 (Kagoshima: Kagoshima-ken ishin shiryō hensanjo, 1980), p. 473.

36. *Shimazu kokushi* (Kagoshima: Kagoshima-ken chihōshi gakkai, 1972), p. 92.

37. Ibid., pp. 129–130.

38. Ibid., p. 97.

39. See notes 2 and 4 above.

40. *Míng shìzōng shílù*, book I:8, vol. 28, entry for 1523 (Jiajing [J. Kasei] 2), Sixth Month, 15th Day, p. 4.

41. For further discussion of the role of pepper in tribute trade between China and the Ryukyu Kingdom during the reigns of Shō Toku, Shō En, Shō Shin, and Shō Sei, see Okamoto Hiromichi, "Minchō ni okeru chōkōkoku Ryūkyū no ichizuke to sono henka: Jūyon jūgo seiki o chūshin ni," *Taiyōshi kenkyū*, 57:4, 1999 and Maehira Fusaaki, "Nanban bōeki to sono jidai," in *Shin-Ryūkyūshi, Ko-Ryūkyūhen* (Naha: Okinawa shinpōsha, 1999), p. 285. For details on the use of local interpreters and brokers, see Nishizato Kikō, "Chūryū kōshōshi ni okeru dotsūji to gakō (kyūshō)," *Ryūkyū kyōiku gakubu kiyō*, 50 (1997).

42. Kamiya Nobuyuki, *Taikun gaikō to higashi Ajia* (Tokyo: Yoshikawa kōbunkan, 1997), pp. 74–76.

43. See Kobata Atsushi, *Zōho chūsei nantō tsūkō bōekishi no kenkyū* (Kyoto: Rinsen shoten, 1993), p. 60.

## *Chapter Four: The Ryukyu Kingdom under the* Bakuhan *System*

1. *Shimazu kokushi* (Kagoshima: Kagoshima-ken chihōshi gakkai, 1972), p. 157.

2. Kamiya Nobuyuki, *Taikun gaikō to higashi Ajia* (Tokyo: Yoshikawa kōbunkan, 1997), p. 80. Hideyoshi's letter can be found in *Miyabe monjo* (Records of the Miyabe Clan), part 1 (Tōkyō Daigaku shiryō hensanjo).

3. Kagoshima-ken Ishin Shiryō Hensanjo, ed., *Kagoshima-ken shiryō, kyūki zatsuroku kōhen 2*, vol. 26, no. 785 (Kagoshima-ken ishin shiryō hensanjo, 1980), p. 518.

4. Tanaka Takeo, ed., *Zenrin kokuhōki, shintei zokuzenrin kokuhōki* (Tokyo: Shūeisha, 1995), p. 376.

5. "Shimazu-ke monjo, Part 3, #1521," in *Dai Nihon komonjo, iewake* [house collections], no. 16, ed. Tōkyō Daigaku Shiryō Hensanjo (Tokyo: Tōkyō Daigaku shiryō hensanjo, 1966), pp. 342–343.

6. For more details on how the Satsuma invasion of Ryukyu unfolded, see Uehara Kenzen, *Bakuhansei keiseiki no Ryūkyū shihai* (Tokyo: Yoshikawa kōbunkan, 2001); and Uehara Kenzen, *Shimazu-shi no Ryūkyū shinryaku—mō hitotsu Keichō no yaku* (Ginowan: Yōju shorin, 2009).

7. Kagoshima-ken Rekishi Shiryō Sentaa Reimeikan, ed., *Kagoshima-ken shiryō, kyūki zatsuroku*, book 2, part 4, vol. 64, section 594 (Kagoshima: Kagoshima Prefecture, 1984), pp. 226–227.

8. Kimura Taka'atsu, ed., *Butoku hennen shūsei*, part 2 (Tokyo: Meichō shuppan, 1976), vol. 58, p. 134.

9. For the text of the actual pledge, see "Ryūkyūkoku Chūzan-ō Shōnei kishōmon," in *Shimazu-ke monjo*, nos. 5–7 (Tōkyō Daigaku Shiryō Hensanjo collection). [Translator's note: Note 5 above cites a volume from the *Dai Nihon komonjo, iewake* series, which includes material from the large *Shimazu-ke monjo* collection held by Tokyo University's Shiryō Hensanjo. This particular document, a National Treasure, is not among those in the published series, though it can be found online.] See also *Kagoshima-ken shiryō, kyūki zatsuroku*, book 2, part 4, vol. 66, section 862, p. 518; for further background, see Umeki Tetsuto, "Ryūkyūkoku no kishōmon," in *Kinsei Ryūkyūkoku no kōzō* (Tokyo: Daiichi shobō, 2011), pp. 277–296.

10. For more information on the *bakufu*'s diplomatic stance toward Ming China after the invasion of Ryukyu, see Kamiya Nobuyuki, "Edo bakufu no tai-min seisaku to Ryūkyū," in *Bakuhansei kokka no Ryūkyū shihai* (Tokyo: Azekura shobō, 1990), pp. 23–29.

11. "Nanpo bunshū," in *Sappan sōsho 2* (Kagoshima: Sappan sōsho kankōkai, 1906), p. 12.

12. Ishin Sūden, *Ikoku nikki—Konchi-in sūden gaikō monjo shūsei* [facsimile edition] (Tokyo: Tokyo bijutsu, 1989), p. 76.

13. *Minshi* (Ch. *Míng Shǐ*) 5, vol. 323, Collective Biographies (Retsuden 列伝) section #211, Foreign Countries (外国 Gaikoku) 4 (Taipei: Kōshi shuppansha [Ch. Hóngshì chūbǎnshè], 1975), p. 8367.

14. Kagoshima-ken Rekishi Shiryō Sentaa Reimeikan, *Kagoshima-ken shiryō, kyūki zatsuroku*, book 2, part 4, vol. 72, section 1388, p. 637.

15. For a more detailed examination of the suppression of Christianity and the *sakoku* policy, see Kamiya Nobuyuki and Kimura Naoya, eds., *Kaishi to sakoku*, Tenbō Nihon Rekishi 14 (Tokyo: Tōkyōdō shuppan, 2002).

16. Maehira Fusaaki, "Sakoku keiseiki no kirishitan kinsei to Ryūkyū—Tokugawa seiken no Manira shuppei keikaku no haikei," in *Sakoku Nihon to kokusai kōryū*, vol. 1, ed. Yanai Kenji (Tokyo: Yoshikawa kōbunkan, 1988), p. 337.

17. For more on the supervision of foreign shipping, see "'Sakoku' (kaishi) taisei no kakuritsu to Ryūkyū," in Uehara Kenzen, *Bakuhansei keiseiki no Ryūkyū shihai* (Tokyo: Yoshikawa kōbunkan, 2001), pp. 313–348.

18. The characters for signal fires [J. *hidatemō*]: 火立毛.

19. For information on Ryukyu assessments, see "Kokudakasei no kōzō—Nōmai/deki oyobi zaisei," in Umeki Tetsuto, *Kinsei Ryūkyūkoku no kōzō* (Tokyo: Daiichi shobō, 2011), pp. 118–168.

20. *Kagoshima-ken shiryō, Kyūki zatsuroku*, book 2, part 4, vol. 66, section 855, pp. 342–343; and *Kagoshima kenshi*, vol. 2 (Kagoshima: Kagoshima Prefecture, 1940), p. 679.

21. *Kagoshima-ken shiryō, kyūki zatsuroku*, book 2, part 5, vol. 87, section 756 (Kagoshima: Kagoshima-ken rekishi shiryō sentaa reimeikan, 1985), p. 444. The text in kanbun: 薩摩大隅両国并日向国諸県郡都合六拾万五千石[目録在別紙]、此外琉球国拾弐万三千七百石事全可有領知之状如件.

22. See *Ryūkyū kuniezu shiryōshū 1—Shōhō kuniezu oyobi kanren shiryō* (Naha: Okinawa-ken kyōiku iinkai, 1992); *Ryūkyū kuniezu shiryōshū 2—Genroku kuniezu oyobi kanren shiryō* (Naha: Okinawa-ken kyōiku iinkai, 1993); and *Ryūkyū kuniezu shiryōshū 2—Tenpō kuniezu oyobi kanren shiryō* (Naha: Okinawa-ken kyōiku iinkai, 1994).

23. For the circumstances surrounding Satsuma's designating the Ryukyu king as a *kokushi*, see Kamiya Nobuyuki, "Satsuma kokushu to Ryūkyū kokushi," in *Taikun gaikō to higashi Ajia* (Tokyo: Yoshikawa kōbunkan, 1997), pp. 59–63.

24. For more on the use of the term *Nihonkoku taikun* in diplomatic situations outside of Japan, see Tomiyama Kazuyuki, "Ryūkyū ōkoku no gaikō to ōken," in *Taikun gaikō to higashi Ajia*, ed. Kamiya Nobuyuki (Tokyo: Yoshikawa kōbunkan, 1997), pp. 112–142.

25. Ryukyu Kingdom documents used the term Edo-*dachi* (departing for Edo), which did not include the connotation of going to a higher (i.e., more important or powerful) place that was implicit in the term "going up to Edo" (Edo *nobori*).

26. Hayashi Fukusai, ed., *Tsūkō ichiran* (Tokyo: Kokusho kankōkai, 1912), pp. 24, 40. This is a collection of documents related to Japanese diplomatic history, covering 1566–1825.

27. For more on Edo *nobori*/Edo-*dachi*, see Yokoyama Manabu, *Ryūkyūkoku shisetsu torai no kenkyū* (Tokyo: Yoshikawa kōbunkan, 1987); and Miyagi Eishō, *Ryūkyū shisha no Edo nobori* (Tokyo: Daiichi shobō, 1982).

28. *Kagoshima-ken shiryō, kyūki zatsuroku kōhen 4*, vol. 66, section 860 (Kagoshima: Kagoshima Prefecture, 1984), pp. 344–345.

29. Kuroita Katsumi, ed., *Shintei zōho kokushi taikei, Tokugawa jikki*, 3rd edition (Tokyo: Yoshikawa kōbunkan, 1976), p. 720.

30. Uehara Kenzen, "Bōeki no tenkai," in *Shin Ryūkyūshi, Kinseihen*, vol. 1, ed. Ryūkyū Shinpōsha (Naha: Ryūkyū shinpōsha, 1989), p. 126.

31. For more information on Ryukyu's office (Ryūkyū *kariya*) in Satsuma, see Kishaba Kazutaka, "Satsuma-han no Ryūkyū tōchi kikō," in *Kinsei satsuryū kankei no kenkyū* (Tokyo: Kokusho kankōkai, 1993), pp. 217–253; and Tokunaga Kazunobu, "Ryūkyūkan no setchi to

tenkai," in *Satsuma-han taigai kōshōshi no kenkyū* (Fukuoka: Kyūshū daigaku shuppankai, 2005), pp. 3–27.

32. For more on Chinese goods that Satsuma obtained through Ryukyu's trade missions to China, see Uehara Kenzen, *Sakoku to hanbōeki—Satsuma-han no Ryūkyū mitsubōeki* (Tokyo: Yaedake shobō, 1981).

33. Kishaba Kazutaka, *Kinsei Satsuryū kankei no kenkyū* (Tokyo: Kokusho kankōkai, 1993), p. 235.

34. Ibid., p. 457.

35. Kamiya, *Taikun gaikō to higashi Ajia,* p. 143.

36. "Straw-wrapped goods": 俵物.

37. For a discussion of the competition between Satsuma and Nagasaki as gateways for Chinese goods, see Kuroda Yasuo, "Satsuma-han no tōbutsu shōhō to Nagasaki kaijo," *Nantōshigaku* 33 (April 1989): 1–19.

38. The work known as *Ka-i hentai* includes a collection of twenty-two hundred reports (called "Tōsen fūsetsugaki") from ship captains involved in trade with China between 1644 and 1717. The Japanese National Archives contains one of the most complete editions.

39. Maehira Bōshō, "Kaigai jōhō to Kumemura," in *Kumemura—Rekishi to jinbutsu,* ed. Ikemiya Masaharu, Odo Kiyotaka, and Dana Masayuki (Naha: Hirugisha, 1992), p. 42. (Note: Kumemura was pronounced Kuninda in Okinawan, but most bibliographies and libraries list it under the reading Kumemura.)

## *Chapter Five: Reform and Sinification of the Kingdom*

1. Kagoshima-ken Ishin Shiryō Hensanjo, ed., *Kagoshima-ken shiryō, kyūki zatsuroku kōhen 4,* vol. 77, section 1855 (Kagoshima: Kagoshima-ken ishin shiryō hensanjo, 1984), pp. 818–819.

2. The characters used to write these words are easy to misinterpret for those who know Japanese history. *Shi* was written with the character 士, which means "warrior." But in the case of Ryukyu, it referred simply to the elite class. Likewise, for Ryukyu, though the character for *nō* (農) implies "farmer," the term refers more generically to commoners, that is, nonelites.

3. Genealogies of families connected to Kumemura can be found in Naha Shishi Henshū Iinkai, ed., *Naha shishi, shiryōhen,* series 1, part 6, Kafu Shiryō 2, sections 1 and 2 (Naha City: Naha shishi henshūshitsu, 1981). Genealogies of families connected to Shuri can be found in Naha Shishi Henshū Iinkai, ed., *Naha shishi, shiryōhen,* series 1, part 7, Kafu Shiryō 3 (Naha City: Naha shishi henshūshitsu, 1982). Genealogies of families connected to Naha and Tomari can be found in Naha Shishi Henshū Iinkai, ed., *Naha shishi, shiryōhen,* series 1, part 8, Kafu Shiryō 4 (Naha City: Naha shishi henshūshitsu, 1983).

4. Translators' note: Monobugyō might be loosely translated as "Ministry of Works," but Mōshikuchihō defies translation. One meaning might be "petitioning," but the functions of this ministry were far more extensive. The characters used to write *mōshikuchi* (申口) may also be interpreted as "West Entrance" (the character 申 representing West Southwest in the Chinese system), but we have found no evidence that this ministry was housed in that quarter of the palace compound. We have decided to leave the two terms unstranslated.

5. Kamiya Nobuyuki, *Taikun gaikō to higashi Ajia* (Tokyo: Yoshikawa kōbunkan, 1997), pp. 137–138.

6. Sai Taku et al., eds., *Saitaku-bon chūzan seifu* (Naha: Okinawan-ken kyōiku iinakai, 1973), p. 67. [Note: The "Saitaku-bon *chūzan seifu*" is the original version of the text, compiled by a team led by Shitahaku Tenshō (1645–1725; Chinese name: Sai Taku), the father of Sai On, who made later emendations.]

7. *Ryūkyūkoku yuraiki,* vol. 1, in *Ryūkyū shiryō sōsho,* vol. 1 (Tokyo: Tōkyō bijutsu, 1972), p. 10.

8. The "Seiden" (Main Hall) of Shuri Castle was rebuilt in 1712, after the complex had burned down in 1709, but some fifty years later, it had fallen into disrepair, and between 1766 and 1768, a reconstruction was undertaken, which was dedicated in 1768, Tenth Month, 18th Day. The *Momourasoe udun fushin ni tsuki miezu narabi ni ozaimoku sunpōzu* records the architectural plans for this project. The plans are held in the Geijutsu Shiryōkan of the library of the Okinawa Prefectural Museum University of Arts (Okinawa Kenritsu Geijutsu Daigaku).

9. For details on the geomancy (*feng shui*) of Shuri Castle, see Shimajiri Katsutarō, "Okinawa no fūsui shisō," in *Okinawa no fūsui,* ed. Kubo Noritada (Tokyo: Hirakawa shuppan, 1990), pp. 3–13.

10. For more on the compilation of *Chūzan seikan* and *Chūzan seifu,* see Dana Masayuki, "Shisho wo amu: *Chūzan seikan, chūzan seifu,*" in *Okinawa kinseishi no shosō* (Naha: Hirugisha, 1992), pp. 1–24. For information on the compilation of *Kyūyō,* see Dana Masayuki, "Shuri ōfu no shisho hensan wo meguru shomondai—*Kyūyō* wo chūshin ni," in *Kyūyō ronsō,* ed. *Kyūyō* Ronsō Kankō Iinkai (Naha: Hirugisha, 1986), pp. 179–214.

11. The characters are 馬, 蔡, and 毛, respectively.

12. Regarding family ties and genealogies, see note 3 above.

13. *Ryūkyūkoku yuraiki,* vol. 1, p. 129.

14. 石巌(敢)当.

15. The *Taijō kannō hen* (Ch. *Tàishàng gǎnyìngpiān*) is a Daoist *kanzensho* (book promoting good deeds) purported to have been compiled from the teachings of Taishang Lǎojūn (Lǎo zě) by Lǐ Shí (Chāng Líng) in the early Song dynasty. The theme of the book is that good deeds will gain for people long life, whereas evil deeds will lead to an early death. This book was transmitted to Ryukyu in the early nineteenth century, and a copy made by Kishaba Seigen in 1841 spread through the aristocracy, many of whom made copies for themselves.

16. *Rekidai hōan,* revised edition, part 1, vol. 6, section 1-06-13, p. 196.

17. Xià Zǐyáng, *Shǐ Liúqiúlù* (Taipei: Xuéshēng shūjú, 1969), p. 190. There is also an edition annotated in Japanese by Harada Nobuo: Kai Shiyō, *Shi Ryūkyūroku* (Ginowan: Yōju shorin, 2001). There is another, earlier work bearing the same title. It was written by the emissary Chin Kan (Ch. Chén Kǎn), and is referenced in Chapter Seven.

18. *Kumemura nikki* is no longer extant, but parts of it are cited in Shimabukuro Zenpatsu, *Naha hensenki* (Naha: Okinawa shoseki, 1930), pp. 142–144; and the entry for "Kumemura" in *Okinawa daihyakka jiten,* vol. 1 (Naha: Okinawa Times, 1983), p. 980.

19. *Ryūkyūkoku yuraiki,* vol. 9, p. 185. Tōei (written with the characters 唐営 and later 唐栄) was the early name of Kumemura. See, in Chapter Three, the section titled "Naha Port: Hub of International Trade."

20. *Rekidai hōan* (revised edition), part 2, section 1-35-10, pp. 417–418.

21. Wén Qìng and Lǐ Zōngfǎng, eds., *Qīndìng guózǐ jiānzhì,* book 1, vol. 18 (Beijing: Běijīng gǔjí chūbǎnshè, 2000), p. 294.

22. The *Rikuyu engi* (Ch. *Liùyù yǎnyì,* Six Dicta, or Six Injunctions) was first commissioned by the Hongwu emperor in 1398, with the purpose of spreading the "six dicta" to the masses. What Tei Junsoku brought back to Ryukyu was a 1708 edition revised by Fàn Hóng (J. Hankō) and printed by the Ryukyukan in Fuzhou in 1708.

23. For more information on the working-students system, see Fukazawa Akito, *Kinsei Ryūkyū chūgoku kōryūshi no kenkyū* (Ginowan: Yōju shorin, 2011), pp. 161–194.

24. For more on the Shuri royal government's "policy of concealment," see Kishaba Kazutaka, "Kinseiki Ryūkyū no taigai inpei seisaku," in *Kinsei satsuryū kankei no kenkyū* (Tokyo: Kokusho kankōkai, 1993), pp. 255–275.

25. "Sasshūsen Shinkoku hyōryū dan," in *Edo hyōryūki sōshū,* vol. 1, ed. Yamashita Tsuneo (original editor Ishii Kendō) (Tokyo: Nippon hyōronsha, 1992), pp. 209–212.

*Chapter Six: The Ryukyu Kingdom's Tribute Trade*

1. In this chapter, details on preparations for the China voyage, and the roles of the various participants, are drawn from the following sources:

Maehira Fusaaki, "Ryūkyū ni okeru kashindan hensei to bōeki kōzō," in *Kyūshū to hansei*, part 2, ed. Fujino Tamotsu (Tokyo: Kokusho kankōkai, 1984), pp. 443–479.
Maehira Fusaaki, "Ryūkyū ni okeru shinkō bōeki no junbi katei: *Tasaku chikudun Pēchin totō junbi nikki* no ichi kōsatsu," in *Kinsei shomondai shiriizu*, parts 2–4 (Urasoe: Urasoe-shi kyōiku iinkai), 1985, pp. 76–81.
Fukazawa Akito, "Kinsei Ryūkyū no Ryūkyū shisetsu wo meguru shōmeishogun ni tsuite—Fumon, zhizhao, huzhao," in *Urasoe shiritsu toshokan kiyō*, 10 (Urasoe: Urasoe-shi kyōiku iinkai, 1999), pp. 43–54.
Fukazawa Akito, "Kinsei Ryūkyū ni okeru totō shisetsu no hensei—Jūkyū seiki no jirei wo chūshin ni," in *Okinawa bunka kenkyū*, 26 (Tokyo: Hōsei daigaku okinawa bunka kenkyūjo, 2000), pp. 23–109.

2. Information on the 1844 mission to Beijing comes from several sources: (a) "Shinkōsen shidashi nikki" (a record of the preparations leading up to the dispatch of the tribute ship), in *Ryūkyū ōkoku hyōjōsho monjo*, vol. 1, ed. Ryūkyū Ōkoku Hyōjōsho Monjo Henshū Iinkai (Urasoe: Urasoe-shi kōiku iinkai, 1988); (b) entries in *Rekidai hōan* that record correspondence between the kingdom and Fujian officials; and (c) reports to the imperial government in Beijing from various provincial officials regarding the progress of the envoys, which can be found in the following Chinese-language sources: *Qīngdài zhōngliú guānxì dǎngàn xuǎnbiān* (Zhōnghuá shūjú, 1993); and *Qīngdài zhōngliú guānxì dǎngàn xùbiān* (Zhōnghuá shūjú, 1994).

3. For more on the rituals associated with the China crossing and the tribute protocols, see Ikemiya Masaharu, "Totōsen no junbi to girei," in *Dainanakai Chūryū rekishi kankei kokusai gakujutsu kaigi ronbunshū* (Taipei: Chūryū bunka keizai kyōkai, 1999), pp. 518–546.

4. Editor's note: This morphing of Mazu/Maso into a Buddhist Bodhisattva begs for scholarly attention but that is outside the scope of this book.

5. Ono Masako, Satoi Yōichi, Tomiyama Kazuyuki, and Maehira Fusaaki, "'Naimushō monjo' to sono shōkai," *Shiryō hensanshitsu kiyō*, no. 12 (Naha: Okinawa kenritsu toshokan, 1987), document 99, p. 73.

6. Tei Heitetsu (Kuwae Katsuhide, ed.), *Kyūyō* (Tokyo: San'ichi shobō, 1971), p. 289.

7. A section of the palace for initially receiving visitors; the Chinese characters 御番所 can be read in Japanese as *gobansho* or *obandokoro*, or, in Okinawan, *ubanju*.

8. Hokama Shūzen and Saigō Nobutsuna, eds., *Omoro sōshi*, vols. 1–2 (Tokyo: Iwanami shoten, 1972, 2000), p. 274.

9. *Shinan kōgi* (handwritten copy of the block-printed Chūgoku Keiga Jūen'eki edition, 1708; University of the Ryukyus Library, Nakahara Zenchū Collection). The Ryukyu University Library produced a facsimile copy of this volume in 2001.

10. For more information on the Ryūkyūkan in Fuzhou, see Yonekura Jirō, "Fukushū no Ryūkyūkan," *Shirin* 22-1 (1937): 187–193; Kobata Atsushi, "Fukushū 'rouyuanyi' [jūen-eki] ni tsuite," in *Shisetsu Nihon to minami Shina*, ed. Takamura Shōhei (Tokyo: Noda shobō, 1942), pp. 113–126; Umeki Tetsuto, "Fukushū 'rouyuanyi' [jūen-eki] to Ryūkyū-chūgoku kankei," in *Fukkenshō-Ryūkyū rettō kōshōshi*, ed. Fukkenshō Ryūkyū Rettō Kōshōshi Kenkyū Chōsa Iinkai (Tokyo: Daiichi shobō, 1995), pp. 95–179; and Fukazawa Akito, "Fukushū Ryūkyūkan no kōzō to kaishū," in *Ryūkyū ōkoku hyōjōsho monjo*, 16, ed. Urasoeshi Kyōiku Iinkai (Urasoe: Urasoeshi kyōiku iinkai, 2000), pp. 5–77.

11. For scholars, the Chinese characters are 柔遠駅.

12. Gāo Qí, *Fújiàn shìbó tíjǔ sīzhì* (Publisher unknown, 1939), section entitled "Ryukyu House" (Róu Yuǎnyì).

13. The expression 開館貿易 (open house trade period) is rarely encountered in Japanese historical records, so its reading is not certain, but presumably it is *kaikan bōeki* in Japanese.

14. For more information on the *Teihin bunshū* [Ch. *Chéngbǐng* wénjí], see Itokazu Kaneharu, "*Teihin bunshū* ni tsuite," in *Daigokai Chūryū rekishi kankei gakujutsu kaigi ronbunshū* (Fújiàn jiàoyù chūbǎnshè [J. Fuken kyōiku shuppansha], 1996), pp. 29–56.

15. Akazaki Teikan, *Ryūkyaku* (or *Ryūkaku*) *danki* (Kan-ekidōban, Sakamaki/Hawley Collection, University of Hawai'i, Hamilton Library), p. 3. A digitized version is now available on the University of Ryukyus Library Web site: http://manwe.lib.u-ryukyu.ac.jp/d-archive/s/viewer?&cd=00061110. (The passage cited here is on p. 12.)

16. Much of this discussion of the route taken by Ryukyuan missions when they left Fujian and headed toward Beijing is derived from Gi Gakugen, *Fukken shinkyō suiriku rotei,* in the collection of Hōsei Daigaku University's Okinawa Bunka Kenkyūjo. Gi Gakugen (1793–1843) was from Kumemura and went to China as a student in 1815.

17. For more information about the tribute missions' activities while in Beijing, see Chén Jiéxiān, "Qīngdài Liúqiú shǐjié zàihuá xíngchéng yǔ huódòng lüèkǎo," in *Dainikai Ryūchū rekishi kankei kokusai gakujutsukaigi ronbunshū* (Naha: Chūryū bunka keizai kyōkai, 1989), pp. 95–142. For information about the mission residence, the "Kaidōkan," see Matsuura Akira, "Min Shin jidai Pekin no kaidōkan," in *Shinchō to higashi Ajia—Kanda Nobuo Sensei koki kinen ronshū,* ed. Kanda Nobuo Sensei koki kinen ronshū hensan iinkai (Tokyo: Yamakawa shuppansha, 1992), pp. 359–379; Gē Bīn, "Shindai no Ryūkyū kansha no kenkyū," in *Dainikai Ryūkyū chūgoku kōshōshi ni kansuru shinpojiumu ronbunshū* (Naha: Okinawa Prefectural Library, 1995), pp. 1–24; and Kamiya Nobuyuki, "Pekin no Ryūkyū shisetsu," in *Higashi Ajia no naka no Ryūkyū to Satsuma-han* (Tokyo: Azekura shobō, 2013), pp. 241–251.

18. Gim Yeongseon, *Yeonwonchiji,* in *Yeonhaengnokjeonjip* 71 (Seoul: Dongguk University Press, 2001), p. 268.

19. During the Qing dynasty, the *Almanac of Standard Time* issued by the Astronomical Bureau [J. Kintenkan, Ch. Qīntiānjiān] in Beijing was given to the Ryukyuan mission in Fujien, which in turn entrusted it to the returning mission to take back and present to the Ryukyu royal government. As noted in the following paragraph, there was a time lag during which the Ryukyuan Kingdom used a rather generic calendar until such time as the new arrived. There are no known extant copies of the almanacs sent to Ryukyu from China.

20. *Kyūyō,* p. 238.

21. *Rekidai hōan* (revised edition), part 13, section 2-183-18, p. 296.

22. Kobata Atsushi, *Shisetsu: Nihon to minami Shina* (Tokyo: Noda shobō, 1942), pp. 123–124.

23. Higashionna Kanjun, "Reimeiki no kaigai kōtsūshi," *Higashionna Kanjun zenshū,* vol. 3 (Tokyo: Daiichi shobō, 1979; first edition 1941), p. 628.

24. Information on the return to Ryukyu of the Beijing legation, as well as the officials who remained in Fuzhou to conduct trade, comes from several sources: the *Rekidai hōan* tells some of the story from the Ryukyu perspective, while on the Chinese side, administrative records (*tōan*) held in the Chūgoku Rekishi Tōankan in Beijing, as well as the Palace Museum and the Academia Sinica in Taibei, provide information on the exact itinerary of the travelers. For more information on the ceremony to receive the imperial rescript, see Ikemiya Masaharu, "Jōhyōwatashi to chokushomakae no gishiki," in *Dairokkai Chūryū rekishi kankei gakujutsu kentōkai bunshū* (Chūgoku daiichi rekishi tōankan, 2000), pp. 287–297.

Documents related to that ceremony can be found in *Sakuhōshi torai no toki no oboegaki,* in the Ryukyu University Library.

*Chapter Seven: The Imperial Investiture System and the Ryukyu Kingdom*

1. *Míng shǐ,* vol. 67, Treatises (Shi 志) section 43, Sumptuary Regulations (Yofuku 輿服) 3 (Taipei: Kōshi Shuppansha [Ch. Hóngshì chūbǎnshè], 1975), p. 1655.

2. *Rekidai hōan* (revised edition), part 1, vol. 1, section 1-01-15, p. 15.

3. For historians, the Chinese characters for these two items are: 大紅素皮弁服 and 五章絹地紗皮弁服, respectively.

4. 駝鈕鍍金銀印. Ch. *tuóniǔ dùjīnyín yìn.*

5. Chin Kan (Ch. Chén Kǎn), *Shi Ryūkyūroku* (Ch. *Shǐ Liúqiúlù*), in *Shi Ryūkyūroku, sanshu,* part 1, ed. Taiwan Ginkō Keizai Kenkyūshitsu (Taipei, 1970), p. 7. There is also an edition annotated in Japanese by Harada Nobuo: Chin Kan, *Shi Ryūkyūroku* (Ginowan: Yōju Shorin, 1995).

6. Extant records of missions are as follows (since all are accessible through Japanese sources, the authors and titles are also Romanized in Japanese): Chén Kǎn, *Shǐ Lliúqiúlù* (1534) [Chin Kan, *Shi Ryūkyūroku*]; Guō Rǔlín, *Chóngbiān shǐ Liúqiúlù* (1561) [Kaku Jorin, *Jūhen shi Ryūkyūroku*]; Xiāo Chóngyè and Xiè Jié, *Shǐ Liúqiúlù* (1579) [Shōsūgyō and Sha Ketsu, *Shi Ryūkyūroku*]; Xià Ziyáng, *Shǐ Liúqiúlù* (1606) [Ka Shiyō, *Shi Ryūkyūroku*]; Zhāng Xuélǐ, *Shǐ Liúqiújì* and *Zhōngshānjì lüè* (1663) [Chō Kakurei, *Shi Ryūkyūki* and *Chūzan kiryaku*]; Wāng Jí, *Shǐ Liúqiú zálù* and *Zhōngshān yángézhì* (1683/1684) [Ō Shū, *Shi Ryūkyū zatsuroku* and *Chūzan enkakushi*]; Xú Bǎoguāng, *Zhōngshān chuánxìnlù* (1721) [Jo Hokō, *Chūzan denshin-roku*]; Zhōu Huáng, *Liúqiú guózhìlüè* (1756) [Shū Kō, *Ryūkyūkoku shiryaku*]; Lǐ Dǐngyuán, *Shǐ Liúqiújì* (1800) [Ri Teigen, *Shi Ryūkyūki*]; Qí Kūn and Fèi Xīzhāng, *Xù Liúqiúguó zhìlüè* (1808) [Chō Shin and Hi Sekishō, *Zoku Ryūkyūkoku shiryaku*]; and Zhào Xīn, *Xu Liúqiúguó zhìlüè* (1866) [Chō Shin, *Zoku Ryūkyūkoku shiryaku*].

7. Lǐ Dǐngyuán, *Shǐ Liúqiújì* [Ri Teigen, *Shi Ryūkyūki*], in *Jìndài Zhōngguó shǐliào cóngkān,* no. 48, ed. Shěn Yúnlóng (Taipei: Wénhǎi chūbǎnshè, 1970), pp. 479–480.

8. Zhào Bǎochū, "Tàihú zhào shìjiājí cóngkè," in *Jìndài Zhōngguó shǐliào cóngkān,* no. 59, ed. Shěn Yúnlóng (Taipei: Wénhǎi chūbǎnshè, 1970), pp. 585–589.

9. For more detailed information on the tribute ships, and the ceremonies connected with their dispatch, see Harada Nobuo, *Sappōshiroku kara mita Ryūkyū* (Ginowan: Yōju shorin, 2000).

10. The term historians use is *hyōka* (Ok. *hangaa*) *bōeki* [評価貿易]. Some English-language scholars use the term "valuation."

11. For the kingdom's response to trade assessments [*hangaa bōeki*], see Tomiyama Kazuyuki, "Kansen bōeki ni tsuite ikkōsatsu: Junbi taisei o chūshin," *Daisankai Chūryū rekishi kankei kokusai gakujutsukaigi ronbunshū* (Taipei: Chūryū bunka keizai kyōkai, 1991), pp.109–162.

12. For more on the relationships between Ryukyu, Japan, and China in the early modern era, see Watanabe Miki, *Kinsei Ryūkyū to Chūnichi kankei* (Tokyo: Yoshikawa kōbunkan, 2012).

*Chapter Eight: The End of the Kingdom*

1. Higashionna Kanjun, "Shōtaikō jitsuroku," *Higashionna Kanjun zenshū,* vol. 2 (Tokyo: Daiichi shobō, 1978), pp. 331–332; and Matsuda Michiyuki, *Ryūkyū shobun,* vol. 1, in *Meiji bunka shiryō sōsho,* 4, *Gaikō-hen* (Tokyo: Kazama shobō, 1987), p. 17.

2. Matsuda Michiyuki, "Ryūkyū kokuō shō tai jōhyō narabi ni kenjōmono" and "Ryūkyū kokuō shō tai o han-ō ni hōji kazoku ni resseraru no chokujō," in part 1, *Ryūkyū shobun,* vol. 4, *Meiji bunka shiryō sōsho: Gaikō-hen* (Tokyo: Kazama shobō, 1987), pp. 17–19.

3. Ibid., pp. 21–23, 47; and Kishaba Chōken, *Ryūkyū kenbunroku* (Tokyo: Shigensha, 1977), pp. 10–11.

4. Mōri Toshihiko, *Taiwan shuppei: Dai-Nippon teikoku no kaimakugeki* (Tokyo: Chūkō shinsho, 1996), pp. 2–18.

5. "Soejima taishi tekisei gairyaku," in Matsuda Michiyuki, *Ryūkyū shobun,* vol. 1, in *Meiji bunka shiryō sōsho, 4, Gaikō-hen* (Tokyo: Kazama shobō, 1962), pp. 33–45.

6. For more on the Japanese government's decision to send troops into Taiwan and treat Ryukyu as part of Japanese territory, see Gabe Masao, "Meiji seifu no seiritsu to Ryūkyū shobun," in *Meiji kokka to Okinawa* (Tokyo: San'ichi shobō, 1979), pp. 25–91.

7. *Nihon gaikō monjo,* vol. 7 (Tokyo: Nihon kokusai rengō kyōkai, 1955), pp. 316–317. The full title is *Nisshin ryōkokukan gokan jōkan.* The characters are 日清両国間互換条款. The English title for this agreement is "Agreement between the High Commissioner Plenipotentiary of Japan and the Chinese Ministers of Foreign Affairs."

8. Matsuda Michiyuki, *Ryūkyū shobun,* vol. 2, pp. 105–107.

9. "Shiryō Kōhon," in *Nahashi-shi, Shiryōhen,* vol. 2, part 4, ed. Naha Shishi Henshū Iinkai (Naha: Naha shiyakusho, 1972), pp. 125–126.

10. Akamine Mamoru, "Shinchō no tainichi Ryūkyū kizoku mondai kōshō to dasshinnin," in *Shindai chūgoku no shomondai,* ed. Ishibashi Hideo (Tokyo: Yamakawa shuppansha, 1995), pp. 264–266.

11. For more detail on Hé Rúzhāng's handling of this situation, see Zhāng Qixióng, "Lùn qīngcháo Zhōngguó chóngjiàn Liúqiú Wángguó de xīngmiè jìjué guān—zhōnghuá shìjiè zhìxù yuánli zhīyī," in *Dainikai Ryūchū rekishi kankei kokusai gakujutsukaigi ronbunshū* (Chūryū bunka keizai kyōkai, 1989), pp. 495–519.

12. "Matsuda taishokikan dainikai hōshi Ryūkyū fukumeisho," in Matsuda Michiyuki, *Ryūkyū shobun,* vol. 2, in *Meiji bunka shiryō sōsho, 4, Gaikō-hen* (Tokyo: Kazama shobō, 1987), pp. 192–193.

13. See note 5 in the introduction regarding the term "Ryūkyū Shobun."

14. Akamine Mamoru, "Ōkoku no shōmetsu to Okinawa no kindai," in *Ryūkyū Okinawa shi no sekai,* ed. Tomiyama Kazuyuki (Tokyo: Yoshikawa kōbunkan, 2003), pp. 245–254.

15. Matsuda Michiyuki, *Ryūkyū shobun,* vol. 3, p. 224.

16. "Liúqiú guózǐ jīnguān Xiàng Déhóng chūcì bǐnggǎo," in *Lǐ wénzhōng gōng quánjí,* Yìshū hángǎo, vol. 9 (Taipei: Wénhǎi chūbǎnshè, 1962), pp. 19–22. (Xiàng Déhóng is the Chinese reading for Shō Tokukō.)

17. Ibid.

18. For more on the movement to restore the Ryukyu Kingdom, see Hiyane Teruo, "Dasshin kōdō no ronri—Ryūkyū fukkyū undō no kiseki," in *Jiyū minken shisō to Okinawa* (Tokyo: Kenbun shuppan, 1982), pp. 95–141.

19. Kinjō Seitoku, *Ryūkyū shobunron* (Naha: Okinawa Times, 1978), pp. 267–275.

20. *Nihon gaikō monjo,* vol. 13, pp. 378–379.

21. For more on Chén Bǎochēn, see Táng Fēnjī, Xú Xiǎowàng, and Huáng Qǐquán, eds., *Chén Bǎochēn yǔ Zhōngguó jìndài shèhuì* (Fuzhou: Chén Bǎochēn jiàoyù jījīn chóuwěihuì, 1997).

22. Yokoyama Manabu et al., eds., *Ryūkyū shozoku mondai kankei shiryō,* vol. 8 (Tokyo: Honpō shoseki, 1980), pp. 902–904.

23. Ibid., pp. 1083–1089.

24. For more on the negotiations at the end of the Qing era between China and Japan regarding where Ryukyu "belonged," see Nishizato Kikō, *Shinmatsu Chūryūnichi kankeishi no kenkyū* (Kyoto: Kyōto daigaku gakujutsu shuppankai, 2005).

25. In 1895, after the outbreak of the Sino-Japanese War in August 1894, the *Ryūkyū shinpō* dispatched two correspondents to cover the war: Goeku Chōi and Moromizato Chōkō. The *Ryūkyū shinpō* assumed a Japanese victory and used the pages of their regular

newspaper, as well as extra editions, to report on Japan's successes in the war, and insisted that rumors spread by the "Obstinacy Party" of China's "Yellow Fleet" were groundless. See Ryūkyū Shinpō Hyakunenshi Kankō Iinkai, ed., *Ryūkyū shinpō hyakunenshi* (Naha: Ryūkyū shinpō, Inc., 1993), pp. 15–19.

26. *Okinawa kenshi,* vol. 1, Tsūshi (Tokyo: Kokusho kankōkai, 1996), p. 355.

27. *Okinawa kenshi,* vol. 13, Okinawa-ken kankei kakushō kōmonjo, part 2 (Tokyo: Kokusho kankōkai, 1996), pp. 630–659.

28. Ibid., pp. 662–673.

29. Ibid., pp. 691–700. The Okinawa Prefecture Land Distribution Law was approved by the Imperial Diet on February 6, 1899.

### *Afterword*

1. Most of China's diplomatic records from the mid-nineteenth century are held in Nanzhing's Historical Records, Building 2, but materials related to the Cairo Summit are housed in Taiwan's National Museum of History. Other materials of value to those doing research on the PRC's policies vis-à-vis Okinawa can be found in Taiwan among the records of the party held in the People's Party History Museum (Guómíndǎng Dǎngshǐguǎn), and diplomatic records held in the Archives of the Institute of Modern History Research in the Academia Sinica.

# Bibliography

*Reference Works and Primary Source Collections*

Akazaki Teikan. *Ryūkyaku* (or *Ryūkaku*) *danki*. Kan-ekidōban, Sakamaki/Hawley Collection, University of Hawai'i, Hamilton Library. Digitized version: http://manwe.lib.u-ryukyu.ac.jp/d-archive/s/viewer?&cd=00061110.

Chōsenshi Henshūkai, ed. *Sin Suk-chu's Kaitō shokokuki*. Keijō: Chōsen sōtokufu, 1933.

*Fukushū ryūkyūkanzō Pekin tōrinshō*. Okinawa kenritsu toshokan Higashionna bunkozō.

Gāo Qí. *Fújiàn shìbó tíjǔ sīzhì*. Publisher unknown, 1939.

Gi Gakugen. *Fukken shinkyō suiriku rotei*. Tokyo: Hōsei Daigaku Okinawa Bunka Kenkyūjo.

*Guójiā dúshūguǎncáng Liúqiú zīliào huìbiān*. Beijing: Beijing dúshūguǎn chūbǎnshè, 2000.

Hayashi Fukusai, ed. *Tsūkō ichiran*. Tokyo: Kokusho kankōkai, 1912.

Ifa Fuyu and Higashionna Kanjun, eds. *Ryūkyū shiryō sōsho*, vol. 1. Tokyo: Tokyo bijutsu, 1972.

Ifa Fuyu, Higashionna Kanjun, and Yokoyama Shigeru, eds. *Ryūkyū shiryō sōsho*, vol. 5. Tokyo: Inoue shobō, 1962.

Ishin Sūden. *Ikoku nikki—Konchi-in sūden gaikō monjo shūsei* [facsimile edition]. Tokyo: Tokyo bijutsu, 1989.

Kagoshima-ken Ishin Shiryō Hensanjo, ed. *Kagoshima-ken shiryō, kyūki zatsuroku kōhen 1–6*. Kagoshima: Kagoshima-ken ishin shiryō hensanjo, 1980–1985.

Kagoshima-ken Rekishi Shiryō Sentaa Reimeikan, ed. *Kagoshima-ken shiryō, kyūki zatsuroku*, book 2. Kagoshima: Kagoshima Prefecture, 1984.

Ka Shiyō (Harada Nobuo, ed.). *Shi Ryūkyūroku*. Ginowan: Yōju shorin, 2001.

Kimura Taka'atsu, ed. *Butoku hennen shūsei*, part 2. Tokyo: Meichō shuppan, 1976, vol. 58.

*Kōraishi*, 3 vols. Tokyo: Kokusho kankōkai, 1908–1909; reprinted 1977.

Kuroita Katsumi, ed. *Shintei zōho kokushi taikei, Tokugawa jikki*, 3rd edition. Tokyo: Yoshikawa kōbunkan, 1976.

Kyūyō Kenkyūkai, eds. *Kyūyō, Okinawa bunka shiryō shūsei*, vol. 5. Tokyo: Kadokawa shoten, 1974.

*Míng shǐ*. Taipei: Hóngshì chūbǎnshè, 1975.
*Míng tàizǔ shílù*. Taipei: Institute of History and Philology, Academia Sinica, 1968.
Naha Shishi Henshū Iinkai, ed. *Nahashi-shi, Shiryōhen*, vols. 1–3. Naha: Naha shiyakusho, 1967–2008.
*Nihon gaikō monjo*, vols. 7 and 13. Tokyo: Nihon kokusai rengō kyōkai, 1955.
*Okinawa daihyakka jiten*, vols. 1–3. Naha: Okinawa Times, 1983.
*Qīngdài zhōngliú guānxì dǎngàn xuǎnbiān*. Beijing: Zhōnghuá shūjú, 1993.
*Qīngdài zhōngliú guānxì dǎngàn xùbiān*. Beijing: Zhōnghuá shūjú, 1994.
*Qīngjì Zhōngrìhán guānxì shǐliào*. Taipei: Zhōngyāng yánjiūyuàn jìndàishǐ yánjiūsuǒ, 1972.
*Rekidai hōan*. Taipei: Táiwān dàxúe, 1972.
*Rekidai hōan, kōteibon*. Okinawa kyōiku iinkai, eds. Naha: Okinawa kenritsu toshokan shiryō henshūshitsu, 1992–.
*Richō jitsuroku*, 56 vols. Tokyo: Gakushūin Daigaku tōyō bunka kenkyūjo, 1953–1967.
*Ryūkyūkoku yuraiki*, vols. 1–2. In *Ryūkyū shiryō sōsho*, vol. 1, edited by Ifa Fuyu, Higashionna Kanjun, and Yokoyama Shigeru. Tokyo: Tōkyō bijutsu, 1972.
*Ryūkyū kuniezu shiryōshū 1 & 2*. In *Shōhō kuniezu oyobi kanren shiryō*. Naha: Okinawa-ken kyōiku iinkai, 1992–1994.
Sai Taku et al., eds. *Saitaku-bon chūzan seifu*. Naha: Okinawan-ken kyōiku iinakai, 1973.
*Sakuhōshi torai no toki no oboegaki*, ca. 1793–1795. Ifa Fuyu Collection, Ryukyu University Library. Digital version: http://manwe.lib.u-ryukyu.ac.jp/d-archive/viewer/en?&cd=00030170.
*Sappan sōsho 2*. Kagoshima: Sappan sōsho kankōkai, 1906.
"Shimazu-ke monjo, Part 3, #1521." In *Dai Nihon komonjo, iewake* [house collections], no. 16, edited by Tōkyō Daigaku Shiryō Hensanjo. Tokyo: Tōkyō Daigaku shiryō hensanjo, 1966.
*Shimazu kokushi*. Kagoshima: Kagoshima-ken chihōshi gakkai, 1972.
Shimonaka Kunihiko, ed. *Ajia rekishi jiten*. Tokyo: Heibonsha, 1962.
*Shinan kōgi*. Nakahara Zenchū Collection. University of the Ryukyus Library (handwritten copy of the block-printed Chūgoku Keiga Jūen'eki edition of 1708). (The Ryukyu University Library produced a facsimile copy of this volume in 2001.)
*Shinkoku gaikō hishi*, vols. 1–10, 1875–1885. Gaimushō gaikō shiryō kanzō.
*Sìbù cóngkān chūbiān suōběn*, vol. 107. Taipei: Taíwān shāngwù yìnshùguǎn, 1967.
Tanaka Takeo, ed. *Zenrin kokuhōki, shintei zokuzenrin kokuhōki*. Tokyo: Shūeisha, 1995.
Tei Heitetsu (Kuwae Katsuhide, ed.). *Kyūyō*. Tokyo: San'ichi shobō, 1971.
Tokyo Daigaku Shiryō Hensanjo, ed. *Dai Nihon komonjo, iewake* [house collections] no. 16, *Shimazu-ke monjo*, part 3. Tokyo: Tokyo University, 1966.
Urasoe-shi Kyōiku Iinkai, eds. *Ryūkyū ōkoku hyōjōsho monjo*, 19 vols. Urasoe: Urasoe City Library, 1988–2002.
Urasoe-shi Kyōiku Iinkai, eds., *Ryūkyū ōkoku hyōjōsho monjo sōsaku-in*. Urasoe: Urasoe City Library, 2011.
Wèi Zhēng et al. *Suí shū*. Beijing: Zhōnghuá shūjú, 1973.
Wén Qìng, Lǐ Zōngfǎng, eds. *Qīndìng guózǐ jiānzhì*, book 1, vol. 18. Beijing: Běijīng gǔjí chūbǎnshè, 2000.
Xià Zǐyáng. *Shǐ liúqiú lù*. Taipei: Xuéshēng shūjú, 1969.
*Xīngchá shèngrǎn* (Survey of Official Voyages, 1436). Digital version, China Text Project: http://ctext.org/library.pl?if=en&res=81929.
Yamashita Tsuneo, ed. (original editor, Ishii Kendō). *Edo hyōryūki sōshū*, vol. 1. Tokyo: Nippon hyōronsha, 1992.

Yokoyama Manabu et al., eds. *Ryūkyū shozoku mondai kankei shiryō,* vol. 8. Tokyo: Honpō shoseki, 1980.

Zhōngguó dìyī lìshǐ dàngàn guǎn, ed. *Qīngdài liúqiú guówáng biǎozhòu wénshū xuǎnlù.* Hefei: Huángshān shūshè chūbǎn, 1997.

Zhōngguó dìyī lìshǐ dàngàn guǎn, ed. *Qīngdài zhōngliú guānxì dàngàn xǔanbiān.* Beijing: Zhōnghuá shūjú, 1993.

Zhōngguó dìyī lìshǐ dàngàn guǎn, ed. *Qīngdài zhōngliú guānxì dàngàn xǔanxùbiān.* Beijing: Zhōnghuá shūjú, 1994.


*Other Primary Sources*


Afonso Dalboquerque (see Birch, Walter de Gray).

Akiyama Kenzō. *Nisshi kōshō shiwa.* Tokyo: Naigai shoseki, 1936.

Birch, Walter de Gray, trans. *Commentaries of the Great Afonso Dalboquerque,* vol. 3. London: Hakluyt Society, 1880.

Cài Xiāng. *Lìīzhi pǔ.* Shanghai: Shāngwù yìnshūguǎn, 1936.

Chin Kan (Ch. Chén Kǎn). *Shi Ryūkyūroku,* edited and annotated by Harada Nobuo. Ginowan: Yōju shorin, 1995.

Chin Kan (Ch. Chén Kǎn). *Shi Ryūkyūroku* (Ch. *Shǐ Liúqiúlù*). In *Shi Ryūkyūroku, sanshu,* part 1, edited by Taiwan Ginkō Keizai Kenkyūshitsu. Taipei: 1970.

Fujiwara no Akihira. *Shin sarugakuki.* In *Tōyō bunkō,* vol. 424, edited by Kawaguchi Hisao. Tokyo: Heibonsha, 1983.

Gim Yeongseon. *Yeonwonchiji.* In *Yeonhaengnokjeonjip,* vol. 71. Seoul: Dongguk University Press, 2001.

Hokama Shūzen and Saigō Nobutsuna, eds. *Omoro sōshi, Nihon shisō taikei.* Tokyo: Iwanami shoten, 1972, 2000.

Jo Hokō [Xú Bǎoguāng] (Harada Nobuo, ed.). *Chūzan denshinroku.* Ginowan: Yōju shorin, 1999.

Kobata, Atsushi, and Mitsugu Matsuda, trans. *Ryukyuan Relations with Korea and South Sea Countries; an Annotated Translation of Documents in the Rekidai Hōan.* Kyoto: self-published, 1969.

Kunaichō Shoryōbu, ed. *Iyōtō Ryūkyūkoku ki.* Tokyo: Kunaichō shoryōbu, 1962.

Lǐ Dǐngyuán. *Shǐ Liúqiújì* [Ri Teigen, *Shi Ryūkyūki*]. *Jìndài Zhōngguó shǐliào cóngkān,* no. 48, edited by Shěn Yúnlóng. Taipei: Wénhǎi chūbǎnshè, 1970.

Lǐ Hóngzhāng, compiler, and Wú Rǔlún, ed., "Liúqiú guózǐ jīnguān Xiàng Déhóng chūcì bǐnggǎo," in *Lǐ Wénzhōng gōng quánjí,* Yìshū hángǎo, vol. 9. Taipei: Wénhǎi chūbǎnshè, 1962.

Matsuda Michiyuki. "Ryūkyū kokuō shō tai jōhyō narabi ni kenjōmono" and "Ryūkyū kokuō shō tai o han-ō ni hōji kazoku ni resseraru no chokujō." In part 1, *Ryūkyū shobun,* vol. 4, *Meiji bunka shiryō sōsho: Gaikō-hen,* pp. 17–19. Tokyo: Kazama shobō, 1987.

*Momourasoe udun fushin ni tsuki miezu narabi ni ozaimoku sunpōzu.* Naha: Geijitsu Shiryōkan, Okinawa Kenristu Geijutsu Daigaku, 1768.

Naha Shishi Henshū Iinkai, ed. *Naha shishi, shiryōhen,* series 1, part 6, Kafu Shiryō 2, sections 1–2. Naha City: Naha shishi henshūshitsu, 1981.

Naha Shishi Henshū Iinkai, ed. *Naha shishi, shiryōhen,* series 1, part 7, Kafu Shiryō 3. Naha City: Naha shishi henshūshitsu, 1982.

Naha Shishi Henshū Iinkai, ed. *Naha shishi, shiryōhen,* series 1, part 8, Kafu Shiryō 4. Naha City: Naha shishi henshūshitsu, 1983.

Naha Shishi Henshū Iinkai, ed. *Naha shishi, shiryōhen,* series 2, part 4, Kōhon. Naha: Naha City, 1972.

Okinawa Kenritsu Toshokan, ed. *Ryūkyū kinsekibun takuhon shūsei.* Okinawa Prefectural Library, 1981.

*Okinawa kenshi,* vol. 1, Tsūshi. Tokyo: Kokusho kankōkai, 1996.

*Okinawa kenshi,* vol. 13. Okinawa-ken Kankei Kakushō Kōmonjo, part 2. Tokyo: Kokusho kankōkai, 1996.

Ono Masako, Satoi Yōichi, Tomiyama Kazuyuki, and Maehira Fusaaki. "'Naimushō monjo' to sono shōkai." *Shiryō hensanshitsu kiyō,* no. 12. Naha: Okinawa kenritsu toshokan, 1987, document 99, p. 73.

Osaka Jinken Hakubutsukan, eds. *Egakareta ikoku iiki: Chōsen, Ryūkyū, ainumoshiri no hitobito.* Osaka: Osaka jinken hakubutsukan, 2001.

Pires, Tomé (Cortesão, Armando, trans. and ed.). *The Suma Oriental of Tomé Pires: An Account of the East, from the Red Sea to Japan, Written in Malacca and India in 1512–1515; and, The Book of Francisco Rodrigues: Rutter of a Voyage in the Red Sea, Nautical Rules, Almanack and Maps, Written and Drawn in the East before 1515,* Hakluyt Society; 2nd ser., nos. 89–90. Nendeln, Liechtenstein: Kraus Reprint, 1967.

Pires, Tomé (Ikuta Shigeru et al., trans.). *Tōhōshokokuki,* vol. 5, *Daikōkai jidai sōsho.* Tokyo: Iwanami shoten, 1982.

Ri Teigen [Lǐ Dǐngyuán] (Harada Nobuo, ed.). *Shi Ryūkyūki.* Tokyo: Gensōsha, 1986.

"Sasshūsen Shinkoku hyōryū dan." In *Edo hyōryūki sōshū,* vol. 1, edited by Yamashita Tsuneo (original editor Ishii Kendō), pp. 209–212. Tokyo: Nippon hyōronsha, 1992.

"Shinkōsen shidashi nikki." In *Ryūkyū ōkoku hyōjōsho monjo,* vol. 1, edited by Ryūkyū Ōkoku Hyōjōsho Monjo Henshū Iinkai. Urasoe: Urasoe-shi kōiku iinkai, 1988.

Shin Shukushū (Tanaka Takeo, ed.). *Kaitōshokokuki.* Tokyo: Iwanami shoten, 1991.

"Tàihú Zhào shìjiājí cóngkè." In *Jìndài Zhōngguó shǐliào cóngkān,* no. 59, edited by Shěn Yúnlóng, pp. 585–589. Taipei: Wénhǎi chūbǎnshè, 1970.

Yasuda Akira et al., eds. *Unpoi irohashū.* Kyoto: Rinsen shoten, 1977.

*Secondary Sources*

Akamine Mamoru. "Dasshinnin no tangansho ni tsuite." In *Daiichizoku chūgokuikigai kanseki kokusai gakujutsu kaigi ronbunshū,* pp. 180–201. Taipei: Liánjīng chūbǎn shìyè gōngsī, 1987.

Akamine Mamoru. "Ōkoku no shōmetsu to Okinawa no kindai." In *Ryūkyū Okinawa shi no sekai,* edited by Tomiyama Kazuyuki, pp. 245–254. Tokyo: Yoshikawa kōbunkan, 2003.

Akamine Mamoru. "Shinchō no tainichi Ryūkyū kizoku mondai kōshō to dasshinnin." In *Shindai chūgoku no shomondai,* edited by Ishibashi Hideo, pp. 263–295. Tokyo: Yamakawa shuppansha, 1995.

Akamine Mamoru. "Shindai no Ryūkyū hyōryūmin sōkan taisei ni tsuite: Kenryū nijūgonen no sanyō iriomote sen no hyōchaku jirei wo chūshin ni." *Tōyōshi kenkyū* 58, no. 3 (1999): 83–109.

Akiyama Kenzō. *Nisshi kōshōshi kenkyū.* Tokyo: Iwanami shoten, 1939.

Araki Moriaki. *Shin Okinawa shiron.* Naha: Okinawa Times, 1980.

Arano Yasunori. *Kinsei Nihon to higashi Ajia.* Tokyo: Tokyo daigaku shuppankai, 1988.

Asato Nobu. *Nihon nanpō hattatsushi.* Tokyo: Sanseidō, 1941.

Asato Susumu. *Kōkogaku kara mita Ryūkyūshi,* vols. 1–2. Naha: Hirugisha, 1990–1991.

Banno Masataka. *Kindai chūgoku seiji gaikōshi.* Tokyo: Tokyo daigaku shuppankai, 1973.

Cáo Yǒnghé, "Míng hóngwǔcháo de zhōngliú guānxì." In Zhōngguó hǎiyang fāzhǎnshǐ lùnwénjí, no. 3. Taipei: Zhōngyāng yánjiūyuàn sānmínzhǔyì yánjiūsuǒ, 1988.

Chén Jiéxiān. "Qīngdài Liúqiú shǐjié zàihuá xíngchéng yǔ huódòng lüèkǎo." In *Dainikai Ryūchū rekishi kankei kokusai gakujutsukaigi ronbunshū*, pp. 95–142. Naha: Chūryū bunka keizai kyōkai, 1989.

Ch'en Ta-tuan (Chin Daitan). "Shindai ni okeru Ryūkyū kokuō no sappū" (Maehira Fusaaki, trans.), *Kyūshū daigaku bungakubu kyūshū bunkashi kenkyūjo kiyō* 33 (1988): pp. 221–262.

China Sadahiro. *Okinawa shūkyōshi no kenkyū*. Ginowan: Yōjusha, 1994.

Dana Masayuki. *Okinawa kinseishi no shosō*. Naha: Hirugisha, 1992.

Dana Masayuki. "Shisho wo amu: *Chūzan seikan, chūzan seifu*." In *Okinawa kinseishi no shosō*, pp. 1–24. Naha: Hirugisha, 1992.

Dana Masayuki. "Shuri ōfu no shisho hensan wo meguru shomondai—*Kyūyō* wo chūshin ni." In *Kyūyō ronsō*, edited by *Kyūyō* Ronsō Kankō Iinkai, pp. 179–214. Naha: Hirugisha, 1986.

Danjō Hiroshi. "Min hatsu no kaikin to chōkō: Minchō sensei shihai no rikai ni yosete." *Min shin jidaishi no kihon mondai*. Tokyo: Kyūko shoin, 1997.

Ding Feng. *Liúhàn duìyīn yǔ Míngdài guānhuàyīn yánjiū*. Beijing: Zhōngguó shèhuìkēxué chūbǎnshè, 1995.

Fujino Tamotsu, ed. *Kyūshū to hansei*, part 2. Tokyo: Kokusho kankōkai, 1984.

Fukazawa Akito. "Fukushū Ryūkyūkan no kōzō to kaishū." In *Ryūkyū ōkoku hyōjōsho monjo*, 16, edited by Urasoeshi Kyōiku Iinkai, pp. 5–77. Urasoe: Urasoeshi kyōiku iinkai, 2000.

Fukazawa Akito. *Kinsei Ryūkyū chūgoku kōryūshi no kenkyū*. Ginowan: Yōju shorin, 2011.

Fukazawa Akito. "Kinsei Ryūkyū ni okeru totō shisetsu no hensei—Jūkyū seiki no jirei wo chūshin ni." *Okinawa bunka kenkyū*, 26 (Tokyo: Hōsei daigaku okinawa bunka kenkyūjo, 2000): 23–109.

Fukazawa Akito. "Kinsei Ryūkyū no Ryūkyū shisetsu wo meguru shōmeishogun ni tsuite—fumon, zhizhao, huzhao." *Urasoe shiritsu toshokan kiyō*, 10. Urasoe: Urasoeshi kyōiku iinkai, 1999, pp. 43–54.

Fukkensho Ryukyu Retto Koshoshi Kenkyū Chōsa Iinkai, ed. *Fukkenshō-Ryūkyū rettō kōshōshi*. Tokyo: Daiichi shobō, 1995.

Fuma Susumu, ed. *Shi Ryūkyūroku kaidai oyobi kenkyū*. Ginowan: Yōju shorin, 1999.

Gabe Masao. *Meiji kokka to Okinawa*. Tokyo: San'ichi shobō, 1979.

Gabe Masao. "Meiji seifu no seiritsu to Ryūkyū shobun." In *Meiji kokka to Okinawa*, pp. 25–91. Tokyo: San'ichi shobō, 1979.

Gē Bīn. "Shindai no Ryūkyū kansha no kenkyū." In *Dainikai Ryūkyū chūgoku kōshōshi ni kansuru shinpojiumu ronbunshū*, pp. 1–24. Naha: Okinawa Prefectural Library, 1995.

Hamashita Takeshi and Karashima Noboru, eds. *Chiikishi to wa nanika*. Tokyo: Yamakawa shuppansha, 1997.

Harada Nobuo. *Sappōsiroku kara mita Ryūkyū*. Ginowan: Yōju shorin, 2000.

Higashionna Kanjun. "Reimeiki no kaigai kōtsūshi," in *Higashionna Kanjun zenshū*, vol. 3. Tokyo: Daiichi shobō, 1979; first edition 1941.

Higashionna Kanjun. "Shōtaikō jitsuroku." In *Higashionna Kanjun zenshū*, vol. 2, pp. 331–332. Tokyo: Daiichi shobō, 1978.

Hiyane Teruo. "Dasshin kōdō no ronri—Ryūkyū fukkyū undō no kiseki." In *Jiyū minken shisō to Okinawa*, pp. 95–141. Tokyo: Kenbun shuppan, 1982.

Hiyane Teruo. *Jiyū minken shisō to Okinawa*. Tokyo: Kenbun sensho, 1982.

Ikehata Setsuho, ed. *Kawaru Tōnan Ajia sizō.* Tokyo: Yamakawa shuppansha, 1994.
Ikemiya Masaharu. "Jōhyōwatashi to chokushomakae no gishiki." In *Dairokkai Chūryū rekishi kankei gakujutsu kentōkai bunshū,* pp. 287–297. Chūgoku daiichi rekishi tōankan, 2000.
Ikemiya Masaharu. "Totōsen no junbi to girei." In *Dainanakai Chūryū rekishi kankei kokusai gakujutsu kaigi ronbunshū,* pp. 518–546. Taipei: Chūryū bunka keizai kyōkai, 1999.
Ikemiya Masaharu, Odo Kiyotaka, and Dana Masayuki, eds. *Kumemura.* Naha: Hirugisha, 1993.
Ikkai Tomoyoshi, Kakehi Kumiko, and Kakehi Fumio. *Kango no sanpodō.* Kyoto: Kamogawa shuppan, 1997.
Irumada Nobuo and Tomiyama Kazuyuki. *Kita no Hiraizumi minami no Ryūkyū,* vol. 5, *Nihon no chūsei.* Tokyo: Chūō kōron shinsha, 2002.
Itokazu Kaneharu. "*Teihin bunshū* ni tsuite." In *Daigokai Chūryū rekishi kankei gakujutsu kaigi ronbunshū,* pp. 29–56. Fujian: Fújiàn jiàoyù chūbǎnshè [J. Fuken kyōiku shuppansha], 1996.
Jo Kyōsei [Xú Gōngshēng] (Nishizato Kikō and Uezato Kenichi, trans.). *Chūgoku Ryūkyū kōryūshi.* Naha: Hirugisha, 1991.
Kamiya Nobuyuki. *Bakuhansei kokka no Ryūkyū shihai.* Tokyo: Azekura shobō, 1990.
Kamiya Nobuyuki. *Higashi Ajia no naka no Ryūkyū to Satsuma-han.* Tokyo: Azekura shobō, 2013.
Kamiya Nobuyuki. "Pekin no Ryūkyū shisetsu." In *Higashi Ajia no naka no Ryūkyū to Satsuma-han,* pp. 241–251. Tokyo: Azekura shobō, 2013.
Kamiya Nobuyuki. *Ryūkyū to Nihon-Chūgoku,* vol. 43, *Nihonshi riburetto.* Tokyo: Yamakawa shuppansha, 2003.
Kamiya Nobuyuki. *Taikun gaikō to higashi Ajia.* Tokyo: Yoshikawa kōbunkan, 1997.
Kamiya Nobuyuki and Kimura Naoya, eds. *Kaishi to sakoku,* Tenbō Nihon Rekishi 14. Tokyo: Tōkyōdō shuppan, 2002.
Kanaseki Hiroshi and Takamiya Hiroe. *Okinawa no rekishi to bunka: Kaijō no michi tankyū.* Tokyo: Yoshikawa kōbunkan, 1994.
Kawazoe Shōji. *Chūsei Kyūshū no seiji to bunka.* Tokyo: Bunken shuppan, 1981.
Kinjō Seitoku. *Ryūkyū shobunron.* Naha: Okinawa Times, 1978.
Kishaba Chōken. *Ryūkyū kenbunroku.* Tokyo: Shigensha, 1977.
Kishaba Kazutaka. *Kinsei satsuryū kankei no kenkyū.* Tokyo: Kokusho kankōkai, 1993.
Kishimoto Mio. *Higashi Ajia no "kinsei,"* vol. 13, *Sekaishi riburetto.* Tokyo: Yamakawa shuppansha, 1998.
Kobata Atsushi. "Fukushū 'rouyuanyi' [jūen-eki] ni tsuite." In *Shisetsu Nihon to minami Shina,* edited by Takamura Shōhei, pp. 113–126. Tokyo: Noda shobō, 1942.
Kobata Atsushi. *Shisetsu: Nihon to minami Shina.* Tokyo: Noda shobō, 1942.
Kobata Atsushi. *Zōho chūsei nantō tsūkō bōekishi no kenkyū.* Kyoto: Rinsen shoten, 1993; first edition 1939.
Kubo Noritada. *Okinawa no fūsui.* Tokyo: Hirakawa shuppansha, 1990.
Kuroda Yasuo. "Satsuma-han no tōbutsu shōhō to Nagasaki kaij." *Nantōshigaku* 33 (April 1989): 1–19.
*Kyūyō* Ronsō Kankō Iinkai, ed. *Kyūyō ronsō.* Naha: Hirugisha, 1986.
Maehira Fusaaki. "Jūgo jūroku seiki ni okeru Ryūkyū—Higashi Ajia bōeki no rekishiteki ichi." *Ryūdai shigaku* 12 (1981): 48–65.
Maehira Fusaaki. "Kinsei Ryūkyū ni okeru kojin bōeki no kōzō." In *Kyūyōronsō,* pp. 239–262. Naha: Hirugisha, 1986.

Maehira Fusaaki. "Kinsei Ryūkyū ni okeru kōkai to shinkō: Tabi no girei wo chūshin ni," *Okinawa bunka* 77; 28, no. 1 (1993): 1–17.

Maehira Fusaaki. "Nanban bōeki to sono jidai." In *Shin-Ryūkyūshi, Ko-Ryūkyūhen,* p. 285n. Naha: Okinawa shinpōsha, 1999.

Maehira Fusaaki. "Ryūkyū ni okeru kashindan hensei to bōeki kōzō." In *Kyūshū to hansei,* part 2, edited by Fujino Tamotsu, pp. 443–479. Tokyo: Kokusho kankōkai, 1984.

Maehira Fusaaki. "Ryūkyū ni okeru shinkō bōeki no junbi katei: *Tasato chikudun Pēchin totō junbi nikki* no ichi kōsatsu." In *Kinsei no shomondai shirīzu,* parts 2–4. Urasoe: Urasoe-shi kyōiku iinkai, 1985.

Maehira Fusaaki, "Ryūkyū shisetsu ni yoru chūgoku kenbun repōto." In *Daiyonkai Ryūchū rekishi kankei kokusai gakujutsukaigi ronbunshū.* Naha: Chūryū bunka keizai kyōkai, 1993.

Maehira Fusaaki. "Ryūkyū shisetsu no ikoku taiken: Chūgoku tairiku sanzenkiro no tabi." In *"Sakoku" wo minaosu,* edited by Nagatsumi Yōko, pp. 94–122. Tokyo: Yamakawa shuppansha, 1999.

Maehira Fusaaki. "Ryūkyū—Tōnan Ajia bōeki no tenkai to kakyōshakai," *Kyūshū shigaku* 76 (1983): 29–57.

Maehira Fusaaki. "Sakoku keiseiki no kirishitan kinsei to Ryūkyū—Tokugawa seiken no Manira shuppei keikaku no haikei." In *Sakoku Nihon to kokusai kōryū,* vol. 1, edited by Yanai Kenji. Tokyo: Yoshikawa kōbunkan, 1988.

Maehira Fusaaki. "Sakoku keiseiki no Ryūkyū zaiban bugyō." In *Ryūkyū no rekishi to bunka: Yamamoto Hirobumi Hakushi kanreki kinen ronshū,* edited by Yamamoto Hirobumi Sensei Kanreki Kinen Ronshū Kankō Iinkai, pp. 141–156. Tokyo: Honpō shoseki, 1985.

Majikina Ankō. *Okinawa issennenshi.* Naha: Ryūkyū shinpōsha, 1974; first edition, 1923.

Matsuda Michiyuki. *Ryūkyū shobun,* 3 vols. In *Meiji bunka shiryō sōsho, 4, Gaikō-hen.* Tokyo: Kazama shobō, 1962.

Matsuura Akira. "Min Shin jidai Pekin no kaidōkan." In *Shinchō to higashi Ajia—Kanda Nobuo Sensei koki kinen ronshū,* edited by Kanda Nobuo Sensei Koki Kinen Ronshū Hensan Iinkai, pp. 359–379. Tokyo: Yamakawa shuppansha, 1992.

Matsuura Akira. *Shindai chūgoku Ryūkyū bōekishi no kenkyu.* Ginowan: Yōju shorin, 2003.

Mǐ Qìngyú. *Liúqiú lìshǐ yánjiū.* Tianjin: Tiānjīn rénmín chūbǎnshè, 1998.

Miyagi Eishō. *Ryūkyū shisha no Edo nobori.* Tokyo: Daiichi shobō, 1982.

Miyata Toshihiko. *Ryū-Min Ryū-Shin kōshōshi no kenkyū.* Tokyo: Bunken shuppan, 1996.

Miyazaki Masakatsu. *Teiwa no nankai daiensei.* Tokyo: Chūō kōronsha, 1997.

Mōri Toshihiko. *Taiwan shuppei: Dai-Nippon teikoku no kaimakugeki.* Tokyo: Chūkō shinsho, 1996.

Nakō Hōshō. *Okinawa bukkyōshi.* Naha: Gokokuji, 1968.

Nishizato Kikō. "Chūryū kōshōshi ni okeru dotsūji to gakō (kyūshō)." *Ryūkyū kyōiku gakubu kiyō,* 50 (1997).

Nishizato Kikō. *Okinawa kindaishi kenkyū.* Naha: Okinawa jiji shuppan, 1981.

Nishizato Kikō. *Shinmatsu Chūryūnichi kankeishi no kenkyū.* Kyoto: Kyōto daigaku gakujutsu shuppankai, 2005.

Okamoto Hiromichi. "Minchō ni okeru chōkōkoku Ryukyū no ichizuke to sono henka." *Tōyōshi kenkyū* 57, no. 4 (1999): 587–621.

Okamoto Hiromichi. *Ryūkyū ōkoku kaijō kōshōshi kenkyū*. Ginowan: Yōju shorin, 2010.
Okamoto Takashi. *Kindai Chūgoku to kaiseki*. Nagoya: Nagoya daigaku shuppankai, 1999.
Ōshiro Tatsuhiro. *Okinawa rekishi sanpo*. Osaka: Sōgensha, 1980.
Ota Yukio. "Futatsu no 'Ryūkyū': Jūsan jūyon seiki no Higashi Ajia ni okeru 'Ryūkyū' ninshiki." Kumamoto University Repository System, March 31, 2009, pp. 201–218. http://reposit.lib.kumamoto-u.ac.jp/bitstream/2298/16119/1/kaA17251007_201-218.pdf.
Pearson, Richard. *Ancient Ryukyu: An Archaeological Study of Island Communities*. Honolulu: University of Hawai'i Press, 2013.
Ryūkyū Shinpō Hyakunenshi Kankō Iinkai, ed. *Ryūkyū shinpō hyakunenshi*. Naha: Ryūkyū shinpō, Inc., 1993.
Ryūkyū shinpōsha, ed. *Shin Ryūkyūshi*, vols. 1–4. Naha: Ryūkyū shinpōsha, 1989–1996.
Satō Tsugitaka and Fukui Norihiko, eds. *Toki no chiikishi*. Tokyo: Yamakawa shuppansha, 1999.
Shimabukuro Zenpatsu. *Naha hensenki*. Naha: Okinawa shoseki, 1930.
Shimajiri Katsutarō. "Okinawa no fūsui shisō." In *Okinawa no fūsui*, edited by Kubo Noritada, pp. 3–13. Tokyo: Hirakawa shuppan, 1990.
Smits, Greg. *Visions of Ryukyu: Identity and Ideology in Early-Modern Thought and Politics*. Honolulu: University of Hawai'i Press, 1999.
Takamura Shōhei, ed. *Shisetsu Nihon to minami Shina*. Tokyo: Noda shobō, 1942.
Takara Kurayoshi. *Ajia no naka no Ryūkyū ōkoku*. Tokyo: Yoshikawa kōbunkan, 1998.
Takara Kurayoshi. *Ryūkyū ōkoku*. Tokyo: Iwanami shoten, 1993.
Takara Kurayoshi. "Ryūkyūshi ni okeru 'kodai.'" In *Shinpan kodai Nihon, 3: Kyūshū, Okinawa*, edited by Tsuboi Kiyotari and Hirano Kunio. Tokyo: Kadokawa shoten, 1991.
Takara Kurayoshi, Tomiyama Kazuyuki, and Maehira Fusaaki, eds. *Atarashii Ryūkyūshizō*. Ginowan: Yōjusha, 1996.
Tanaka Takeo. *Taigaikankei to bunkakōryū*. Kyoto: Shibunkaku shuppan, 1982.
Táng Fēnjī, Xú Xiǎowàng, and Huáng Qǐquán, eds. *Chén Bǎochēn yǔ Zhōngguó jìndài shèhuì*. Fuzhou: Chén Bǎochēn jiàoyù jījīn chóuwěihuì, 1997.
Tei Ryōsei. *Min-Nichi kankeishi no kenkyū*. Tokyo: Yūzankaku shuppan, 1995.
Tokunaga Kazunobu. *Satsuma-han taigai kōshōshi no kenkyū*. Fukuoka: Kyūshū daigaku shuppankai, 2005.
Tōma Shiichi. "Kōko ibutsu yori mita gusuku jidai zengo no kōryū." *Rekishi to chiri* 505 (1997): 1–22.
Tomiyama Kazuyuki. "Edo bakufu gaikō to Ryūkyū." *Okinawa bunka* 65; 22, no. 1 (1985): 22–43.
Tomiyama Kazuyuki. "Kansen bōeki kara mita Ryūkyū ōkoku makki no taishin gaikō." *Ryūkyū daigaku hōbungakubu kiyō, Nihon tōyō bunkaron shū* 6, no. 3 (2000): 137–180.
Tomiyama Kazuyuki. "Kansen bōeki ni tsuite ikkōsatsu: Junbi taisei o chūshin." In *Daisankai Chūryū rekishi kankei kokusai gakujutsukaigi ronbunshū*, pp.109–162. Taipei: Chūryū bunka keizai kyōkai, 1991.
Tomiyama Kazuyuki. "Ryūkyū ōkoku no gaikō to ōken." In *Taikun gaikō to higashi Ajia*, edited by Kamiya Nobuyuki, pp. 112–142. Tokyo: Yoshikawa kōbunkan, 1997.
Tomiyama Kazuyuki, ed. *Ryūkyū-Okinawashi no sekai*, vol. 18, *Nihon no jidaishi*. Tokyo: Yoshikawa kōbunkan, 2003.

Uehara Kenzen. *Bakuhansei keiseiki no Ryūkyū shihai.* Tokyo: Yoshikawa kōbunkan, 2001.

Uehara Kenzen. "Bōeki no Tenkai." In *Shin Ryūkyūshi, Kinseihen,* vol. 1, edited by Ryūkyū Shinpōsha, pp. 119–157. Naha: Ryūkyū shinpōsha, 1989.

Uehara Kenzen. *Sakoku to hanbōeki—Satsuma-han no Ryūkyū mitsubōeki.* Tokyo: Yaedake shobō, 1981.

Uehara Kenzen. *Shimazu-shi no Ryūkyū shinryaku—mō hitotsu Keichō no yaku.* Ginowan: Yōju shorin, 2009.

Umeki Tetsuto. "Fukushū 'rouyuanyi' [jūen-eki] to Ryūkyū-Chūgoku kankei." In *Fukkenshō-Ryūkyū rettō kōshōshi,* edited by Fukkenshō Ryūkyū Rettō Kōshōshi Kenkyū Chōsa Iinkai, pp. 95–179. Tokyo: Daiichi shobō, 1995.

Umeki Tetsuto. *Kinsei Ryūkyūkoku no kōzō.* Tokyo: Daiichi shobō, 2011.

Umeki Tetsuto. "Ryūkyūkoku no kishōmon." In *Kinsei Ryūkyūkoku no kōzō,* pp. 277–296. Tokyo: Daiichi shobō, 2011.

Urasoe-shi Kyōiku Iinkai, ed. *Kinsei shomondai shiriizu,* parts 2–4. Urasoe: Urasoe-shi kyōiku iinkai, 1985.

Wang Lianmo. "Urasoeshi, senshūshi—Sōhō no kankeishi ni kansuru jakkan no mondai ni tsuite no chōsa kōshō." In *Ryūkyū/Chūgoku kōryūsho o saguru: Urasoeshi, senshūshi yūkō toshi teiketsu kinen gakujutsu/bunka tōron hōkokusho,* pp. 40–72. Urasoe City: Urasoeshi kyōiku iinkai, 1988.

Watanabe Miki. *Kinsei Ryūkyū to Chūnichi kankei.* Tokyo: Yoshikawa kōbunkan, 2012.

Watson, Burton, trans. *The Old Man Who Does as He Pleases.* New York: Columbia University Press, 1973.

Xiè Bìzhèn. *Zhōngguó yǔ Liúqiú.* Amoy: Xiàmén dàxué chūbǎnshè, 1996.

Xú Yùhǔ. Míngdài Liúqiú wáng wángǔ. Míngdài Liúqiújiū. Taipei: Táiwān xuésheng shūjú, 1982.

Yamazato Jun'ichi. *Kodai Nihon to nantō no kōryū.* Tokyo: Yoshikawa kōbunkan, 1999.

Yanai Kenji. *Sakoku Nihon to kokusai kōryū.* Tokyo: Yoshikawa kōbunkan, 1988.

Yokoyama Manabu. *Ryūkyūkoku shisetsu torai no kenkyū.* Tokyo: Yoshikawa kōbunkan, 1987.

Yonekura Jirō. "Fukushū no Ryūkyūkan." *Shirin* 22-1 (1937): 187–193.

Zhāng Qixióng. "Lùn qīngcháo Zhōngguó chóngjiàn Liúqiú Wángguó de xīngmiè jìjuéguān—zhōnghuá shìjiè zhìxù yuánli zhī yī." In *Dainikai Ryūchū rekishi kankei kokusai gakujutsukaigi ronbunshū,* pp. 495–519. Naha: Chūryū bunka keizai kyōkai, 1989.

Zhào Bǎochū. "Tàihú Zhào shìjiājí cóngkè." In *Jìndài Zhōngguó shǐliào cóngkān,* no. 59, edited by Shěn Yúnlóng, pp. 585–589. Taipei: Wénhǎi chūbǎnshè, 1970.

Zhuāng Jífā. *Gùgōng dàng'àn shùyāo.* Taipei: Guólì gùgōng bó bóōng bówù, 1983.

# Index

Page numbers in boldface type refer to illustrations.

# About the Author

Mamoru Akamine is a professor in the Department of Languages and Cultures at the University of the Ryukyus, Okinawa, Japan. He received his Ph.D. in history from Taiwan National University and has published articles and books on China's Qing Dynasty, as well as the Ryukyu Kingdom (Okinawa) in relation to both China and Japan in the early modern period. Having expertise in official Chinese-government documents related to China-Ryukyu relations, he participates with other scholars from China, Okinawa, and Taiwan in regular conferences on historical issues connected to China and Okinawa. Akamine also played a key role in establishing a consortium between the libraries of the University of the Ryukyus and the University of Hawai'i to digitize and publicly share their Okinawa-related holdings.